THE
MENTAL
HEALTH
FIELD

THE
MENTAL
HEALTH
FIELD: a critical appraisal

EDITED BY
MORTON LEVITT
University of California at Davis

and

BEN RUBENSTEIN
Marlboro College

PUBLISHED FOR THE
AMERICAN ORTHOPSYCHIATRIC ASSOCIATION

WAYNE STATE UNIVERSITY PRESS

DETROIT/1971

Library of Congress Catalog Card Number 79-135397
International Standard Book Number 8143-1438-4

1626216

CONTENTS

THERAPY

NEW DIRECTIONS

INTRODUCTION

[An occasionally personal history of a few events in the
mental health movement, hopefully written at some distance,
and since the tone is selective and argumentative rather than
encyclopedic, there is no claim made for either objectivity or
subjectivity.]

I

Shortly after World War II I was a rather unskilled member
of a mental health team in a suburban school system. The development of the program was a geographical accident. One
of the few private psychiatric hospitals in the country was located near the community and a few of the adolescent patients attended the high school in town very much on a trial
basis. The school superintendent and the medical director of
the hospital conferred occasionally about these youngsters,
and a loosely organized program came into existence. Meetings with teachers were few, but children with problems were
sent to see the psychiatrist who appeared weekly. I came on
the scene just after this phase ended, but, if memory serves me
rightly, the major theoretical premise of this early effort was
that most educational disorders were related to faulty sexual
information and habits, and therefore the therapeutic thrust
was to straighten out these misapprehensions. A number of
years later I attended a teachers' party where this method-

ology was amusingly lampooned. A pudgy and bearded psychiatrist speaking with an accent straight out of Hans and
Fritz of the Katzenjammer Kids undertook to "treat" a youthful offender by explaining the relationship between "a boy's
pee-nis and a girl's vagin-ia."

By the late 1940s the approach had become much less casual. The professional staff now consisted of a consultant
team—a psychiatrist, a psychologist, and a social worker.
Early efforts to concentrate on the troubled child were replaced first by an experiment which tried to make the teacher
a therapist, then by one which endeavored to make the therapist an educator, and finally by what was soon to become the
established pattern the country over, i.e., each of the mental
health professionals working in terms of his own skills coopera-
tively with the educators in a solid effort to improve the learning climate in the school. The whole experience was very interesting and the reports which came out of the project[1]
attracted some attention, but apparently were not definitive,
for articles reporting much the same conclusions continue to
be found in journals today.

What is more important, however, is that each of the team
members drifted inexorably away from the mental hygiene
clinic into either private practice or medical education, or
combinations of the two, and today none has much to do with
the field of mental health in the sense of being on the firing
line, at least. Nor is this circumstance very unusual currently.
As soon as a person becomes skilled in psychotherapy, he is
likely to elect either to be an educator or a supervisor helping
the newcomers, as it were, to learn the game before they in
turn succeed to the seats of power and/or philosophic detachment. There are major implications to this state of affairs, for
the fact is that the most skilled and best trained of our professionals are farthest removed from the cutting edge of practice,
while the most severely disturbed patients are usually treated
by eager but unseasoned people. But this is not a new argument nor a particularly relevant one, for many things are happening now and have happened recently within the field
which make such comments seem like shallow pedantry.

In an historical sense the modern mental health movement began in the middle 1920s with the concept of interrelated professionals, a contribution uniquely orthopsychiatric in nature. This imaginative wedding of previously separated groups bore small fruit until the war years, for psychiatry remained disappointingly nosologic, psychology rigidly experimental, and social work welfare-oriented throughout the next decade. All of this was changed in the early 1940s when the psychiatric adjustment of the military and civilian population became a high priority item and the need for personnel and facilities brought crash training and building programs in all facets of American life. The period immediately following continued the upswing, as educational and training services of all kinds were created and the general postwar belief in a better life provided the impetus for government-supported programs in the mental health field. Prime examples were supplemented stipends for physicians willing to take psychiatric residencies, and support by the Veterans Administration for graduate students in clinical psychology. Social work, which had become an integral part of the therapeutic mix in service installations, was now dynamically oriented, and case conferences in university clinic and hospital settings were lively affairs indeed as professional lines were set aside and patient welfare became the operative term.

This was a period of immense professional growth with each of the fields expanding rapidly. The size of national organizations increased algebraically (for example, the American Psychological Association grew from something less than 3,000 members in 1939 to more than 13,000 in the early 1950s). Intergroup national conferences were the order of the day with lay persons being openly trained by psychoanalytic societies. The ambience of the period can best be captured by Lawrence Kubie's proposal in 1952 that standard medical training be abolished for those going into psychiatry in favor of a specialized graduate school program centering on the behavioral sciences and leading to a doctorate in medical psychology. Although most clinic directors were medically trained, more than a few psychologists and social workers also held such positions of leadership, and cooperative arrangements in the private practice of psychotherapy were common. Kubie's bold stroke may well have presaged the end of the line, for things began to change shortly. The American Psychoanalytic Association, long a potent force in cooperative endeavors, began to back off. This trend was accelerated by the presidential address of Robert Knight in 1953, in which he clearly outlined the essential differences and responsibilities of the medical psychiatrist and called directly for medical leadership in all mental health matters. The McCarthy era was just subsiding, but there were analogs in the mental health field which were equally frightening. The psychiatrist who had trained lay people was often regarded by colleagues as *persona non grata,* and a few even lost lofty professional positions as a consequence. Similarly, psychologists and social workers who had received such training were asked in some sections of the country to sign letters certifying that they were not using that knowledge to treat patients. Discussions of the "Detroit situation," "the Cleveland situation," or "the Los Angeles situation" usually took place in muted tones, and bills were introduced in a number of states to either strengthen existing medical practice acts or to write new ones making psychotherapy the exclusive province of the physician. Psychologists countered with licensing and certifying acts, some of which made the doctorate the mark of treatment privilege, and as a consequence their long-term rapprochement with social workers was imperiled.

At its best the whole thing seemed like an angry family quarrel which would subside by morning (one colleague professed to view it humorously and constantly tried to persuade others to work with him on a musical comedy which, he assured all, would sell thousands of tickets weekly in New York, where everyone was reported to be in treatment and where each would try to identify his particular therapist in the cast); at its worst it was a bitter and unending civil war (a psychiatrist in charge of a Veterans Administration facility tried to discharge the psychologists in his program because they refused to attend his case conferences and claimed they had nothing to learn from him). Why the struggle did not become a public scandal still puzzles me. Perhaps all the fields were still so busy expanding that no united front was really possible; perhaps clinics had long waiting lists nonetheless, and new facilities were coming into existence so rapidly that there was little time for internecine warfare; but finally perhaps nothing really erupted because there was still one organization, which by both charter and temperament stood for cooperation. The American Orthopsychiatric Association was certainly not untouched by the conflict, for its minutes give evidence of the strain, but there never was, to my knowledge, a major confrontation, and it was the only major association in the country that routinely chose people both for its scientific panels and elective offices with complete disregard for professional affiliation.

How can one explain these curious events, a kind of Hatfield and McCoy mountain feud, where each shooting led to a reprisal, where the only winner was confusion and the only loser was good mental health? Some contestants offer the idea of professional pride, that each group felt it necessary to uphold its own disciplinary ensign while derogating another's. From this stance one could argue that psychiatrists knew little about personality theory, that psychologists always missed organic lesions, that social work training was a hodgepodge of unrelated course offerings which scarcely added up to a professional discipline. This simplistic view is at best one side of a tarnished coin. The other thesis is far less rational but cunningly persuasive. Based upon the old Gallic proverb *cherchez l'argent*, it suggests that professional glory was far less compelling an issue than financial considerations. Nonmedical therapists, formerly relegated to working under supervision with children and for lower fees than charged by psychiatrists, began to create psychotherapeutic enterprises and even associations of their own, and the onetime alliance was thereby doomed. Where does the truth lie? Both arguments are likely to fall under the casuistic label, and I think it is literally impossible, from this distance at least, to make any meaningful judgment. Perhaps the best that can be said is that the times—the social and economic climate of the period—exacerbated some minor issues while simultaneously encouraging honest starts in solving some of the more serious conflicts of our era, the civil rights matter being just one example. The latter question—the impact of social and political events on the field of mental health—will form the basis of the second half of the introduction, but something still needs to be said about the conclusion of the problem described above.

People were still becoming ill in large numbers and the research indicating that country dwellers were not the healthy and happy lot we naively had expected them to be was soon matched by Srole's monumental study on city dwellers in Manhattan, which told of the debilitating psychic effects of urban living. And then from a strange quarter there was the sound of some distant thunder. The National Institute of Mental Health was reported to be evaluating the results of its many million dollar investment in the field of human behavior and coming up with bearish estimates. Had the country's mental health improved? No one apparently knew, for epidemiological research was still rooted in the identification stage, and measures of individual or national mental health were as yet too evanescent to assess. Were there new therapeutic methods being developed? Here too the results were inconclusive. The field of chemotherapy, which Freud had cast longing eyes upon as far back as 1915, was making some progress, but once again the experimental evidence of success was contradictory. Were there more psychiatrists, psychologists, and social workers being trained, and where did they work? The answer to the first part of this question was clearly yes, but the matter of employment was something else. Very few psychiatrists were to be found in anything but private practice, and while comparatively more psychologists remained in institutional settings, those who did treatment worked largely privately and in the traditional one-to-one setting. Social workers were now to be found in large numbers in all settings but were more difficult to categorize as a field than either of the above groups.

Soon the rift between the professions was healing. Among a host of signs of the new times were: 1) the federal government's recognition that there probably would not be sufficient manpower before the year 2000 in any of the psychological fields to solve mankind's emotional problems, and its suggestion that new, nonprofessional classes of therapists and other workers be trained; 2) the willingness of the American Psychoanalytic Association to undertake once again the training of selected lay people; and 3) the delegation by the government of selection responsibility to psychologists in the rapidly expanding and politically exciting Peace Corps.

What is remarkable, nonetheless, is the fact that during this era more patients than ever before were in treatment, and many apparently were profiting from it, despite the annual obituaries in *The New York Times, The Atlantic Monthly, Harpers Magazine,* and such, for psychoanalysis in particular and psychotherapy in general. This latter matter prompted the semi-serious rejoinder by Edward Murray in *Contemporary Psychology:* "If psychoanalysis is dead, why are so many people hacking away at the corpse?"[2] Still and all, many were shaken by Jerome Davis's study at Johns Hopkins that failed to show any significant long-range differences in two matched hospital groups, one given intensive therapy and the other allowed to profit simply from the decontaminated hospital milieu.

Although perhaps the public was not getting a big enough return over the years for its therapeutic dollar (and this is still a moot point), there were many striking contributions being made by the mental health field in the education and research spheres. In the latter category immense progress has been made in the treatment of the psychoses, both in changing therapeutic attitudes toward the patient as well as in the use of drugs as an ameliorating influence. Only recently has the full impact of this research been made explicit. The better mental hospitals today are likely to have eliminated locks on doors, to have drastically reduced patient numbers, and as a consequence, to have freed staff members from previously onerous housekeeping chores to allow them to move freely into the community, now in the practice of comprehensive psychiatry in the fullest sense of the term. Changing social times have created a different set of demands, and experimentation is going on rapidly through the development of walk-in clinics, training programs for mental health aides and rehabilitation workers, and community mental health centers where a full spectrum of psychiatric services are provided, and so on.

All in all, the most solid research in the last twenty years is in studies dealing with the impact of the institutional milieu upon patient mental health. Here the big names have been Menninger, Rees and MacMillan, Hunt and Snow, Bettleheim, Stanton and Schwartz, Redlich, Greenblatt, Rioch, and Stainbrook, all of whom contributed markedly to the new humanizing of mental hospitals. Others who have made major research contributions to the mental health field in physiological studies include Nauta's fine neuroanatomical studies, Ginsberg's work in behavioral genetics, Weisel's studies in the processing of visual information, Levine's work on the effects of neonatal hormones on later behavior, Pribram's studies in neurophysiology and neurosurgery, Bruner's contributions in cognition, and Roberts's studies in neurochemistry. Although the individuals listed above are mostly psychiatrists and psychologists, if we assume that the major research breakthrough was primarily related to those two groups, we look away from the evidence. The mental health community is made up mainly of three classes of professional workers, and all have made significant contributions to the exciting research ferment.

The fields of education and mental health have long been interrelated. It is noteworthy that the key names in this connection were originally Dewey and Freud.

Freud's insights spurred the growth of the mental hygiene movement; Dewey's transformed modern education. Dynamic psychology has, by far and large, provided the impetus and support for the tremendous expansion in both the prophylactic and therapeutic concern with the emotional life of the school child. The results of the expansion can be seen in the vast increase in school clinics and guidance facilities. But this is not all, for it was Freud in psychiatry who was the first to call attention to the importance of early experiences in the life cycle of an individual: "the injunction to love little children and the historic assertion of the supreme importance of human personality, find their strongest support and confirmation in Freud's studies and teaching. Preoccupation with his clinical findings has obscured these implications for education and mental health."[3] If one adds to these lofty ideals the pragmatic efforts to enhance the psychological education of teachers through an emphasis upon human development in college courses, special workshops, etc., the above statements are accurate descriptions of the "mid-years" (1930–1960) of the mental health movement in its continuing engagement with education. Things have moved very rapidly in the last ten years, and the focus has shifted from providing both educationally enriching and prophylactic services to middle class children to becoming frontline soldiers in the struggle against poverty and war. An imaginative education model for the poverty goal was recently offered by Norman Lourie:

> the educational institution should package more of the direct services and we should let it experiment with being the total neighborhood human service agency. Within it we would develop a total service system using uniform problem definitions to account for the broad spectrum of disorders with which all of our systems deal. There would be one intake and one set of centrally administered treatment resources. Diagnosis, treatment planning, service coordination, accountability, and evaluation of results would then be subject to one institutional overview and interpretation. Case registers and rational case management would be more easily possible. Communication between disciplines would be more easily achieved. Disorders could be recognized earlier. Epidemiological studies would be more easily attained. Manpower could be better deployed and evaluations more easily conducted.

> Traditional social welfare and mental health service agencies, in this model, would be packaged in the educational world.

New community agency models would then be free to develop. They would be community oriented and would be the public education, propaganda, and social action arms of the new system. They could educate people, and legislators, about the need for new resources.[4]

The anti-war movement has been centered in the high schools and colleges in recent years, and few will question the fact that social scientists are in the very vanguard of the movement. As early as 1963 the American Orthopsychiatric Association held a meeting on human survival which yielded an exciting volume, *Behavioral Science and Human Survival*, edited by Milton Schwebel, the tenor of which is conveyed by his introduction:

> This book is about life. It is not filled with words about work and play, loving and mating, children and laughter, or nature and beauty. It is not about the stuff of life that the authors write but about the preservation of our lives and those of the generations that are to follow endlessly. They write about the specter that hangs over the world of man, that mushroom-shaped aftermath of a tragic decision to destroy life on our planet, about its effects on our lives, our emotions, our relationship with our fellow men, and about the social, economic and psychological factors that perpetuate conflict. And they write with the deep conviction that man, with his infinitely creative brain, has the capacity to solve the problems of survival.[5]

Student dissent is another area of mounting social concern over the last four years. The sight, strange to this country, of arson and pillage, of police busts, of violence and counter violence, has dismayed some, buoyed others. The journal of this association reviewed this new arena in a for-and-against exchange in 1968; the pro position being held by Alfred Freedman and the con by the editors of this volume.[6] From this heated exchange it was but a small step to the theme for the Association's 46th Annual Meeting in New York this spring which was devoted to "Youth in Transition." This meeting was a true happening for it was replete with pickets, mini-confrontations, and even a monotonic vestige of the Berkeley Free Speech Movement. The exciting events, as well as the papers which apparently inspired them, will make up the next theme volume.

II

> When I first heard the health center was coming, I figured it would be the same old deal: you'd run the services and you'd permit us to provide the illnesses. People think of us as hardcore poverty cases. Well, you can see what we call hardcore social workers, hardcore doctors, hardcore professionals of every kind.
>
> —A resident of the Columbia Point Area in Boston

Would these professional preoccupations (poverty, student dissent, and war) sound strange to the nine founding psychiatrists who called the first meeting of the American Orthopsychiatric Association in 1924: "To unite and provide a common meeting ground for those engaged in the study and treatment of the problems of human behavior. To foster research and spread information concerning scientific work in the field of human behavior, including all forms of abnormal behavior." What would they think of the present committee structure: "Alternatives to War, Law and Mental Health, Mental Retardation, Minority Group Problems, Psychosocial Diagnosis and Classification, Psychotherapy, Research Education, Social Issues, Community Mental Health Centers, Invasion of Privacy, and Legislative Issues in Psychotherapy."[7]

Or the task that awaits one of those committees (Committee to Work With the Joint Commission on Mental Health of Children): "the committee is now in the process of compiling a list of priority issues on which position statements will be formulated and sent to the membership for reaction. Some of the issues on which we have to decide whether to take an official Ortho position include: pregnancy and the civil rights of women; unwanted babies; inadequate prenatal care; foster care of children; programs in the schools; new roles for teachers as preventive therapeutic concepts are integrated with the educational mission; inequalities in the draft."[8] Things have changed mightily in fifty years. Contrast the clean muscular prose of 1924—"to write and provide a common meeting ground;" "to foster research and spread information," with today's preoccupations—racism, black power, Vietnam, poverty, student revolt. How isolated the echo from the past! Nine men sat in a room in the East and planned a forum "to develop a common vocabulary." Could any of them have envisioned a time when they would feel unsafe in the cities, when racial strife became so commonplace that it occupied no more time on the evening telecast than the baseball scores, when an undeclared and unending war resulted in more deaths than any previous conflict in United States history, and when socially progressive mayoral candidates in the nation's large cities were defeated by a white law and order backlash?

Today's community clinics, in urban areas, at least, are likely to be operated through federal funding but under a policy of neighborhood control which is apt to be so restrictive in a color sense that no white man can possibly qualify for employment. At the same time education in the cities seems likely to be controlled by neighborhood boards, often endowed with the right to hire or fire teachers, and there is strong suspicion that such schools will have stronger political overtones than before. No one yet is in a position to identify what impact this latest development will have on mental health programs within the schools. What is certain, however, is that the old model with experts (psychiatrists, psychologists, and social workers) shuttling in and out of neighborhoods on a consultant basis is likely to be a thing of the past. More likely is the Lourie model cited above with specially trained nonprofessionals available on a twenty-four hour basis because they live on the scene, and whose efforts will be truly comprehensive since the school, the hospital, and the neighborhood will indeed be one.

This revolutionary concept will be interesting to follow and will certainly occupy the attention of those who edit the volume dealing with the second fifty years of the mental health movement. Although history shows that the earliest interest was in the hospitalized poor and in delinquent children, most of the recipients of our bounty in this first half century have become the privileged middle class. Celia Deschin put the matter trenchantly when she wrote:

> Social workers themselves are still questioning whether the skills they now have might not best be used in casework service to those who use it "well and with an economy of time"—namely, the middle-class. If the profession does choose the casework emphasis, it should do so without making it appear as if it were serving the whole community by providing consultation to public welfare departments and working with a small number of the poor, the uneducated, the sick and disabled, the underemployed and unemployed on a quasi-demonstration basis. But if, as some in the profession believe, the casework skills our profession has learned can be utilized indirectly as well as directly to help thousands of individuals and families, groups and communities, then we should willingly forego some of the individual satisfaction that goes with helping on a one-to-one or small group basis; we should willingly give up some of our middle-class bias.[9]

Deschin has directed her remarks to social work, and while she is somewhat more sanguine about psychiatry's focus, her criticism really applies as well to all who work in this troubled area. Underlying this changed emphasis is the thesis that community action will make for community change, and in Daniel Moynihan's words, "maximum feasible participation" will improve not only the behavior but also the character of the poor. So here we have in *statu nascendi* something which should be called a "maximum feasible action" program designed to: 1) reduce hardcore unemployment by training some and upgrading others; 2) to improve physical and mental health through comprehensive programs; and 3) to create in the poor a feeling of community which serves both as the glue and as the self-sustaining motivational force for the entire program. Whether this will really provide society with what it needs in a health "flivver"—an inexpensive, useful, sturdy, and low cost vehicle—will soon be put to the test. Cynics are already protesting that the poor neighborhoods have no sense of community nor are they likely to develop one since the poor move so often. Others criticize the idea of the indigenous health professional as naive at best, shortsighted at worst. This second group point out that few physicians practice in poor neighborhoods and those who do are not likely to "live in" in the sense demanded by the community. There is some evidence to support this last assertion; of the approximately twenty-five physicians practicing in the Watts area in Los Angeles, none were willing to participate in the Watts Clinic, organized under community control and under the very distant guidance of the University of Southern California.

No one argues that previous efforts by middle class intellectuals to bring about behavioral change in the poor have been markedly successful. Michael Gorman, executive director of the Nation's Committee Against Mental Illness, has reported (June 1969) that mental illness among children has increased 150 percent in the last ten years, and that while there are at least four million emotionally disturbed children, fifteen states have no facilities of any kind for treatment while twenty-four other states have no public institutions which take in children from lower and middle class groups.[10]

The current contention that people closer to the poor in terms of race and religion, attitude and class, and roles and goals will have better prospects for altering long-standing patterns of behavior contradicts almost two thousand years of human history, but the times are hard and they call for innovative solutions. Like it or not, the community has now become the new professional arena, and success or failure for our efforts in the future may well depend upon how we answer this crucial challenge.

American readers are discovering belatedly the writings of Julio Cortazar, an Argentine expatriate now living in Paris, who for many years has experimented with freshly minted words in an effort to break out of the bonds of automatic acts and responses. Cortazar first identified three categories of people, (famas, cronopios, and esperanzas) in an article reviewing a concert given by the jazz musician Louis Armstrong in 1952. The article was affectionately entitled "Louis: Enormisimo Cronopio." More recently, in a book called *Cronopios and Famas*, Cortazar has defined his categories in a pleasant metaphor:

> When *famas* go on a trip . . . one fama goes to the hotel and prudently checks the prices, the quality of the sheets, and the color of the carpets. The second repairs to the commissariat of police and there fills out a record of the real and transferable property of all three of them, as well as an inventory of their valises. The third fama goes to the hospital and copies the lists of the doctors on emergency and their specialties.
>
> When *cronopias* go on a trip, they find that the hotels are all filled up, the trains have already left, it is raining buckets and taxis don't want to pick them up. . . . The cronopios are not disheartened because they believe firmly that these things happen to everyone. When they manage finally to find a bed and are ready to go to sleep, they say to one another, "What a beautiful city!"
>
> *Esperanzas* are sedentary. They let things and people slide by them. They're like statues one has to go visit. They never take the trouble.[11]

What shall the reviewers say of the next fifty years of mental health? Let us hope that their evaluation will be "Enormisimo Cronopio."

III

> Those who cannot remember the past are condemned to repeat it.
>
> —George Santayana

The forty-fifth annual meeting of this association was entitled "Mental Health: A Critical Review." In the words of one of the participants it was "a time for considering past intentions and future direction, for remembering where we had come from and where we are going." The president of the Association put it less sentimentally: "The past decade has witnessed a growing concern with developing more suitable ways of putting into use the limited knowledge we currently possess to alleviate the distress and waste of psychopathology, while struggling to keep in clearer focus the need for an effective model of social action which can ultimately minimize, if not altogether prevent, the social pathology inherent in the etiology of psychopathology."[12]

It was, nonetheless, a sentimental occasion for three of the original nine founding members were present, and one, David Levy, offered a touching evocation of the past. There was "a philanthropic lady, Mrs. Dummer" who read with horror in her newspaper of juvenile delinquency, and determined to do something about it. She contributed a sum of money to find "a skilled physician" (her words) to make "a proper investigation of this malady." William Healy was selected and the Juvenile Psychopathic Clinic of Chicago was born. Also born was the scientific method for the study of delinquents, the clinic environment as a locus, and in Levy's words: "The child guidance movement was then fully established." The whole effort smells pleasantly of lavender and old lace and is presented first in this collection of papers from that commemorative meeting in Chicago in 1968.

The second and third papers arrive in the present in one large leap. The editors of this volume review normality in the light of present-day reality. Suggesting that the water in which the fish swims has something to do with his characteristic coloration, they reprise some past controversies about the definition of normality and conclude that "those who can effect some accommodation between the two (personality and environmental) forces, or who can work constructively to change the balance, can probably be considered to be in good health." On the way, however, considerable attention is paid to changing dimensions of assessment.

The second work in this section is by a social psychologist, James Tedeschi, who argues that 1) all models require an acceptance of some value theory as a preface to a definition of normality; and 2) therapists should attempt to minimize value assumptions and adopt scientific criteria and goals. Tedeschi ends by viewing psychotherapy as a prolegomena rather than a determinant of an individual's selection of values, and the psychotherapist as a social scientist rather than a social engineer.

The next collection of papers relates to social issues, and ranges from theoretical arguments about man's condition in society to the LSD subcultures. Other station stops are violence, the military establishment (both pro and con), abortion, and mental health for Negroes. Amitai Etzioni relates what he calls man's "inauthentic" condition to resistance to making affluent societies more responsive and to opening the society to extensive participation. Pointing out that the opposition to these efforts is both real and symbolic, Etzioni concludes: "Should the mobilization of the uninvolved lead to a gradual transformation . . . inauthenticity—the mark of the affluent society—will be much reduced." Victor Gioscia has spent considerable time examining the "acid" scene, and his consultants have been both "trippers" and their therapists. What emerges is a fascinating picture of the dark side of the moon. There is indeed an acid subculture with well defined roles and goals, and with many more citizens than we used to think there were. Try this disquieting conclusion for a late Sunday night sedative: "In an age where conscience permits the napalm flames of war to engulf civilian women and children scarcely two decades after millions were burned in ovens throughout Europe, the suspicion that terms such as 'neurosis' and 'psychosis' may become political weapons cannot be regarded as outrageous. Perhaps, in such an age, some of those who seek some form of ultimacy in mind-changing chemicals deserve neither to be 'treated' nor to be subjected to 'criminal' process." The next two papers are a set piece. Roger Little describes Project 100,000, an attempt by the military to give basic education to young men from deprived backgrounds. He analyzes some of the elements of military life and training, the skill structure, cultural climate, and the social context to determine whether civilian society may profit from this experiment. His conclusion that the project was successful offends no one, but his extension of the argument into a metaphor which compares the military with a residental treatment center for disadvantaged minority groups, and a more successful one at that, creates some controversy. At least part of the storm comes from Marc Pilisuk, who immediately questions the practice of military socialization and its acceptance by Little. Objecting to the portrayal of military training as rehabilitative rather than destructive, Pilisuk characterizes the military as "an organization which is incapable of tolerating discussion and dissent within its ranks, particularly because its main function of inflicting extreme malevolence on a national foe is one which requires an equally extreme form of discipline." The set-to is not a very friendly one, but the arguments are provocative and worthwhile.

Not entirely unrelated is Herbert Schiller's paper, which takes the broad view of violence and suggests that a major part of this country's problem stems from the resistance, both economic and psychological, that has been created deliberately against the social application and utilization of modern technological and natural resources. The inability of American society to adapt its institutions to meet the enlarged social tasks that confront the nation produces domestic chaos and international violence. The war in Vietnam, seen in this perspective, is symptomatic of the general effort to prevent structural change, internationally or domestically, that might improve the human condition.

The next article in this section discusses a central position in the struggle for women's rights in the last several years. Alice Rossi is notably unimpressed with "the more children the better" argument, for she is convinced that this stance looks away from the important social considerations of fertility control and population growth. Her conclusion sounds a stark and tragic commentary on modern life: It will not be enough to support those women who do not want any more children. It will also become necessary to study and think through the means whereby women and men will be encouraged to reduce the number of children they want.

The next section of the book is concerned with what must be regarded as one of the major issues in the field today, the role of the mental health professional in the rapidly changing world. Leonard Duhl, writing from the post of Special Assistant to the Secretary of Housing and Urban Development in the Johnson Administration, really provides the keynote address in his paper, which examines the pressures for change within and without the mental health world. He concludes that if we are to carry out our responsibility for society's health, we must 1) straighten out our professional ideology; and 2) examine our training institutions, research programs, and community services in terms of this new ideology.

The next two papers offer commentaries on Duhl's charge. Irving Berlin takes a realistic approach to the possibility of change and comes up with a somewhat less sanguine trial balance. He acknowledges the fact that a rapidly changing society requires the establishment of more responsive models of theory and practice, but notes that mental health professionals resist totally new models because of fears about reduced status, financial return, work satisfaction, and feelings of loss of competency. Berlin suggests that the reaction may be ameliorated by the satisfaction of community involvement which may well bring its own particular satisfactions to mental health professionals. Freeman and Gertner are also less optimistic about the same problem, and see those alterations envisioned by Berlin as only a temporary means of meeting political and social demands for change. They offer the thesis that the strategy of adopting an equalitarian set of role relationships within the mental health consortium may simply be a transitional one, with the next step being a vertical structuring which maintains organizational arrangements. This paper takes a refreshing look at some of the therapeutic issues described in the first part of this introduction.

Richard Williams writes about the sometimes muddied relationship among the three professional groups that make up the mental health consortium, adds the psychiatric nurse to the group, and develops them further in line with changes throughout the country. Making some comparisons with the mental health movement in France in each of the professional categories, Williams concludes that "the traditional approach of using only very highly skilled professionals has not only limited the supply of helpers, but has also produced gaps in communications and transactions generally between them and those who need help."

Diana Tendler directly confronts one of the major professional issues of our time, the partly trained nonprofessional mental health worker. Beginning with a quick look at the usual initial enthusiasm that greets such revolutionary innovations, Tendler constructs a "who, what, when" trilogy that tries to sort out the circumstances under which this exciting stratagem may work. She concludes that the key to facilitating important changes for the nonprofessionals involved, in terms of the contribution they can make to the activities and goals of the helping professions as well as their own destinies, requires a hard look at present and emerging questions.

The final article in this section, by sociologists Robert Kleiner and Seymour Parker, is notably skeptical of medical models of mental disorder. They propose instead social interaction and cognitive consistency theories which lend themselves more readily to prediction and empirical evaluation. The authors maintain that these alternatives emphasize the need to study both the individual and the social networks in which he participates.

Paul Wender provides an interesting review of studies on the factors in the etiology of schizophrenia. Recognizing that the developmental mix obscures the possibility of assessing either experiential or genetic elements in the disease process, the author utilizes adoptive children to provide a separation factor and shows that genetic factors play an important role in the etiology of schizophrenia as well as in other psychiatric illnesses.

Nancy Waxler looks at the same problem from another vantage point. Her interest is also in schizophrenia, but she is more concerned with the process by which family research is philosophically conceived. Her search is for a transactional model which will offer a set of concretely stated relationships open to further test and refinement. For readers with an interest in theoretical conceptualization the article provides a kind of inner dialogue about how a researcher thinks about research.

The next section includes three articles on treatment. They are an interesting mixture. One deals directly with classic treatment updated by metaphoric interpretation, the second has a markedly social class—caste sound, and the third is full of poetic hope and promise. Rudolf Ekstein's skillful interweaving of the social scene, psychoanalytic theory ("the child's mental health is defined as his capacity to live and learn"), and a treatment case provides a most revealing study of an analyst at work. The second paper by McDermott and others is one of a series emerging from a long-range psychiatric investigation of social class factors in psychiatric practice at a university medical center. A number of surprising things are reported in the discussion, which deals with the real or apparent differences perceived in the therapeutic response of children of the various social classes, the relation of duration of treatment to improvement among the various social groups, as well as the varying implications of the principles of planning and carrying out psychotherapy with children of different social classes. John Schimmel's paper describes twenty adolescents treated psychoanalytically in an urban area. The patients all suffered from what the literature calls an "identification crisis" and most of the group improved markedly in therapy. The simplicity of the presentation is attractive, and although much of it sounds today like a period piece, there is surely something to be said for one-to-one treatment setting even in this changing world.

The last section of the book contains three papers which point to new directions in mental health conceptualization.

Kahn and Arbib introduce and illustrate some aspects of cybernetics, communications theory, and systems theory which may prove relevant to the efforts of the mental health worker in the future. Theoretical material is touched on lightly, and no mathematical formulations are involved. Rather, behavior is seen as the end product of an internal process—as a symptom rather than as the disease. Analogic, digital, and meta-informational roles in information processing are defined and placed in developmental context, and infantile autism and childhood schizophrenia are used as developmental models.

Harley Shands's frame is both philosophic and behavioral, and his paper presents a broad view of the learning process. His conclusions are that learning is specifically dependent upon acting and that only in the course of overt activity does learning occur, and that the major task of education is to train learners to minimize overt activity while retaining the capacity to be alert and process data. His paper makes an interesting bridge between the Kahn and Arbib articles and the Schon paper. This last article in the collection should be read carefully, for it provides both a reprise as well as a broad prospective glance. Schon discusses social change from a variety of parameters and his conclusion can well stand as paradigmatic for the next fifty years of the mental health field: "The pressures for change and the loss of the stable state, press all these toward a variety of responses: revolt (an attempt at total rejection of the past, while letting in a literal or distorted form of the past through the backdoor); reaction (a futile attempt to return literally to the past); or diversions or attempts at escape from the problem—such as in the mindlessness associated with infatuations with machines, with violence, or with drugs. To the question, 'What can I be if I am not what I am?' the answer must always take the form, a transformation of what I have been—not a rupture with the past."

As in all such collections of program papers, one fact must be recognized. This selection is limited to papers presented at an annual meeting, and this is almost certain to ensure some areas of neglect. The collection of papers in this volume, nonetheless, deals with the professional concerns of the American Orthopsychiatric Association at the midcentury of the mental health movement.

NOTES

1. M. L. Falick, *et al.*, "Some Observations in the Psychological Education of Teachers," *Mental Hygiene*, 38:374-86 (July 1954); M. L. Falick, Morton Levitt, and Ben Rubenstein, "A Critical Evaluation of the Therapeutic Use of a Group in a School-based Mental Health Program," *MH* 38:322-36 (July 1954); M. L. Falick, M. Levitt, and B. Rubenstein, "Diagnosis and Therapy in School Mental Hygiene Clinics," in *Orthopsychiatry in the Schools*, ed. M. Krugman (New York: American Orthopsychiatric Association, 1958), pp. 46-59.
2. "Psychology's Paperbacks," *Contemporary Psychology*, 9:10-17 (1964).
3. Lawrence Frank, "Preface," in Morton Levitt, *Freud and Dewey on the Nature of Man* (New York: Philosophical Library, 1960), p. 172.
4. Norman Lourie, "Orthopsychiatry and Education," *American Journal of Orthopsychiatry*, 37:836-42 (1967).
5. *Behavioral Science and Human Survival* (Palo Alto: Science and Behavior Books, 1965).
6. Alfred Freedman, "Responding to Student Protest," *AJO*, 38:780-83 (1968); Levitt and Rubenstein, "The Children's Crusade," *AJO*, 38:591-98 (1968).
7. 45th annual meeting, American Orthopsychiatric Association, March 20-23, 1968.
8. Walter Kass, "Business Meeting," *AJO*, 37:994-1003 (1967).
9. "Future Direction of Social Work," *AJO*, 38:9-17 (1968).
10. "Report to Nation's Committee Against Mental Illness," June, 1969.
11. "Cronopios and Famas," *The New York Times Book Review*, June 15, 1969, pp. 20-23.
12. Eliot H. Rodnick, 45th annual meeting, American Orthopsychiatric Association.

Beginnings of the Child Guidance Movement*

DAVID M. LEVY

The child guidance movement started in Chicago in the field of delinquency. A simple story. A philanthropic lady, a Mrs. Dummer,** was appalled by accounts in newspapers about juvenile crime and contributed money to make possible a proper investigation of this malady by the "skilled physician"—her words. A committee was formed, a search was made for the "skilled physician," and there at the appropriate moment William Healy emerged. Why Chicago? Why Mrs. Dummer? Why Dr. Healy?

Most likely it was because in 1906, when ideas about the study and treatment of delinquency were evolving, Chicago

*This paper appeared in slightly revised form in the *American Journal of Orthopsychiatry*, *38*: 799-804 (October 1968).

**I wish to express my appreciation to Dr. Marian Kenworthy, herself a pioneer in the child guidance movement, for letting me know that Mrs. Dummer had willed her correspondence at the Women's Archives of Radcliffe College. It included a number of personal letters, both from Dr. William Healy and Mrs. Dummer, which proved to be a valuable source of information.

was in the forefront of progressive legislation and civic betterment activities. It was ready historically for the next step. This historical readiness might well be amplified. I need only mention the Cook County Juvenile Court, an essential laboratory for Healy's future investigations, and Judge Pinckney, a friend and protector of the new project. Such a project needed a high degree of official cooperation, especially for the necessary followup studies. According to Healy, "only by such a method of self-criticism and prolonged observation can the observer or his science grow." Healy expressed his philosophy clearly in *The Individual Delinquent*. He wrote: "Our main point of view is to ascertain from the actualities of life the basic factors of disorders and social conduct."[1]

In addition to the juvenile court and correctional institutions which put an end to the incarceration of children with adults, there was an amazing group of people in Chicago in 1906—social workers, lawyers, professors, doctors, and civic and political leaders. They were identified with Hull House, a social settlement, and its founder, Jane Addams. Mrs. Dummer was a member of the Hull House group. Her knowledge of delinquency was gained as a member of the Board of the Juvenile Protective Association and as observer of children brought to the juvenile court. She had the advice and help of Jane Addams (to receive the Nobel Peace Prize in 1910), Julia Lathrop (later to be the first head of the Children's Bureau in Washington), and George H. Mead, head of the department of philosophy at the University of Chicago. Mrs. Dummer's husband was helpful in every stage of the enterprise, even drafting letters for his wife and working out the legal papers for the disbursement of funds which were donated mostly by the Dummers.

The Juvenile Psychopathic Institute, a name proposed by Healy, was organized in April 1909. Mrs. Dummer, Jane Addams, Dr. Frank Churchill, and Mrs. Emily Dean signed the certificate of incorporation. The selection of a director for the new undertaking followed a number of meetings at Hull House and at the home of Mrs. Dummer. Professor Mead wrote to some friends in the East—to Adolf Meyer and to William James. Both recommended William Healy.

The original letter, written by Mr. Dummer in January 1909 after discussions with the committee and with Mrs. Dummer, who signed it, follows:

> It is desired to undertake in Chicago an inquiry into the health of delinquent children in order to ascertain as far as possible in what degree delinquency is caused or influenced by mental or physical defect or abnormality and with the purpose of suggesting and applying remedies in individual cases whenever practicable as a concurrent part of the inquiry.
>
> A fund for the purpose has been guaranteed for a period of five years, and a medical director is to be appointed, whose salary will be probably $4,500 yearly.
>
> The organizing committee wishes to secure a director who shall have the requisite interest and ability. It believes that he should be a physician with special experience in mental and nervous diseases in children and with an understanding of the methods of modern psychology.
>
> The committee recognizes the experimental character of the inquiry. However its general need is so obvious and has been brought home in Chicago with special urgency from a preliminary inspection of the results of the inquiry into juvenile delinquency made in 1907-8 by the Research Department of the Chicago School of Civics, and by the work of the Childrens Hospital Society Clinic at the detention home.
>
> The Committee fully understands that the value of the proposed inquiry will be measured entirely by the quality of the director, and accordingly begs to bespeak your earnest consideration in suggesting any suitable person of your acquaintance, who might desire such appointment.

By "the methods of modern psychology" Mrs. Dummer evidently meant the methods of psychoanalysis. She sat with Dr. Healy when he interviewed a delinquent girl for the juvenile court. This is Mrs. Dummer's own account:

An early astonishing case of stealing was by a girl doing well in her lessons. Dr. Healy asked: "What do you think about just before you take something?" The answer was: "The name John. If I see it in my reading lesson I must take something." Dr. Healy listened and there came to the child's conscious memory an experience which had apparently passed below the level of awareness: a condition which at the time Dr. Healy called the sub-conscious. A little boy had made suggestions to her which she had resisted, but she had gone with him to a store and stolen some fruit. The astonishing result of recalling this incident to consciousness was the immediate cessation of the stealing habit.

1626216

After several sessions of this type the girl's delinquency ended. It was an unusual case, quite dramatic. Healy's utilization of the analytic method, as we shall see from his own account, was necessarily limited. They were classified as mental-conflict cases and are contained in his book *Mental Conflict and Misconduct*.[2] This case impressed Mrs. Dummer very strongly, and it was this she referred to as the "new psychology." She was intrigued by her reading of Freud. As a deeply religious person, she found Freud's theory of sublimation to be a most satisfactory explanation of spiritual values and of social service as a transformation of sexual energies into higher ones. She saw in Healy a deeply religious person, an apostolic one.

In 1923 Mrs. Dummer wrote a foreword to Professor W. I. Thomas' book *The Unadjusted Girl* (1925):[3] "Modern psychology is throwing so much light upon human behavior that concerning delinquency one cannot do better than follow the teaching of Spinoza, 'Neither condemn nor ridicule but try to understand.' Such an attitude led to the establishment of the first mental clinic in connection with a court where Doctor William Healy revealed astonishing facts regarding causes and cures of delinquency." The juvenile court (and the boys' division of the municipal court of Chicago) had originally been thought adequate to handle delinquency, provided only the officers of the court and, particularly, the judges were well chosen. The shortcomings of this court, fully recognized by the excellent Judge Pinckney, spurred the new venture. Julia Lathrop and Allen Burns were quick to find its weakness. How, they asked, can a judge prescribe wisely for the delinquent child when he knows very little about the child's personality or the factors in his life experience that explain the delinquency.

In 1908 Miss Lathrop, Burns, and Healy met at Hull House to hear Healy outline his plan to study delinquents at the juvenile court. As a neurologist working for a clinic, he had many patients referred for "conduct difficulties," including delinquency. Among them were cases of head injury, chorea, epilepsy, and hysteria. As in the clinic, his plan for the court included a careful physical examination, special school reports from teachers, and interviews with parents and relatives to ascertain "heredity, developmental personality peculiarities, family relationships, and much else." He added "study of the delinquents during their period of detention."

That same year under his first grant from Mrs. Dummer, Healy traveled throughout the country visiting psychiatrists, psychologists, and judges, all of whom agreed on the value of an appropriate clinic. No such clinic existed at the time, but he found two clinics that were thought to be adequate. One was at the University of Pennsylvania—Witmer's Clinic for retarded children, where testing plus a physical examination were done. The other was Goddard's laboratory for mental measurement of the feebleminded at Vineland, New Jersey. Neither had developed anything like the case studies he had in mind.

Miss Lathrop, who was influenced by William James's recommendation more than by the others, urged Healy to head the project he had outlined so carefully. Healy wrote later that at the time he had not the slightest idea of accepting the job. He was forty years old; he had a good practice; it would be a real sacrifice. Nevertheless, "the scientific quest was enticing" and the vision of clinics for behavior problems of children overcame all "hesitations."

The Individual Delinquent, published in 1915, was the first book of its kind. In his introduction Healy stated he found "astonishingly little" to help him in his work. There was no lack of theories, but they gave no help in attaining clear understanding of the individual. As he analyzed more than 800 cases, he weighed factor after factor in terms of its relevance to delinquency and came up with a "theory" of multiple causes. He found no special quality of abnormality or degeneracy, no born criminal. He disproved Lambroso's theory in a statistical survey. He wrote: "In view of the immense complexity of human nature in relation to complex environmental conditions, it is little to us even if no set theory of crime can ever be successfully maintained."

There are many firsts in Healy's book. They include a battery of intelligence tests, study of focal infections in relation to delinquency, and the routine search for early emotional traumata. The book had an amazing influence on legal procedures, on sociology, anthropology, psychology, and especially psychiatry. The fact that the child guidance movement started in the field of delinquency made necessary the utilization of a team—psychologist, psychiatrist, and social worker. Even if not in the form of a team, these three disciplines are now authentic units in most mental hospitals.

I have written previously on the course of child guidance practices as they varied through the years. At first the distance from its medical origins and from the hospital was increased. After forty years the trend began to reverse itself, and there are now more child guidance clinics in the outpatient departments of medical schools and hospitals.

After Healy wrote *The Individual Delinquent*, the commissioners of Cook County took over the Juvenile Psychopathic Institute. Within two years no funds were available. The prospect of losing Healy to the Judge Baker Foundation stirred up a great protest, but a plea for more funds failed. Healy left for Boston to become director of the foundation and was succeeded by Herman Adler, previously director of the Boston Psychopathic Hospital. The Chicago Juvenile Psychopathic Institute became the Illinois Juvenile Psychopathic Institute under a statewide organization (1917).

In 1920 when I became a member of the Illinois Institute for

Juvenile Research, a new name for the Psychopathic Institute, I was assigned for one day a week to the Cook County Juvenile Detention Home, the same three rooms which Healy had occupied from 1909 to 1917. In reviewing a number of his case records I noticed that in the more recent years physical examinations had become briefer. At the time I was there two psychologists were in attendance; that was the staff. Presumably they were to call for others when needed. Did it mean that when personnel was scarce in this field, and it was for some time, you could spare anyone except the clinical psychologists? A letter about a delinquent to the juvenile court that did not include the child's I.Q. was by that time unheard of. For the physical, there was a hearing test (watch tick), a test for vision (Snellen charts), and the knee jerks (performed by the psychologists). The personality was described with the usual rubrics, the patient's "own story," a school report, and his delinquency record, if any, from the court. In time this was all remedied.

In Boston, Healy had the advantage of retaining a much better facsimile of the old Juvenile Psychopathic Institute. At Chicago, in addition to the central headquarters at the Institute for Juvenile Research, we had a statewide organization with traveling clinics, numerous assignments to the custodial institutions at Geneva (delinquent girls) and St. Charles (delinquent boys), and surveys in penitentiaries and other institutions, including baby health surveys at county fairs. There were a wealth of opportunities and a large staff. These were all under the directorship of our first state criminologist, Herman Adler.

By 1918 Healy's interest in neurology was reawakened by an epidemic of encephalitis, with its aftermath of personality disturbances. The next year our facilities in Chicago were strained by the same problem, a problem which more than any other factor stimulated the development of in-patient services for children.

Healy was an unusual man, receptive to new ideas—the true eclectic—ready to put any new theory to the test of practice, without a trace of bias except possibly an optimistic hope that he would find something of special benefit for his multitude of troubled children. It took a person like Healy, free of the professional pecking order, to make of himself and his coworkers in psychology and social work an authentic unit. The Institute for Juvenile Research was the successor to Healy's institute. The difference, as in the later Child Guidance Institute, was a relatively smaller percentage of cases of delinquency and referrals from the juvenile court. The research projects included biochemical studies (Rich's chemical study of personality), neurological studies (the postencephalitis prevalent in Chicago in 1919), and child development studies, besides the usual psychological testing and case study investigation. Herman Adler, successor to Healy, was incisive, energetic, stimulating, cynical, and brilliant. Unfortunately, as state criminologist, he had an overwhelming job and almost no time for writing the books he had in mind.

Since its start in 1917 the Institute for Juvenile Research has continued to this day. The Child Guidance Demonstration Clinics, organized in 1921-1922, used Healy's Juvenile Psychopathic Institute and the Institute for Juvenile Research as their first models. The child guidance movement was then fully established.

NOTES

1. William Healy, *The Individual Delinquent* (Montclair, N.J.: Patterson, Smith Publishing Corporation, 1969).
2. William Healy, *Mental Conflict and Misconduct* (Montclair, N.J.: Patterson, Smith Publishing Corporation, 1917).
3. W. I. Thomas, *The Unadjusted Girl* (Boston: Little, Brown, 1925).

An Assessment of Current Mental Health Models: normality in the light of present-day reality

MORTON LEVITT AND BEN RUBENSTEIN

The Committee, a satirical drama group in San Francisco, performs a skit about the plight of a man who finds that the bar in which he is sitting is peopled entirely with homosexual men. Pursued aggressively by one man who insists on buying him a drink, our "innocent abroad" tries to appear nonchalant. In the face of his own mounting terror he blurts, "How do you like being ah . . . ah . . . ah . . . homosexual?" His would-be drinking partner answers drily, "How do you like being ah . . . ah . . . ah . . . whatever it is *you* are?"

This paper speculates on the fact that the water in which the fish swims has something to do with his characteristic coloration. For example, children reared on kibbutzim are uniformly described as hard-working and responsible citizens, devoted to their settlements and their country. They are also free, it is reported, from the noxious influence of drugs, homosexuality, and delinquency, and in addition, as the summer of 1967 has shown, they can also be successful in modern warfare. These facts are of some current interest because the Israeli culture raises its children in clusters, far removed for most of the day from the influence of their parents. Behavioral scientists certainly do not need to be told of the corrupting influence of this state of affairs. When changes in parental role become necessary, we are committed to the idea that those adults responsible for the surrogate care of young children shall be kept as permanent as possible. Yet here, too, Israeli children apparently differ, for the adults who rear them are often replaced, and youngsters have to adapt to new faces and expectations. Bruno Bettelheim has summarized the results as follows: "The kibbutz example has shown that it is possible in a single generation to create a healthy personality that is entirely different from that of the parents."[1] But all of this, mildly interesting as it is, is not the point of this introduction. What is important is that American scientists, who had been invited observers to this new style of developmental rites, quarreled with the results, indeed refused to accept the kibbutz as a way of life as natural as their own. And here we are quickly at the nub of one of the issues which concern us: what is the impact of any given culture upon the concept of normality?

This is, of course, a very old question. Two factors, almost too trite to require repetition, need some brief acknowledgment at the outset. The first is that concern about normality has routinely been a second step which develops after the excitement about pathology has begun to die down. The second factor is that most definitions of normality differ only in the degree of obeisance paid to the separate elements in the "nature plus nurture equals behavior" formulation.

Only recently has there been some effort to factor out in a scientific fashion the elements that make up normality. This new interest has been a reaction against the traditional descriptions which relate, in the main, to either 1) the symptom-free concept or 2) what has become known as the centrist construct, a statistical average of normally distributed characteristics.

Over the past twenty years definitions of normality have tended to cluster around the idealist position which provides for variation through recognition of "complex cultural activity, symbolization, and altruism."[2] It has been stated that behavior is positive or integrative to the extent that it reflects the unique attributes of the human animal. The positively valued traits specified by a variety of authors are cited below:

> Acceptance of self, others, and of nature; spontaneity; the quality of detachment; autonomy; democratic character structure; creativeness; resistance to enculturation; freedom to focus energy on main purposes; ability to work and love with ease and to achieve happiness and efficiency somewhat in proportion to circumstances; self-control; personal responsibility; social responsibility; democratic social interests and ideals; emotional independence and self-reliance; balance between giving and getting; relative freedom from egotism, inferiority feelings and excessive competitiveness; conscience; constructive aggressiveness; solid sense of reality; and flexibility and adaptability.

Believing that such a compendium of traits based upon the particular value system of the individual author illustrates the uselessness of the concept of normality, at least one psychologist, Friedes, opted out. This occasioned an interesting reply from Maurice Korman, who agreed that there was much confusion about normality, but who felt that this should drive us toward a more operational definition which "would have the essential character of a theoretical construct."[3] It is important to note that Korman feels the idea of normality has therapeutic relevance as "a gross predictor of a person's future behavior."

This last matter is not really of small import, for there exists a substantial body of opinion which holds that normality is central to clinical practice, and that one measure by which distinctions can be drawn between normal and pathological is through the comparison of patient and nonpatient groups. This idea, attractive as it seems at the outset, turns out to be a complicated one upon consideration of the range of problems for which various patients come into treatment, as well as the complex set of factors that motivate both patient and therapist in treatment decisions. It is certainly easy to say that the element of suffering is found in all who present themselves, but this thesis hardly stands the test of experience when one considers children, the perversions, character disorders, individuals who want draft deferments, and so on. Moreover, one large segment of child therapy is based upon the prevention of severe psychopathy by judicious intervention at the time of a reactive crisis. To classify all who are helped by brief, situational aid as pathological hardly serves to define the borders.

Even when we look at this problem from the other side of the table, there is scarcely more light. Maybe the best that can be said is that clinicians take patients into treatment when there is some consonance between patient and therapist on expectations. The complexity of this last issue perhaps can be illuminated by Edward Glover's classic work in 1932, which defined normality from the psychoanalytic point of view.[4] This piece was particularly necessary and timely, since psychoanalysis was moving from a concern with unconscious manifestations to a growing interest in ego psychology. Freud made very few references to the ideal psychic state; concern with the institution of normality seems to coincide with the shift described above. Glover maintained that the use of such commonplace terms as "normality" or even "ego strength" required an equal understanding of such terms as "abnormality" and "ego weakness," and stated further that all psychoanalysts make use of working standards of normality that differ widely from their clinical colleagues. His suggestions, still relevant even today, are outlined below:

1) The advent of psychoanalysis made it impossible to exclude a capacity for personal happiness and peace of mind from the professional categories of normality.
2) There can be no adult normality without an infantile psychosis, i.e., "children are not more ignorant or more stupid than adults, but differ in the *way* they think."
3) Adult normality is the end product of child defense.
4) The pleasure-pain principle is seen to be the most primitive measure of normal reaction for the infant; but it cannot become an adult measure until it has undergone that slow

process of modification during childhood which converts
it into the reality principle.

5) In the present state of Western civilization, we have no
grounds for assuming that normality and complete reality
adaptation are identical, and

6) Normality may be a form of "madness" which goes un-
recognized because it happens to be a good adaptation to
reality.

The whole matter is then summed up in Glover's well known
definition of normality: ability to love, ability to work, relative
freedom from mental conflict, and freedom from physical
symptoms. Perhaps it is sentiment, perhaps the nostalgia of
middle age which promotes an attachment to this definition,
but attached to it we are.

Glover's efforts were probably viewed with interest by
Freud, who saw normality as "an ideal fiction." Ernest Jones,
writing at about the same time as Glover, and Kurt Eissler in
1960, both made serious efforts to flesh out the bare psychoanalytic bones, but each leaves much to be desired; Jones because
his concepts are almost impossible from an assessment point
of view, and Eissler because he ties his effort to therapy and
ends up with the conclusion that the healthiest person is the
best candidate for analysis.[5]

Other psychoanalytic precincts have made similar efforts
with mixed results. Melanie Klein speaks out very clearly for
the concept of integration, with love seen as the glue which
unites the unknown with the known parts of the personality.
Erikson postulates mastery of developmental tasks leading to
a mature identity. Kubie speaks for personality flexibility, with
illness depicted as "the freezing behavior." Fromm-Reichmann
spoke of freedom from fear, anxiety, and the entanglements of
greed, envy, and jealousy. Hartmann[6] offers the intriguing
concept of ego autonomy, i.e., the strength of the ego determining the degree of stability and adaptation. Existential analysis is another matter. Apparently substituting the concept of
authenticity for adjustment, such analysis suggests that this
norm is to be approached by lively participation in all human

experience including values, activities, and all other aspects of life.

Perhaps some of the confusion can be eliminated by an examination of the kind of adjustment expected by psychotherapists from patients who have been successfully treated. Surely the clinician has some goals in mind as he assays the progress of his patient. Nunberg's article written in 1954 is most interesting.[7] The author states simply that the experienced analyst is deeply committed to the alteration in ego reaction, a change in character structure which makes cure of symptoms dependable. Nunberg's emphasis is on the balance in economic factors in personality adjustment, and his description of cure as signified by the patient's readiness to work and to love bears close relationship to Glover's ideas. Roger E. Money-Kyrle, writing a few years later, identified self-knowledge as the ideal treatment goal, but concludes that all is relative since complete self-knowledge is never to be attained.[8]

Most therapists do deal in one manner or another with the problem of normality. Such assays most frequently revolve around the matter of optimal gain, but the basis for comparison often involves the contrasting of the patient with other patients, as well as with the therapist's own self-evaluation. This last is of crucial import, for if this assessment depends upon the therapist's judgment, how can we assume that it is reliable? This whole confusing state of affairs—psychotherapists defining standards of normality—requires more than a passing glance. It presumes that a detachment exists in the therapist which must place him close to the summit of Olympus, while in fact the present and past literature abounds in discussions of the perils of counter transference. Moreover, there is more than a little feeling that therapists as a group include some individuals whose normality may be questioned, this in spite of something which approaches a public fetish of overestimation of the therapist's character.

Even if we assume that psychotherapists as a group are normal individuals, it is clear that the range of normality is both elastic and variable and that it must perforce include many idiosyncratic levels of adjustment. Stated simply, all human beings, including those within and without the therapeutic commonwealth, approve of people who apparently hold to the same set of values as themselves and who respond positively to their suggestions. This is certainly true within the more exhortative or active therapies which bear descriptive labels such as suggestion, persuasion, reeducation, rational, or implosive therapies. While it is obviously less true in psychoanalysis where the analyst goes out of his way to avoid any semblance of persuasion or exhortation in his patient relations, all of us who work analytically must continuously struggle to avoid our own biases in the selection of patients, within treatment options, and termination goals. Even here in what we have come to regard as the most detached observational platform of all, a well defined value system obtains. We require certain traits in our patients (the ability to be reflective, to be able to internalize, to free associate, to feel pain). Each requirement, try as we will, places a premium on one particular set of values instead of another. These are the things we encourage patients to do; ergo, these are the things we value. Notably two of the more attractive ideas advanced for treatment goals have little to contribute to the usual academic definitions of normality. They come from far distant vantage points; one from a novel and one from neurology. In the first an analyst commonly supposed to be Freida Fromm-Reichman is quoted as saying to a recalcitrant patient: "I never promised you a rose garden. I never promised you perfect justice . . . and I never promised you peace or happiness. My help is so that you can be free to fight for all of these things."[9] Equally poetic is Kurt Goldsteins' statement about treatment goals which is paraphrased as not freedom from anxiety, not freedom from conflict, not freedom from problems, but a life worth living.

Much more could be said in this regard, but space does not permit. The therapist's ideas about normality are certainly of considerable interest, but here as elsewhere, the elements of self-interest have to be examined carefully. Finally, both therapists and the group with which they have expertise come almost entirely from the middle and upper classes, and observations deriving from this group are likely to have limited relevance to the much larger group who comprise the so-called basement of our society.

One of the things that apparently has changed these days, or perhaps been relegated to the background, particularly with regard to middle class normality, is Freud's idea of genital primacy. Formerly viewed as central to normal development, it is little heard today. Love in the generic sense is part of most current definitions of satisfactory adjustment, but this is hardly what Freud had in mind when he stated in markedly direct fashion that: "Inhibitions in the course of its development (genital primacy) manifest themselves as the various disturbances of sexual life."[10]

References to the issue appeared in profusion in the psychoanalytic literature of the 1920s to the 1940s but have almost disappeared today. What can have happened over the years? Can it be that the ability to relate sexually in an enjoyable and mutually gratifying fashion is out of vogue?

It is interesting to speculate on what this tells us about culture. Admittedly, these discussions were at some variance from Victorian times when the characteristic arrangement was that "existence of a whole universe of sexuality and sexual activity was tacitly acknowledged and actively participated in, while at the same time one's consciousness of all this was, as far as possible, kept apart from one's larger, more general, and public consciousness of both self and society."[11] Writing in 1909, Freud suggested that: "The most striking distinction between the erotic life of antiquity and our own no doubt lies in the fact that the ancients laid the stress upon the instinct itself, whereas we emphasize its object. The ancients glorified the instinct and were prepared on its account to honor even an inferior object; while we despise the instinctual activity in itself, and find excuses for it only in the merits of the object."[12]

Today we are confronted by what is apparently a mirror image, i.e., an emphasis upon the forms of sexual experience becoming a prominent part of our behavioral pattern without any corresponding development of depth. Seen in this light, several dozen casual experiences in youth involve as much emotional investment today as a single major love affair in the past, and most of the current youthful sexual exuberance seems to have a mocking quality.

A recent report made to the American Psychiatric Association contains some additional dispiriting news. Data from an interdisciplinary study conducted by Golden, Mandel, and Glueck find the normal man rather unremarkable.[13] He is described as stable and well adjusted, and unhampered by serious marital discords, job dissatisfactions, or particularly high aspirations. Anticipating the pitfalls which lay ahead, the researchers boldly ask: "Does 'normality' necessarily imply a lack of creativity, imagination and spontaneity?" Their answer is an equally forthright yes.

Disciplines other than psychiatry, psychoanalysis, or psychology approach the problem of normality differently, as might be expected. There has been considerable interest within anthropology, and here the prime names are Ralph Linton and Ruth Benedict. In anthropology the issues relate to approaches which make behavioral assessments relative to the culture in which the act is performed, as well as to the functionalist premise which looks more closely at the total economy of the personality. Irrespective of these matters, the field has stressed the cultural determinants of behavior. Contrariwise, sociology has really expressed very little interest in normality, and with the exception of Robert Merton, who has recently become interested in medical education and Kai Erikson, who comes by psychoanalytic interests in a familial way, concern with normality in the field is dormant.

Lastly, a word needs to be said of the work of Thomas Szasz who, although speaking from a psychiatric and psychoanalytic background, usually attacks stereotypes in both fields. Arguing that mental illness is a myth, Szasz has little more sympathy for its opposite. His particular hobbyhorse is the confusion between medical and legal values, and he finds that ethical values contaminate society's judgment of normality.

We have touched lightly on a large body of knowledge, and our own biases are, of course, apparent in the selection. The reader is referred, however, to the monumental review *Normality* by Offer and Sabshin, published in 1966.[14]

We now want to return to some more contemporary concerns which have come into focus in the past few years. Behavioral theorists represent Western European and American middle class cultures and are largely of Anglo-Saxon background. In an expanded general sense most ideas of normality reflect a view of man deriving from the Judeo-Christian tradition. Thus, painful as it occasionally is, most of us can relate to the exaggerated adolescent rebellion as it expresses itself in efforts to break away from academic models and standards. These movements reflect feelings which we all have experienced, and the crucial differences are in the ways we have chosen to manage such impulses. Similarly, we can react sympathetically to resistance to the Vietnam conflict. Historians remark that World War II was our only popular war, and most of us have struggled at one time or another with related feelings about the uselessness and hopelessness of such resolutions.

The matter of race strife is, however, a very different matter. James Baldwin's quiet voice of yesteryear calling attention to the fact that the black man cannot trust the white man now sound like sweet reason. The events of the last few summers still have stunning impact, and there is little reason to feel sanguine about the immediate future. In the light of these facts, what can we say about normal behavior of ghetto children, of black adults, of the black middle class, of white homeowners in threatened neighborhoods, of Southern policemen, of prosperous restaurant owners, or of any one of several million people whose lives or whose treasured prejudices have been threatened by the recent racial cataclysm? Some fascinating questions can be raised regarding some relatively fixed notions about normal adjustment, and perhaps the passage of time will help us to think constructively about some very puzzling contemporary matters.

We cannot turn away from this issue without a word about

another cultural-economic arena that, although less dramatic than the one referred to above, is nonetheless a persistent source of concern. We here refer to the impact of the Establishment—defined as corporate management—upon concepts of mental health. This group has displayed little real interest in those human beings who have no value as workers and consumers. The unemployed, the unemployable, and the underemployed are often viewed as the slag heaps which follow in the wake of bulldozers uncovering veins of coal in strip mining. The government is expected to care for such excess waste, but corporations often attack welfare programs as socialistic. The recipients of alms are held responsible for their own condition, ADC mothers are judged to be promiscuous, unemployed men are described as shiftless and irresponsible, and youth of welfare families are blamed for crime on the streets.

In a monograph which we edited for this organization entitled *Orthopsychiatry and the Law* numerous articles document the manner in which our society forces members of the other America into psychopathy and anti-social behavior.[15] After judicial proceedings, which usually have a pejorative cast, such individuals are often sentenced to prison and subsequent oblivion.

Thus we have identified three groups at least—adolescents in conflict, blacks, and the poor of any color—whose plights seem to fall so far out of the range of normal adjustment that some new way of perceiving their behavior seems necessary. These are unquestionably a different group from those who bare their souls to paid friends in darkened little rooms in buildings on Park Avenue, Michigan Boulevard, or Roxbury Drive in Beverly Hills. We certainly do not mean to denigrate those single voices which recite a catalog of agonies or a rosary of ancient sorrows to an objective listener. We do, however, wish to suggest that standards of normality which neglect the matter of those who "turn on and tune out," who defecate in the offices of university presidents, who riot, burn, and pillage in our cities, or who have not been employed for several years, as in the case of the male population of Saint Michael, Pennsylvania, tend to overlook a fairly sizable portion of our populace.

Even in regard to the great middle class—traditionally the spawning ground for definitions of normality—all goes not well. At the 1963 meeting of this group we offered the idea that "breakdowns or attenuations of the synthetic function of the ego have increased as a result of difficulty in integrating the growing absurdities and contradictions in modern society," and that "the consequent ego accommodations are normal adjustments to our culture." And finally that "alienation and depersonalization can be seen as expressions of an era in which external forces exert a profound influence on the individual's feelings, orientation, and identity."[16] These mild statements created some havoc at that meeting as well as later in Southern California where some individuals took umbrage at the pessimistic nature of our conclusions. The strength of these reactions made us review our material more carefully, but the final conclusions remain the same.

The seasoned diplomat, George F. Kennan, was recently quoted as saying: "Never has there been an era when the problems of public policy even approached in their complexity those by which our society is confronted today, in this age of technical innovation and the explosion of knowledge. The understanding of these problems is something to which one could well give years of disciplined and restrained study, years of the scholar's detachment, years of readiness to reserve judgment while evidence is being accumulated."[17] There has always been a discrepancy between the stated and practiced values of any given society. Each culture through its institutions consciously and unconsciously makes known the acceptable standards. The gap between stated and practiced values in our culture has incredibly widened, some say beyond any point of synthesis. Various segments of the population have made clear by their behavior that they cannot function in what they call our sick society. Other groups contend with equal intensity that life is better today than ever before. The philosopher Herbert Marcuse refuses to be bought off by optimism. He contends: "The fact that the vast majority accepts this

[American] society does not render it less irrational and less reprehensible. Individuals identify themselves with the existence which is imposed on them and . . . are indoctrinated by the conditions under which they live and think and which they do not transcend."[18]

Perhaps the time has arrived to define the standards basic for mental health in modern society. Such standards and values are not absolutes but are intended to help a given culture survive in a healthy fashion. As health professionals we must accept the responsibility for defining social values which are fundamental to emotional health. From a variety of sources we offer some related, very generalized ideas. Someone has suggested that a healthy society is one which accepts and extends affection, concern, and love to all its members, values people above objects, and refuses to accept a class and caste system of have and have-nots. Another authority suggests such values as the rediscovery of a coherent view of life, the achievement of intellectual and effective communication between people and groups of people, and the encouragement of voluntary action, both alongside and within public administration.

Our own views begin and currently end with some reasonable consonance between the taught values of childhood and the actual values of adult life. Our list can go on and on, for never has it been more necessary to find a philosophy suitable for conditions in our wildly changing world. M. V. C. Jeffreys, the English educator, asks: "Shall we be able to rise to the challenge of our times and will the true nature of man prevail? Or shall we fall victims of the civilization we have made and of our own fear of freedom? That is a question which can be answered only in action. Only history can answer it—and history as yet unmade at that. But the kind of history that we make will be influenced by our understanding of the questions that cry for an answer.[19] If the *bouillabaisse* offered above has proven confusing to the reader, it is no more than we expected. One last task, however, remains. We would like to speculate, at least a little, about what might constitute normative patterns of behavior in our country today. Along with most of life, mental health assessment must operate stereoscopically. One lens should focus upon the individual in a crudely diagnostic sense, with checkpoints involving temperament, intelligence, reaction to frustration, and so on. The other lens should focus upon the milieu and evaluate such analogous criteria as economic or educational opportunities, emotional climate, and opportunity for expression of feelings. Those who can effect some comfortable accommodation between the two forces, or who can work constructively to change the balance, can probably be considered to be in good health.

From the material cited earlier our model is likely to be a very different figure from those of preceding eras, for role functions change today at a dizzying pace. Writing in 1963, Roy Grinker related mental health to individual flexibility, and suggested that it was necessary in the contemporary world to adapt to many different environments almost simultaneously. We refer to an editorial appearing in *The New York Times* on December 27, 1967. This was one week after President Johnson visited Vietnam, the Pope, commanders in the Pacific and troops in California, and attended the funeral of the Australian prime minister.

> Thus he indicates to the American generals in South Vietnam that he rejects compromise and shares their conviction that military victory is possible. Then he flies to Rome to protest to the Pope that he is ready to lay aside military means and seek peace by negotiation—which, by definition, implies compromise. Do the military urge increased bombing of North Vietnam, as they did last summer over the opposition of Secretary McNamara? Then there is verbal support for Mr. McNamara, but within weeks the bombers strike at many of the targets the Defense Secretary has opposed. Does the Pope urge a halt in the bombing? Mr. Johnson is ready. All he asks is that Hanoi make a reciprocal gesture in advance, a condition that, however reasonable it may sound, is not likely to be fulfilled.

Surely here is a picture of the man who made ready changes, who accommodated to differing expectations, and who stayed on top of complexities which stagger the mind of more contemplative types. He has not been in psychiatric treatment and has overcome a physical handicap (a severe coronary) which has turned some heroes toward timidity. He was not confused by contradictions, scarcely paying heed to anything other than the central issue of the time as he saw it, the spread of Communism. In physical appearance he sometimes resembles a Wall Street banker, sometimes a Perdenales River gambler, sometimes a hardheaded politician determined to get his way. Despite the carping of some critics whose defects he sarcastically exposes in broad strokes, he continued to forge ahead with his master plan for the Great Society and for world peace. His solemn reassurances were to be heard on all sides, and, truly the medium here *is* the message.

Although he protested the impossibility of his job, its hours, its terrible responsibilities, its lack of personal satisfaction, and its loneliness, the captain stood ready until late in his term to continue at the helm for another voyage, for his is the long view of the horizon. Undeflected by small riptides of large storms, and obliged to be all things to all people, he succeeded very well indeed, and only the occasional news analyst, historian, or political rival professed to see uneasiness behind the mask. Although a credibility gap was known to exist, (and his personal popularity was reported to be falling), his views and acts received support from strong men, and despite a late winter thaw, there was a majority who believed that he would be invincible in the fall election. His very deficiencies force a grudging admiration upon many, and history may well record that Lyndon B. Johnson was the man for all seasons in the second fifty years of the twentieth century.

And so we finally come to the end. We frankly admit we have raised more questions than we settled, that in fact we have written an "imposition" paper rather than a position paper.

The submission of these thoughts to the program committee brought an interesting query from someone with a bright idea to possible publicity. His question was: "Are you fellows serious about Lyndon Johnson?" This brings to mind the joke in which one man asks another: "How's your wife?" The second man asks: "Compared to whom?"

Do we really regard Lyndon Johnson as the man for all seasons? The answer is the same: "Compared to whom?" For this is the real issue which must be resolved, is it not? Normal compared to whom?

NOTES

1. *The New York Review of Books,* October 6, 1966, pp. 12-15.
2. D. Friedes, "Toward the Elimination of the Concept of Normality," *Journal of Consulting Psychology,* 24:128-33 (1960).
3. "The Concept of Normality," *JCP,* 25:267-69 (1961).
4. *Medico-psychological Aspects of Normality, On the Early Development of Mind* (New York: International Press, 1956).
5. Jones, Ernest, "The Concept of the Normal Mind," *Our Neurotic Age,* ed. S. D. Schmalhausen, (New York: Farrar and Rinehart, 1931), pp. 65-81; Kurt R. Eissler, "The Efficient Soldier," *The Pschoanalytic Study of Society,* ed. Warner Muensterburger and Sidney Axelrod (New York: International Universities Press, 1960).
6. Melanie Klein, "On Mental Health," *British Journal of Medical Psychology,* 33:237-41 (1960); Erik H. Erickson, "The Problem of Ego Identity," *Journal of American Psychoanalytic Association,* 4:56-121 (1956); Lawrence S. Kubie, "The Distortion of the Symbolic Process in Neurosis and Psychosis," *JAPA,* 2:739-48 (1954); Frieda Fromm-Reichman, "Remarks on the Philosophy of Mental Disorder," *Psychiatry, 19*: 293 (1946); Heinz Hartmann, "Towards a Concept of Mental Health," *BJMP, 33*:243-48 (1960).
7. Herman Nunberg, "Evaluation of the Results of Psychoanalytic Treatment," *Readings in Psychoanalytic Psychology,* ed. Morton Levitt (New York: Appleton-Century-Crofts, 1959), 311-20.
8. "Psychoanalysis and Ethics," *New Directions in Psychoanalysis,* ed. Melanie Klein *et al.* (New York: Basic Books, 1957).
9. Hannah Green, *I Never Promised You a Rose Garden* (New York: New American Library, 1964), 106.
10. Sigmund Freud, *An Outline of Psychoanalysis, 30-33* (New York: Norton, 1949).
11. Steven Marcus, *The Other Victorians: A Study of Sexuality and Pornography in Mid-Nineteenth-Century England* (New York: Basic Books, 1966).
12. Freud.
13. Emma Harrison, "Normal Man Sits for His Portrait," *The New York Times,* May 12, 1961, pp. 53-55.

14. Melvin Sabshin and Daniel Offer, *Normality* (New York: Basic Books, 1966).

15. Morton Levitt and Ben Rubenstein, eds., *Orthopsychiatry and the Law* (Detroit: Wayne State University Press, 1968).

16. Morton Levitt and Ben Rubenstein, "Some Observations on the Relationship Between Cultural Variants and Emotional Disorders," *American Journal of Orthopsychiatry, 34*(3):423-535.

17. "Rebels Without a Program," *The New York Times Magazine*, Jan. 21, 1968, pp. 22-23, 60, 69-71.

18. Marshall Edelson, "A Dynamic Formulation of Childhood Schizophrenia," *Diseases of the Nervous System, 27*:612-15 (1966).

19. Eugene Talbot and Stuart C. Miller, "The Struggle to Create a Sane Society in the Psychiatric Hospital," *Psychiatry: Journal for the Study of Interpersonal Processes, 29*:165-71 (May 1966).

What Goal for Therapy: normality or the apprehension of reality?

JAMES T. TEDESCHI

As I look out upon the areas of psychiatry and clinical psychology I see an argument about what criteria should be used to establish that an individual is mentally ill or abnormal. My viewpoint as a clinical outsider is as social psychologist, and when it comes to an argument, I prefer to have scientific criteria for whatever position I adopt.

The statistical definitions, the competence or mastery model, the contented-cow approach, the disease entity medical analogy, biochemical reductionism, and the social learning model are being reexamined. When each model is examined carefully, we find that each requires an acceptance of some value theory as a prolegomena to a definition of normality. Thus at the very starting point, problem identification, and at the endpoint, therapeutic goals, the field of science is left for the murky depths of ethical philosophy and metaphysics. I will argue that therapists should attempt to minimize value assumptions insofar as possible and adopt scientific criteria and goals.

The statistical definition of normality assumes some measure of central tendency for a behavior in a population as the standard; deviations are considered abnormal. The problem with this definition is that clinical practitioners must discriminate between those deviations which are considered good and those which are considered bad. Also, it is necessary to identify precisely the degree of deviation that will be said to be abnormal—for instance, a cutoff point of minus 1.67 standard deviations. Statistical criteria for defining normality obviously are laden with value judgments.

The competence model, sometimes referred to as the mastery model, assumes that individuals have internal needs that can be satisfied by "successfully" adjusting to or manipulating the environment. Some forms of the model assume genetically-based potentialities which can somehow be encouraged to develop so that the individual can master his own destiny. It is clear to me that practitioners do not have scientific criteria and consequently do not agree on which copings are good and which are bad; nor can they agree about the determination of the criteria for judging whether a genetic potentiality has been fulfilled—people have the potential to kill and lie as well as to love and tell the truth. The competence model therefore requires extrascientific value criteria for determining good adjustment or good actualizing.

The so-called contented-cow approach to defining normality suggests that the individual makes his own judgments about his mental health. If the individual's subjective report is that he is contented and happy, then he should be considered normal. However, if the patients' introspective report is used as a criterion, we are left with the ideals of conformity, comfort, and the absence of stress just at a time in the history of social science when stress is assumed as a normal part of life and the generator of creativity. Thus, the contented-cow approach does not get us away from the need for a value theory from which the criteria for normal conduct are derived.

Some practitioners attempt to escape the problem of values by adopting some version of a medical analogy. One version, which has been called the disease entity approach, pieces to-

gether bits of behavior called symptoms into categories of
illnesses. This approach has practical problems related to the
fact that the categories established lack homogeneity, reli-
ability, and validity. In any case, in the identification of symptoms in the disease entity, medical analogy uses criteria
adopted from some other model, since identifying symptoms
require that a bit of behavior be in some fashion considered
different or unusual. By reverting to other models for its
criteria, the disease entity approach is confronted with the
need for some theory of ethics as a basis for defining normality.

The biochemical medical model is frankly reductionistic
and assumes that reduction to smaller and smaller units located within the organism will necessarily improve prediction.
This model further implies that as we move from molar to
molecular we get closer to the "true" causes of behavior.
Many criticisms have been made of the biochemical reduc-
tionist which are not relevant to the topic of discussion here.
Asking the physiologist to handle such predictive problems as
the causes of racial discrimination and prejudice is about as
reasonable as asking a social psychologist to predict refractory
periods of neurons from knowledge of social attitudes. In any
case practitioners who use the biochemical model must first
look at the molar behavior and define it as normal or abnormal
before breaking it down into the molecular units of biochem-
istry. In order to make the molar discrimination between normal and abnormal, people who utilize the biochemical model
accept some other model's criteria. As a consequence, they
must adopt the value criteria associated with those other
models.

The social learning model sees human culture in its simplest
terms as reducible to broad prescriptions and proscriptions.
Reduced to its fundamentals, human culture tells us what we
shall want and how we should go about getting it. Implicit
in each prescription is the negative proscription—what we
should not want and how we should not proceed. Problems of
pathology are viewed as arising out of the personality-situa-

tion context. A technical mapping is made of the prescriptions and proscriptions of the culture or subculture, and then those who violate the rules are considered to be abnormal. Therapy consists of assisting the offender achieve conformity within the existing society. The therapeutic goal accepts an extreme cultural relativism; whatever exists is accepted as valid. Unfortunately, it is well known that the actual rules of a society are never very precise, always admit of exceptions, and may come into conflict with each other. Furthermore, the prevailing rules are typically conservative, not affirmative or constructive or creative. Both insiders and outsiders can evaluate the rules of any particular society as bad, immoral, or wrong. The social learning model then also relies on value theory for its criteria for normality.

Value judgments are nonscientific in nature in that there is no experimental way of ascertaining their truth value; they are judgments made on a good-bad dimension. There is no way to escape value judgments, but there may be ways to minimize their nondeliberate influence on both the methods and goals of therapy. The clinical practitioner can escape choosing an ethical theory and involving himself in the complex and technical problems associated with such a choice and maximize the scientific criteria he uses.

Developing veridical or true concepts that reflect reality is a scientific goal relatively free of value judgments. The perception of physical reality is said to be veridical or accurate when verbal reports from the person correlate with the controlled observations and theories of natural scientists. If a stick in water is perceived as bent, a perceptual illusion occurs, because the physics of refractory light plus geometrical measurements tell us that the stick is straight. Similarly, the apprehension of social reality must be compared with the best theories and evidence in social science. If there are competing theories of reality available from equally competent assessments, then we must live with the uncertainty, holding on to our conceptions most tentatively.

The clinical practitioner in my view must be a generalist in

the area of social science and should take as his major therapeutic goal the development in the patient of true concepts of
reality. There is an implied criticism of present training programs associated with this goal, since they more narrowly train
practitioners in the medical school tradition. I should point out
that multidisciplinary aspects adhere to most applied sciences.
For example, in medicine, the physician draws upon everything from physics to entymology and psychology. Similarly,
the psychiatrist and clinical psychologist should be familiar
with the basic concepts and theories of sociology, economics,
political science, theology, philosophy, and social psychology.
Otherwise, the practitioners, whom I conceive of more as
teachers than as doctors, are in no position to help patients develop veridical conceptions of reality.

Therapists are gatekeepers of information about the nature
of reality, much as are newspaper reporters, television com-
mentators, or school teachers. A patient who believes that he
is Napoleon has a faulty notion about the nature of reality. He
must learn enough about history so that his biographical time-
space identifications can match up with historical analysis. An
hysteric patient has false notions about the functions of his
body. A person with a phobia has an unrealistic fear. A psychotic has difficulty distinguishing his inner realities from external realities. In each of these cases the goal of therapy
should be to bring the patient to recognize the true nature of
reality. The therapeutic goal has a true-false scientific dimension rather than a good-bad value dimension. Sometimes, as
Robert Lindner has pointed out, the patient is so convincing
about his version of reality that he reshapes the therapist's phenomenological world.

Teachers have many techniques of transmitting information.
Presumably the therapist is capable of using any or all techniques of helping his patient to achieve veridical perceptions
of physical and social reality. Insight therapy and behavioral
therapy use different techniques, but I think they share the
same goal. Which techniques should be used can be judged by
the pragmatic criterion of which best serves the particular

need. Thus, if a patient has a functionally paralyzed arm and if behavior therapy teaches the person that he can use that arm, then that would be the best technique to use to instruct that patient about the reality of his bodily functioning. If a person lacks purpose or finds life meaningless and insight therapy allows him to develop a more profound grasp of the universe, then that would be the best tactic to employ. In this manner the split between insight and behavior therapies would be bound into a single objective and would be seen to buttress and support one another.

Scientists well understand that emotional biases and special interests interfere with objective judgments about the nature of reality. They take elaborate precautions to compensate for such biases through careful design of experiments, precise measurements, sampling techniques, and other methodological factors. Great teachers often reveal their values openly so that students know what kinds of filters information about reality pass through. The teacher's biases can then be discounted or compensated for. Similarly, clinical practitioners should express their values freely in the therapeutic interview. After all, the therapist's values are part of the social reality of the immediate situation. This is not to say that the therapist should impose his values; only that their existence and nature be revealed in the general process of exploring reality.

The therapist and patient should concentrate on the existing phenomenological world of the patient. Unlike his education colleague, the therapist is restricted to correcting what exists; the teacher tries to construct what as yet does not exist. Both inevitably get into the other's business. The internal states of the patient are also more the concern of the therapist than of the educator. Questions related to the norms and rules of society, the pathways and manipulanda of the physical and social environments, contingencies which relate rewards and punishments to behaviors, the question of how values are connected to actions and the causal structure of the environment, are scientific in nature. Such scientific questions require scientific answers in the form of evidence and theoretical explanation.

Perhaps there is a role for the inculcator of values in society. Certainly indoctrination is carried out in our schools and churches. Correctional institutions and rehabilitation centers often attempt to reshape the value systems of their inmates. But let us be frank about it: This kind of brainwashing is more subtle than that used in Orwell's *1984*, but it carries us very far from the therapeutic goal I am advocating. If the legal or political structure of society requires such inculcation, a new profession could be developed to handle the job. New professionals would be as different from current clinical practitioners in their goals as are advertisers from Madison Avenue.

An explicit goal for therapy would be present-day reality as an implied criterion for concepts of normality. A legitimate question arises as to what value leads me to say that the veridical apprehension of reality by the patient should be the goal of psychotherapy. My answer lies at the very basis of all value theory. Values are made by and for men. If the human species should become extinct, then all values would disappear from the earth. Thus the supreme value of men is that their species survive. If the assumption is made that veridical perception of reality is prerequisite to survival, then it follows that veridical perception should be diligently pursued.

Present-day reality does present the human species with survival problems of great magnitude. Sometimes the person who is caught up with such problems is considered a deviant individual in society, going so far at times as to engage in civil disobedience and other disorderly or unlawful conduct. If that person's construction of reality is veridical with the best that present-day science can give to us, then he must be considered more normal than someone who has a more parochial version of reality or a distorted conception of it.

Clearly the reality criterion of normality is not without its value judgment. But the species survival criterion of normality is a grossly general value commitment which could fit any particular ethical or value theory. Furthermore, all value theories require that an individual who makes value judgments claim a consensus for his view, but there is no requirement that the individual bow to the judgment of the majority. The individual does not claim an actual consensus, but only that on Judgment Day his position will be concurred in by those who freely and clearheadedly review the relevant facts from a moral point of view. The individual must be autonomous in order to judge for himself; he may be mistaken, but like Luther, he cannot do otherwise. What I am suggesting is that we take as our criterion of normality the factor that allows an individual to choose most freely his value system. He must be free, informed, clearheaded, impartial, and willing to universalize. If others disagree with his judgment, he must reconsider, but if he is openminded and tolerant and disagreement persists, he must claim to be right. A person whose phenomenological space is incongruous with reality could not be informed; would be unable, even if willing, to universalize; would have limited freedom because freedom requires knowledge of alternative ends and means; and, consequently, could not be impartial. Thus psychotherapy could serve as a prolog to an individual's selection of values, but it would not determine them. The clinical practitioner would be a social scientist and not a social engineer.

Man and Society: the inauthentic condition

AMITAI ETZIONI

Sociologists and social psychologists hold the concept of basic human needs in low regard. Alex Inkeles, in reviewing the field, has said:

> Man's *original nature* is seen largely in neutral terms, as neither good nor bad. It is rather, a potential for development, and the extent to which the potential is realized depends on the time and society into which a man is born and on his distinctive place in it. If it does not quite treat him as a "tabula rasa," modern sociology nevertheless, regards man as a flexible form which can be given all manner of content. Socialization, the process of learning one's culture while growing out of infant and childhood dependency, leads to internalization of society's values and goals. People come to want to do what from the point of society they must do. Man is, therefore, seen, in his inner being, as mainly moral, by and large accepting and fulfilling the demands society makes on him.[1]

Albert K. Cohen stated: "Nobody has ever been able to formulate an inventory of original or unsocialized tendencies that has commanded more than scattered and temporary agreement. In the second place, the very meaning of "original human nature," in any other sense than a range of possibilities, each of them dependent upon specific experiences for its development or maturation, has always proved exceedingly elusive and obscure."[2] This is not to suggest that the disciplines do not recognize the existence of tensions between social roles (modes of conduct which are socially prescribed and reinforced) and personal needs or preferences. But the discrepancies between a person's inclination and that which is socially expected are accounted for by imperfect socialization, inadequate social control, or conflicting social demands—all social factors. True, the sociologists and social psychologists will concede, we do encounter what seems like a conflict between a person's private self and his public self (or between a person and his fellow men), but since the private self is shaped by previous socializations, this conflict really amounts to a clash between the social past and the present. One cannot even retreat, grant that private selves are socialized and that all that is socialized is by definition a social product, and suggest that unsocialized elements in the infant's conduct are indicative of basic human needs. This is because sociologists and social psychologists will be quick to point out that unsocialized conduct is animal-like (illustrated by studies of children adopted by a wolf or left in attics) or like a free-floating libido, which has no shape of its own. The human element, they stress, is socially provided, and the animal needs—the physiological requirements for nourishment, liquids, and slumber—can be provided for in such a wide variety of socially approved ways that they set only very lax limits on that which is socially feasible. This is where the collective wisdom of mainstreams of modern sociology and much of social psychology stand; the concept of basic human needs cannot be used to account for tensions between specific attributes of private and public selves.

The counter arguments—and we are dealing with debates among schools rather than with findings of critical experiments—advance the proposition that human nature is significantly less malleable than these disciplines tend to assume, that unsocialized beings have specific needs. When social arrangements run counter to these needs, human beings can be made to adapt to them, but the fact that adaptations had to be made can be learned from the level of personal costs inflicted, such as mental disorganization and psychosomatic illness. Modern industrial society is often depicted as such a frustrating structure, one which causes various kinds of neurosis, interpersonal violence, and craving for charismatic leadership. Excessively instrumental (or cold), it is said to provide only inadequate opportunities for expressive (or warm) relations.

A second set of costs is social rather than personal. It manifests itself, we suggest, in that efforts which must be spent to socialize man into roles or cultures which are unresponsive to basic human needs are much greater than those needed to socialize men into more responsive roles. The same holds with regard to the costs of social control, those expenditures required to keep man in frustrating roles and to prevent them from being altered are higher than those which would be required to keep man in less frustrating roles. It seems more costly to educate a man to be a good bureaucrat (for instance, one who disregards family, friendship, and political bonds and allows his decisions and acts to be governed by abstract and universalistic criteria) than to be a public servant who follows the opposite rules. That is, we suggest that it is more natural to be particularistic.[3] The same difference is expected to be found between roles which require substantial deferment of gratification, and those that allow more frequent gratification, even if there is no difference in the sum total of rewards.

Evidence that some social roles and cultural patterns are less natural as compared to some others may be gleaned from cross-cultural comparative studies, which show that certain modes of required conduct generate frustration in many types of societies, suggesting that such conduct violates a universal set of human needs. The frustration found could not be caused by a specific socialization, cultural pattern or institutional structure of any one society, for these vary greatly among the societies compared. Austerity, for instance, is found objectionable (and generates pressure to overcome it) in as different situations as the U.S.S.R. a decade after the revolution, contemporary Israeli kibbutzim, and Catholic orders a generation after their founding.

The implications for critical view and social research of these two divergent views of the malleability of human nature are extensive. By the first view persons who do not accept the social prescriptions are deviants. Even when no moral connotations are attached to the term, attention focuses on the factors which generated the deviance and the ways these factors can be altered to engender conformity to social prescriptions. In contrast, the second view implies that a society is the deviant if it sets prescriptions which are contrary to human nature. According to this view, society ought to be altered to make it more responsive to man.

While this debate is often viewed as one between the integration school (of which G. H. Mead and Talcott Parsons are main proponents) and the conflict or alienation school (whose representatives are numerous), scholars of the Marxist branch of the conflict school tend to reject human nature conceptions even more resolutely than those of the integration school. The reason is that they see the concept of a universal set of basic human needs as ahistorical. Conflicts, the Marxist writers stress, are determined by technological and economic relations which have grown apart from other social relations in the process of history. They are not the results of personality variables. Actually the notion of basic human needs and of historical processes can be reconciled quite readily. Human needs, such as that for regular and frequent affection and recognition, may be universal, while the social conditions, which determined the degree to which they are satisfied, may be historically shaped.

If we ask the extent of responsiveness of society in the present historical stage, and limit our answer to Western societies, we find the suggestion of a rather central transformation from past stages. This is the transformation from scarcity and the alienation generated by instrumentality toward rising inauthenticity of affluence and pseudo-expressive relations. Before the trend can be explored, we should note the place of participation in our conceptual scheme. Of the many definitions of alienation the following seems the most essential: a social condition is alienating if it is unresponsive to the basic needs of men in that condition; if it is beyond their understanding and control. The question arises as to how a responsive social structure may be generated. How are the members' needs and preferences to be related to societal forms? The answer seems to us to lie in the members' participation in shaping and reshaping these forms. Maximal societal responsiveness will be attained under the utopian condition in which all the members participate in the shaping of all aspects of their societal life. Even this condition would be expected to encounter some alienation (which Marcuse refers to as irreducible),[4] resulting from the fact that not all members' needs are mutually complementary, and hence the compromises inevitably worked out leave each less than fully satisfied. Participation, however, provides the most effective way to reach such compromise; any other procedure, for instance, a wise and openminded monarch taking his country's needs into account, would be expected to leave a greater residue of alienation than broadly based participation. This is because under such a system, upward communication of members' needs would be both more accurate and more powerful as compared to any other system. While maximal participation is utopian, we may compare social systems in terms of the extent to which they are participatory, and expect that the more participatory will also be the less alienating.

This brings us to the historical stage and situation in which we find ourselves. In contrast to previous ages of scarcity the contemporary period has been characterized as one of abundance for industrialized societies (at least for the private sector and the upper two-thirds of the members). The lower the level of scarcity, the lower the extent of irreducible alienation. More basic needs of members can be satisfied without necessarily depriving anyone.

When a society lives close to the subsistence level, existing allocative patterns often entail the deprivation of the most basic human needs to some categories of members—baby girls or minorities, for instance. Here reallocation aimed at improving the lot of these members may entail inflicting such deprivation on some other segment of the membership. In the age of affluence, reallocation is aimed at creating a society which satisfies the basic needs of all members and which does not inflict deprivation of basic needs on any member; it can draw on slack. That is, rather than redistribute the burden of societal alienation, the total level can be reduced. Moreover, not only can material needs be more widely satisfied, but also more time and energy can be freed for expressive pursuits. For example, all other things being equal, the mother who need not labor to add to the family's income will find it easier to provide affection for both her husband *and* her children, reducing the rivalry between them over this ever scarce "commodity." In this period of affluence the role of participation becomes more crucial; if alienation is not reduced here, this can be attributed more to exclusion and unresponsiveness than to objective inability to respond, as compared to much less affluent earlier periods or other societies.

The difference between our own and earlier societies, it may be argued, is much smaller than we suggest, because scarcity is a state of mind as well as of the economy. For a suburban matron inability to acquire a new fur coat, when all her friends acquire one, may be as frustrating as a Burmese village matron's inability to fill her rice bowl. But, even if there are no "real" (physiological) differences, and if the status race has no level of satiation, the basic reason that the suburban matron is caught in a status race is lack of authentic expressive relations, while the sources of hunger in the Burmese village are at least in part economic and technological. The suburban scarcity can be treated to a large extent by providing for authentic participation; the hunger in Burma can be so treated only to a very limited degree.

The resistance to making affluent societies more responsive, to reallocating resources and to opening the society to extensive participation, has both real and symbolic sources. In part the resistance draws on existing privileged power and economic positions which would be undermined in such a societal change. And while there is on the one hand an increase among the deprived collectivities in societal consciousness and in the capacity to act politically as a result of mass education and communication, there is also in contemporary industrialized society an increasing capacity of those in power to manipulate. The communication revolution and the growing utility of social science, especially market and voting research, have aided these developments. Aside from sustaining the existing pattern of privileges and restricted participation, mass manipulation is said to provide for the unloading of the ever increasing produce the affluent economy manufactures. The ultimate manipulation, about which some empirical evidence is cited below, is the sustaining of the legitimacy of a system that is unresponsive to the basic needs of its members, in that it offers a sense of participation—and, more broadly, of responsiveness—where there is only a pittance.

In pursuing the idea of alienation with the eyes of a sociologist, our attention focuses first on the array of societal institutions. In earlier writings on unresponsiveness, attention usually focused on work and economic institutions as the sources of alienation. But in seeking to understand the affluent age, the emphasis should be on the main source of inauthentic participation, the politics of pluralistic democratic societies. On the face of it, the structure of the government interests and the values of all members assure authentic democracy. It is asserted that these interests and values can find their way into the political give-and-take, out of which consensus policies and acceptable structures emerge. Such claims tend to minimize or view as temporary the unresponsiveness of the political system to those significant segments of the population which have no effective vote, the role played by the mass media and the elites in producing endorsement of unresponsive policies (policies which are against the interests of the members and which they would reject if they were better informed and less tranquilized), and the fact that the political alternatives among which choice is offered constitute a narrow range which excludes many options—especially for fundamental changes leading to increased responsiveness on the total society level. The 1964 choice between the Vietnam policy that Senator Goldwater advocated and the rather similar one that President Johnson followed up to the election (let alone after it) is a case in point.

Pluralism by itself, without substantial equality in power among the political contenders, does not provide for a responsive political system. Groups of citizens (such as classes or ethnic groups) have a say in accordance with their assets, power, and above all, the extent of their organization for political action, such as lobbying and campaigning. As these resources are unevenly distributed among groups of citizens, the consensus produced is about as responsive to the needs of the weaker members as an agreement between an international oil company and a streetcorner gasoline pump owner. Pluralism works not mainly via elections, but via private and public interest groups.[5] New administrative policies and major pieces of legislation are "cleared" with the relevant groups, for example, labor and management, the church and civic associations. In the process those interests which are not organized (and part of their deprivation is their relative lack of the educational background and experience which organization requires) are neglected. Farmhands, excluded from minimum wage legislation in the United States, are a typical case.

Inauthenticity occurs in other institutional areas. Studies of education show that stress is placed on a uniform personality format, the "rounded personality" capable of the smooth handling of others. This format first does not provide for expression of the variety of personality needs young men exhibit and second promotes relations among men which are devoid of deep affection and adequate releases.[6] Studies of suburbia have shown the pseudo quality of the gemeinschaft generated. Here, reports state, the instrumental orientation penetrates even the relation between mother and child, the mother using the child to score points in a status race, disregarding the child's deeper needs (to get dirty sometimes), and failing to provide authentic unconditional affection.[7] Studies of human relations training programs for management reveal programs aimed at teaching supervisory personnel to provide underlings with a sense of participation in the industrial decision making without real sharing of power or interest in responsiveness,[8] and of labor unions which are so committed to industrial peace and cooperation that they serve much more as a mechanism of downward control ("part of the labor relations department of the plant"), than of upward representation of workers' needs.[9]

Inauthenticity in one area sustains that in others. "Rounded" education prepares for pseudo participation in the realm of work (with "don't rock the boat" as the prime tenet). Consumer races provide an outlet for an avalanche of products which answer no authentic need, but produce the demand to work, even at alienating conditions, in order to obtain them. Inauthentic politics close the circle by not providing an opportunity to mobilize for fundamentally different systems, and the mass culture provides escapes which drain protest and which in turn serve to conceal the flatness[10] of the mass society consumption-and-work world.

The total effect is a society which is not committing, to which members are not cathected, one which provides no effective channels for expression of frustrations, grievances, and needs. Hence the rise of demonstration democracy, as men take to the streets to express, release, or communicate feelings upward; the rise in wildcat strikes, as labor unions become part of the managerial structure;[11] the rise in middle class dropouts among students; and the rise in the number of demonstrators and the increasingly "respectable" kinds of social groups which take to the streets (teachers, social workers, and at least in one case, doctors—who demonstrated in New York City against unsafe automobiles.) More deeply, the high rate of alcoholism, neuroses, divorce, addiction, and other such symptoms seem traceable in part to the noncommitting social world. The best evidence that lack of involvement is a major factor in causing these personal costs and societal problems is that when social life becomes more committing—as with members of a social movement—there is a sharp decline in the symptoms.[12] It seems that not only are members of such movements less likely to be alcoholics, have fewer breakdowns and such when compared to less involved citizens of similar class, ethnic, and educational background, but also that the same persons—for instance, Malcolm X—experience a sharp decline in particular symptoms and/or asocial behavior when they are authentically activated.[13] In final analysis even the members of a social movement are, of course, not free of their society, and only a society which would become more active, less inauthentic, could expect to overcome these problems on a broader base.

Shifting from a sociological focus to a psychological one, we find that the difference between alienation and authentic involvement seems to lie primarily in the difference between having a clear and external target for aggression and keeping aggression at least partially bottled up inside. The purely alienated person—barred from voting, joining a labor union, or attending a university—may feel shut out, as if facing a heavy locked door in a passage he seeks to travel. He can, with relative ease, identify an enemy and release part of his frustration by anger and even physical violence against the bosses, the Establishment, and so forth. The inauthentically involved person can vote, organize, join; but all of this does not make the system more responsive to his needs. It is like being caught in an invisible net. He is often unable to identify the sources of his frustrations. He frequently has a sense of guilt, because had he not played along, he could not have sustained the system and he would not have ended up being manipulated. His resentment against being caught is in part a resentment against himself for allowing himself to be taken.

Rejection, which lies at the root of both conditions, is much more impersonal and hence less psychologically damaging in the pure alienating situation than in the inauthentic one. Jews, usually excluded during the Middle Ages from the political and economic power centers of society, could make a comparatively healthy psychological adjustment by focusing their identity on the in-group and limiting their expressive ties to other Jews. But with emancipation, as Jews were allowed, for instance, to study at German universities, they lowered their defenses and moved emotionally closer to non-Jews. When rejection came here, it was often more damaging to self-identity and emotional security.[14] Similar experiences now affect educated Negroes in the United States. More technically, pure alienation may be said to exist when the social distance scale is great and encompasses all the major expressive relations; authentic relations reduce the scale to a minimum; inauthentic ones stand midway on the scale and are uneven, allowing for closer relations in some expressive areas and less in others, a particularly strained imbalance. We need to find out much more about the differences in the psychological problems and dynamics of persons who live in the two kinds of social conditions. Are there differences in psychosomatic illness, for instance? Do alienated persons have more speech defects, while inauthentic ones have more asthma and ulcers?

In conclusion, I offer a brief note on the conditions under which alienation and inauthenticity may be reduced. In part these are structural conditions as, for instance, those under which a more equal distribution of political power among the members of society can be brought about. These, in turn, are prerequisite of more widely distributed opportunity for participation and thus for a more broadly based responsiveness. Here the central question is: does not the very structure of inequality which generated excluded and underprivileged groups also prevent their effective mobilization for societal change which such a redistribution of power would constitute? The answer, which cannot be spelled out here, seems to be that while the existing structure does make it more difficult for some groups to mobilize themselves, if only because of differential access to education, other factors prevent control from being watertight. The spread of education (which the economy's needs foster) and the unbalanced upward mobility of those groups which did gain admittance (for example, the Jews in the United States) are among the factors.[15]

76   *The Mental Health Field*

In addition, there are psychological factors. The fear to challenge the existing social structure or its rhetoric, for example, has some roots in the reality of experiences in earlier periods or even present ones (for instance, where political activity on the side of change causes loss of one's job, land, or life as in parts of the South); but it may also be grossly magnified because of internal weakness or absence of a tradition of collective action.[16]

Attempts by those who share similar fears, underprivileged statuses, *and* the social sources of alienation to confront their difficulties serve first to reduce the inauthenticity by more clearly marking the true opportunities for participation and by pointing out the false ones. They then serve to make the system less alienating by promoting some reallocation of resources and power, which in turn makes society somewhat more participatory and responsive. Whether this leads to a continual reformation of society until it gradually becomes highly responsive or leads to full-fledged confrontation between the rising collectivities and those who see their interest in preserving the status quo, is too early to answer. In either case, should mobilization of the uninvolved lead to a gradual transformation or showdown, inauthenticity—the mark of the affluent society—will be much reduced.

NOTES

1. *What is Sociology?* (Englewood Cliffs: Prentice-Hall, 1964), p. 50.
2. *Deviance and Control* (Englewood Cliffs: Prentice-Hall, 1966), p. 60.
3. Talcott Parsons, *The Social System* (New York: Free Press, 1951).
4. Herbert Marcuse, *Eros and Civilization* (Boston: Beacon Press, 1955).
5. Grant McConnell, *Private Power and American Democracy* (New York: Knopf, 1966).
6. Edgar Z. Friedenberg, *Coming of Age in America* (New York: Random House, 1965).
7. John R. Seeley, *Crestwood Heights* (New York: Basic Books, 1956).
8. Reinhard Bendix and Lloyd Fisher, "The Perspectives of Elton Mayo," in *Complex Organizations*, ed. Amitai Etzioni (New York: Holt, Reinhart, and Winston, 1961), pp. 113-26.

9. W. F. Whyte *et al.*, *Money and Motivation* (New York: Harper, 1955), pp. 149-65.

10. Herbert Marcuse, *One-dimensional Man* (Boston: Beacon Press, 1964).

11. On the nature of wildcat strikes, see A. H. Raskin, "Why Labor Doesn't Follow Its Leaders," *The New York Times*, Jan. 8, 1967, p. 21. For engineers on the picket line, see *American Engineer News*, Jan., 1968, p. 13.

12. Federal Bureau of Narcotics, "A Study of Narcotics Addiction Among Negroes in the United States for a Decade," *The New York Times*, March 6, 1967; Kenneth Clark, *Dark Ghetto* (New York: Harper and Row, 1965), p. 216; Edward Druz, *The Big Blue Line* (New York: Coward, McCann, 1967), p. 131; George Rude, *The Crowd in History* (New York: John Wiley, 1964), pp. 195-268; Donald D. Reid, "Precipitating Proximal Factors in the Occurrence of Mental Disorders: Epidemiological Evidence," *Causes of Mental Disorders: A Review of Epidemiological Knowledge, 1959* (New York: Milbank Memorial Fund, 1961).

13. Malcolm X, *The Autobiography of Malcolm X* (New York: Grove Press, 1965).

14. Louis Wirth, *The Ghetto* (Chicago: University of Chicago Press, 1928).

15. Amitai Etzioni, *The Active Society: A Theory of Societal and Political Processes* (New York: Free Press, 1968).

16. James Q. Wilson, *Negro Politics* (New York: Free Press, 1960).

LSD Subcultures: acidoxy versus orthodoxy

VICTOR GIOSCIA

There is no need to document what everyone knows—there are a lot of young people whose special use of psychedelic substances is part of their special relation to contemporary culture. The special set of values, attitudes, and opinions of this LSD subculture were the focus of my participant observation in London, New York, and San Francisco during the past three years. Interviews with hundreds of users reveal that an acid subculture is comparably to be found in many other world cities, such as Copenhagen, Jerusalem, Tokyo, Paris, and Berlin.

Less well known is the fact that there is a growing tension between the subculture of LSD users and what might be called the subculture of therapists. The following paragraphs describe some aspects of the tension, written as much to solicit as to share insight into a phenomenon which increasingly troubles professionals in the therapeutic community.

In addition to their use of psychedelic substances which precipitate experiences of a sort radically different from those with which the midrange of therapeutic personnel are familiar, hippies (yippies and many others) are outspokenly anti-familial (dropouts), anti-psychiatric (proparanoid), and anti-bureaucracy (radical politics). They deplore wealth as alienating (the Digger Free Store), cleanliness as neuroticism ("clean is a hang-up"), and prefer free sex ("group grope") to the marital practices sanctioned by society. They refuse the counsel of rationality (the bomb is rational—the Pentagon is rational) and they insist that "doing my thing" is healthier and saner than going to war or programming computers. They regard the trip as a unique experience, communes as better than traditional family life, and look forward to the replacement of violence with love and education with ecstasy.

They are increasingly regarded as social pariahs, public health menaces, political pests, and as a degenerate generation, labels which are said to earn them the right to treatment. Yet treatment programs face a number of very practical problems in addition to the value differences described above when they try to offer service to this population. Few are willing to become patients voluntarily. Even if a given therapist has attempted to manage his counter transferences to a patient who regards him as ignorant of the trip experience, biased in favor of family life, militaristic because he offers therapy instead of politics, an impersonal bureaucrat because he is an agent of an agency, "hung-up on loot" because he works for a living, and a puritan because he is clean and (relatively) monogamous and heterosexual, a therapist must still confront a number of perplexing problems. For example, in attempting to cope with a patient experiencing a bad trip which may last for ten or twelve hours, what is to be done about scheduling? When the patient is a sixteen-year-old who has run away from home and does not wish to speak to his or her parents, of what use is family therapy? Or, if one wants to treat the natural group (or social network, in the sense used by Ross Speck) of significant others, does one suggest that the whole commune come in? Is a bad trip an emergency? Does thorazine mollify a bad trip? Does niacinamide?

Faced with these kinds of questions, an increasing number

of therapists are reexamining their treatment rationales, so that convictions developed over long years of experience are now sometimes regarded as value-assumptions which may require some modifications.

In our interviews we explored five areas: 1) subcultural differentiation: we wanted to know what trippers and therapists thought of each other; 2) status: we wanted to know whether the *avant garde* nature of the acid scene "threatened" orthodox therapists; 3) relevant experience: we wanted to know whether the trip is a unique experience; 4) sex: we wanted to know if traditional family sex and trip sex differed; 5) religion: we wanted to know whether tripping involved religious experiences. Our findings were as follows.

With respect to subcultural differentiation we found a continuum of attitudes which rendered our dichotomy of trippers versus therapists useless. Although we spoke with trippers who regard therapists who have not dropped acid as hopelessly out of it, we also spoke with trippers who were in therapy with nonusing therapists, who felt that the course of therapy contained learning experiences for both parties. However, trippers whose therapists had had an LSD experience were uniformly envied by trippers whose therapists had not.[1]

Self-administered massive dosages may result in good or bad trips. Good trips engendered in this way will ordinarily not send a tripper to a therapist. Bad trips engendered in this way might, if the tripper panics and has no one else to "talk him down." In this case, the acid-experienced therapist will know how to talk his patient down, if he has a number of hours available. The acid-inexperienced therapist usually does not know that a patient in a bad trip *can* be talked down, and may resort to medication (thorazine, niacinamide). In this case, in the words of one respondent, "then you have both the thorazine and the bum trip to handle." A particular danger is the possibility that the bad trip is not due to LSD but to STP, because the combination of STP and thorazine is believed to be fatal. The role of the inexperienced therapist who fails to make this crucial distinction is not an enviable one.

It is not surprising, therefore, that trippers prefer therapists who have had relevant experiences. Like the heroin addicts of yesteryear,[2] acid heads know that there is no sure way of knowing the strength of a "cap" of acid when they receive it. Nor is it surprising that trippers feel confined to their own resources and not a little disdainful of the therapist subculture, which by and large (but especially in the United States) is an acid-inexperienced subculture.

Perhaps the most important finding of our interviews is that the experienced trippers regard inexperienced trippers who seek the help of acid-inexperienced therapists as fools because of the high likelihood that acid-inexperienced therapists are not only unable to help but are unwilling to help, resulting as much from their alleged moralistic alliance with an anti-acid society as from their fear that "acid is better than analysis" (a fear expressed by a number of therapists). More often therapists said that they would "like to try some," but legal concerns prevented them. A few therapists said they were able to learn a good deal about LSD from patients who began treatment with them before they began experimenting with LSD, but that they feel limited in their ability to empathize with the experience.

Many of the interviewed protagonists of the LSD experience, both trippers and therapists, do not regard the experience as fitting in neatly with psychoanalytic paradigms, and in their view LSD should not be regarded simply as either a defense dissolver or as an ego builder because such views are uncomfortably psychologistic. The social nature of the experience has also been noted by many investigators, notably by Becker and Cheek[3] who have shown that social groups selectively define aspects of the drug experience as real and unreal. Our respondents repeatedly referred to the sociopolitical dimensions of the experience, reminding us, in the words of one young girl, that "dropping acid and dropping out are really very similar, because, you know, in an insane world, counter-insanity is saner than plain insanity." Thus, many users inquire more deeply into the therapist's political views than into his therapeutic credo, often believing them to be more intimately related than the therapist himself does. We have interviewed therapists who do this to patients.

A number of conclusions about the relative status of the acid subculture emerged from our interviews. First many therapists felt that sooner or later they will have to learn more about the LSD experience because they believed the number of users to be increasing and expect them to need help eventually. Some therapists thought that they would eventually try using LSD, and others (usually the younger ones) eagerly looked forward to the experience.

One finding was paradoxical. Before the popularity of acid, therapists who preferred the organic viewpoint to the psychogenic one were regarded by many as oldfashioned. Some smiled knowingly at those who did not employ the then fashionable terms derived from psychoanalytic theory. Now the shoe seems to be on the other foot. Those who attempt to reduce the acid-induced experience to psychoanalytic terms are regarded as conservatives who resist the new orthodoxy. Terms like "synaesthesis" are in; interpretations like "identifying with the object" are out, at least among those we interviewed. This does not mean that psychoanalytic investigators are not researching the acid scene. Clay Dahlberg, at the William Alanson White Institute in New York, is among those highly regarded, although he is seen as cautious in both method and dosage levels.[4]

Some who resort to LSD find their particular pathologies temporarily masked or even alleviated by the experience, but acid is no leveler. In fact, the contrary seems often true, and experienced users have an ability to distinguish what is generically due to acid and what is specifically due to idiosyncracies of the individual. Again, we found our initial dichotomy to be naive. The question is not whether acid dethrones orthodox diagnostic categories: the real question seems to be which personality types respond to acid in which ways. The work of Linton and Lang is particularly instructive in this regard, as is the work of Blum and his associates.[5] They find different personality patterns at varying dosage levels.

Psycholytic therapy is gaining in popularity in Europe as a professionally administered modality. In the United States in the absence of legal availability it must be reported that self-administered massive dosages are on the increase, especially now that incidents of chromosome damage have been reported, then contradicted, then rereported, so that even professionals in touch with the literature state that the controversy has not yet been resolved.[6]

The status of the LSD subculture is in rapid flux. Hippies in the Village, in the Haight, and in Soho are now avoiding the harsh glare of publicity because they know that it leads to ridicule and persecution. They resent the commercialization of their way of life, their music, and their art, because it is used for cheap imitation by faddists. Nor do they wish to be put in the mobility race and competed with for status. Many of our respondents were very seriously concerned with freedom, both inner and outer, and would be much happier if they were not cast in the role of criminal violators of the American way of life; bucolic emigration for those who are is becoming increasingly attractive.

From the point of view of relevant experience there is almost uniform agreement—the trip is unique. LSD, of course, is not the only psychedelic drug, and mescaline and peyote are favorites, as are psylocybin and psilocin. Other psychedelics have been in use for centuries, but they are not ordinarily found in the training experiences of therapists, and there are few, if any, comparable experiences in the orthodox psychoanalytic encounter. Alcohol is not comparable, nor are tranquilizers, sedatives, depressants, and stimulants found in the psychiatric arsenal. William James' famous experience with nitrous oxide (laughing gas) is well known, and his reaction was very much his own. Others find this chemical quite delightful. One of our respondents prefers it to LSD. But acid, like sex, is hard to compare with other experiences. The psychedelic experience seems to be regarded as a unique one, except for those who have used psychedelic substances before the name was invented.

In a much-quoted interview in the September, 1966, edition of *Playboy Magazine* Timothy Leary stated that the real secret behind the acid scene was LSD's fantastic aphrodisiacal properties, which, for example, enabled women to have "hundreds" of orgasms during a trip. If one takes the term orgasm literally (that is, biologically), our respondents contradict Leary's assertions. However, if one takes a more metaphorical meaning, our respondents indicate that the statement is true, by which they seem to mean that moment after moment is filled with delights of the most sensuous and rapturous sort and that for hours on end in what seem to be vastly extended spans of time, wholly satisfying releases of ecstatic bliss are attained with magnificent ease.

Some claim that LSD is not specifically aphrodisiacal, but has that effect because it heightens the exquisiteness of perception across the entire sensorium, so that if sex is what one is experiencing, it is a heightened and exquisitized sex one will experience under LSD.

Our respondents told us that there were three ways in which LSD heightened the sexual experience: 1) it dissolves defensiveness and anxiety, thus enabling one to enter fully into the experience; 2) it extends the sensations associated with sex so that stroking and orgasm are spread over large regions of the body; 3) it extends experience time (as opposed to clock time) so that one seems to have more time in which to luxuriate. Thus, even though the clock is running, one can play at one's own pace. "Since a short time seems to last a long time, it's better," is the way one of our respondents put it.

We were also specifically interested in another aspect of psychedelic sexual behavior, namely, what one of our respondents called the "group grope" in which a number of individuals of both sexes participate in what might be termed an orgy. We were told that group sex does not derive its impetus mainly from LSD, but from the political rejection of the notion of private property and from the practical unattainability of privacy in the urban commune: that acid only served to disinhibit those who already had the wish to "love together."

It is instructive to observe that psychedelic sex differs markedly, however, from narcotically disinhibited sexuality, since the latter becomes increasingly impossible as dosages climb. Hence, a sharp distinction should be drawn between psychedelic sex, which is improved, and narcotic sex, which is depressed. Nevertheless, LSD users said that group sex is part of the new political philosophy of community with which they are attempting to replace older political philosophies of proprietary (commodity) sexuality. We were told that acid and group sex, in combination, are both aspects of a new political philosophy which is emerging in the youthful acid subcultures around the globe, and that proper initiation into this subculture involves far more than acid and group sex.

Of interest to us was the relation between the communes in which group sex is often practiced, and the family processes characteristic of the more permanent communes. If, for example, a certain girl functioned as the mother of a given commune, did she also function as a group sex partner? If so, what about incest taboos, and if not, why not? We were told that roles were frequently reallocated within communes, so that this month's mother might be next month's daughter, and that there were major differences to be found among rural versus urban communes, the latter experiencing a more rapid change of personnel. We were further informed that group sex was not the rule but was not precluded by rule either so that if the spirit happened to move them on any given occasion, it might occur. The fact is that dyadic pairings are by far more common. We were repeatedly told that LSD was not the *sine qua non* of group sexuality. One of our informants reminded us that several accounts existed in anthropological literature describing similar practices among adolescents in preliterate societies, and that "drugs were not prerequisites there either."

Hypothesizing that there might be some relation between the anti-familial values of the LSD subculture and anti-conformist sex roles, we asked dropout users whether they were consciously and deliberately engaging in sexual behaviors that were specifically opposite to the kinds of sex practiced in their families of orientation. Again we were given responses which accused us of psychologistic reductionism, suggesting that we were hopelessly out of touch with the generational nature of contemporary youthful rebellion, which did not consist exclusively or even principally of an anti-familial revolt but of a rebellion against all of the major institutions of urban-industrial societies. We were politely informed that it was not simply with the family that youth was unhappy, but with schools, jobs, wars, governments, businesses and bureaucracies, indeed, the whole complex of cultural institutions of which urban-industrial societies are comprised. "This," we were forcibly reminded, "is a cultural revolution, not simply an anti-family experiment." In this way, our hypothesis of reaction-formation received its demise. We concluded that the acid subculture may not solely be understood in psychological terms and that newer models for its comprehension need to be devised.

We alluded previously to William James's masterpiece, *The Varieties of Religious Experience*. Masters and Huston have written what may be a minor masterpiece which they call *The Varieties of Psychedelic Experience*[7] in which they address themselves to the relation of psychedelic and religious experience. Their orientation is exploratory, and they attempt to make sense out of the religious statements made by subjects who report on their LSD sessions. Some of their subjects report theistic experiences and some do not, but many report feelings which they regard as religious.

We inquired about religious experiences under LSD. Some subjects responded that they had had experiences which they would call religious if they were religious persons, but they were not religious. Other subjects said that the trip was the "most profound experience" they ever had and, like the Masters and Huston subjects, described the experience in esthetic terms. Others described the experience as one of "immense unity" and "in touch with the All." That Tibetan, Hindu, and other religious vocabularies are widely employed by LSD users is also well known. Such languages describe what Tillich must have had in mind when he spoke of "ultimate concern," or what John Dewey described as a "genuine religious experience." That such experiences were not commonly described by our respondents in theistic terms should thus not be surprising.

We were interested in the extent to which acid serves as a ritual initiation into a subculture, having investigated this hypothesis in the narcotic scene.[8] In the present study we wanted to know whether the profound nature of the LSD experience might serve as a ritual initiation into what may legitimately be termed a cult, a band of believers united in common observance of religious ritual.

It is difficult to classify the responses to questions in this area. Some respondents denied the idea of religious ritual, while others said it was "convenient" to share a Tibetan or Hindu language. Others (a Feuerbachian proletariat?) said that what was once called religion is "what they were into." We regarded this response as the least defensive one given and found no reason to doubt its veracity.

As with narcotics users, acid users almost instantly strike up a rapport with each other. It is as if there were a "community of the alienated."* For example, those who read Ronald Laing's *The Politics of Experience*[9] insist that the final chapter, "The Bird of Paradise" is a trip and that Laing "must have dropped some acid" to write it. Thus, acid may well serve to initiate members into a mystical cult which promises deliverance from an age gone mad by suggesting that there is a realm of peace above and beyond the falterings of an imperfect civilization. It is not necessary that those to whom such deliverance is given also be required to have an acceptable academic theory of it.

Our conclusions from this exploratory study are as follows. First there is an LSD subculture. It is sharply critical of orthodox therapy and places itself in a paranoid opposition simply

---

*I am indebted for this phrase to Harry Silverstein of the New School of Social Research.

because there is a uniqueness to the trip experience with
which many inexperienced therapists nonetheless claim professional familiarity. Such therapists are often cast, sometimes
undeservedly, into the role of middle class police whose duty
it is to eliminate an allegedly monstrous drug. Not a few therapists refuse this role. Others experiment with LSD in both their
private and professional lives, but at present they are in the
United States a decided minority. Therapists who do not regard a bad trip as a moral outrage do not quickly reach for
tranquilizers when confronting one, since they see it as an
experience with which they can deal empathically, and hence,
effectively. Among users, professional or not, there exists a
bond of empathy which many regard as a prerequisite for effective treatment, not of acid, but, perhaps, even with it.

Second, LSD related attitudes represent in many ways only
the surface of a new emergent ideology and therefore enjoy
the status that all new and promising things are accorded in
a world in need of miracles. Possibly in the near future the
drug aspects might become prophetic. For, in our view, what
is new about acid is not its ideology of the absolute dignity
of the individual's experience, nor its conviction that love is
the only sane response to a violently destructive world. What
is new about acid is its centrality to a generation of people
who will not mouth beliefs they do not actually live. With this
experience, we hope the professional therapist can feel a
kinship.

Third, it was Freud who taught us that sex is not always
sex. The LSD subculture seems to be trying to teach us that
lesson again, since we seem to have forgotten it. Perhaps poly-
morphous perversity is an infantile and unsociological creed.
Perhaps it is a stage of development which is better tran-
scended. But perhaps, as play, it incarnates values which are
less destructive than wars of another sort, and perhaps for the
young who occasionally experience group sex in experimental
communes, it is a necessary experiment seeking new answers
to old questions.

Fourth, in an age where conscience permits the napalm

flames of war to engulf civilian women and children scarcely two decades after millions were burned in ovens throughout Europe, the suspicion that terms such as "neurosis" and "psychosis" may become political weapons cannot be regarded as outrageous. Perhaps in such an age some of those who seek some form of ultimacy in mind-changing chemicals deserve neither to be treated nor to be subjected to criminal processes.

NOTES

1. Here it is necessary to distinguish, as Hanscar Leuner does, between psychedelic therapy, which involves massive doses of LSD in one or two breakthrough sessions, and psycholytic therapy, which involves repeated lower dosages at regular intervals as adjuncts to the therapeutic process. It is additionally necessary to distinguish the self-administered from the professionally administered trip, since they may differ markedly in the experiences thereby engendered. "Present State of Psycholytic Therapy and Its Possibilities," *The Use of LSD in Psychotherapy and Alcoholism*, ed. H. Abramson (New York: Bobbs Merrill, 1967).
2. Richard H. Blum *et al.*, *Utopiates* (New York: Atherton Press, 1964).
3. Howard S. Becker, "History, Culture and Subjective Experience: An Exploration of the Social Bases of Drug Induced Experiences," *Journal of Health and Social Behavior* 8:163-76 (1967); Frances E. Cheek, "Exploratory Study of Drugs and Interaction," *Archives of General Psychiatry*, 9:566-74 (1963).
4. R. Mechaneck *et al.*, "Experimental Investigation of LSD as a Psychotherapeutic Adjunct" paper read at American Orthopsychiatry Association meeting, March 1967.
5. Harriet B. and Robert J. Linton, and R. Lang, "Subjective Reactions to LSD-25," *AGP*, 6:352-68 (1962); Blum.
6. Samuel Cohen, personal communication, March, 1969.
7. R. E. L. Masters, and Jean Huston, *The Varieties of Psychedelic Experience* (New York: Holt Rinehart and Winston, 1966).
8. Victor Gioscia, "Adolescence, Addiction, and Achrony," *Personality and Social Life* ed. R. Endleman (New York: Random House, 1967), pp. 325-52.
9. (New York: Penguin, 1967).

Basic Education and Youth Socialization in the Armed Forces*

ROGER W. LITTLE

The armed forces have long been thought of as offering a "second chance" to youngsters from lower class backgrounds, a second chance for education and personal development for those who did not have access to appropriate schools and for those who had access but failed. Because of the limited effectiveness of public education in the inner city, this paper deals with the question of whether there are any organizational and procedural lessons to be drawn from military training and life by civilian agencies concerned with basic education and youth socialization for the most deprived groups in our society.

In the popular image the military serves as an agency of basic education because it operates a vast number of technical and vocational schools. There can be no doubt that the military is the largest vocational training institution in the United States, but it is important to recognize that only a small proportion of enlisted personnel receive any advanced or complex technical training. The military serves as an agency of educa-

*This paper appeared in slightly revised form in the *American Journal of Orthopsychiatry*, 38:869-76 (October 1968).

tion precisely because it uses unskilled manpower. It is to the skill structure of the armed forces that we must first look to help explain their contribution to basic education and youth socialization.

By skill structure we do not mean merely the particular technical and professional requirements which are essential for the military service. We mean the logic of the organization, including the rules by which it operates in the allocation of its manpower. The military is an organization into which new cohorts of young men enter each year. Once individuals are admitted into the institution, there is no question but that the organization must incorporate them into functioning roles. In this sense, despite its complex skill structure, the military is a primitive or a noneconomic organization. In this sense all its members are equal; all its members are basically soldiers.

The new recruit need not have any doubt as to whether there is a place for him in the institution. This does not assume that all new members adjust to the system or that the institution does not seek to reject some persons. But by comparison with most civilian institutions, and particularly by comparison with the public education system, the army is an organization based on the complete availability of opportunity plus a basic acceptance of each member.

The logic of full incorporation works precisely because a pervasive element of reality is involved. The military is a highly complex organization. But in his day-to-day assignments each soldier quickly recognizes that he has real work to perform and that he has a real capacity to assist or retard the function of his immediate group. A diffusion of operational responsibility exists throughout the institution. Even the rifle-man, who is located on the bottom of a vast organization, has a sense of competence—not only because of the power of his weapon, but because in the modern military, concepts of team and group authority make him rapidly aware of his individuality. Regardless of the hierachical features of the system, effectiveness requires not simply compliance with orders, but positive participation.

Second, the military operates with a set of training procedures that assume maximum potentials for personal growth.
The very notion of basic training implies a set of skills which
all members of the institution can and must know. Basic training is required of all members as a mechanism of assimilation.
Prior social characteristics are deemphasized during this period,
particularly social disabilities accumulated during civilian life,
such as delinquency and academic records.

But even more importantly the training procedures operate
on the assumption that each person has the potentiality of
mastering the contents of basic training; or that it is up to the
system to teach each young man the essentials for success in
basic training. This does not mean that there are no failures
in basic training, but rather that those who manage the training develop the perspective that they can teach almost anyone.

Without the benefit of the educational psychologist, the
basic training systems of the armed services have incorporated
many so-called "advanced" procedures. The services use no
ability groupings, and all recruits are mixed together, so that
the heterogeneous character of the group will create the optimum conditions for learning and group support. The training
cycle is based on the equivalent of the nongraded or continuous educational development scheme. The recruit is not
graded at the end of the course with a pass or fail, but at the
end of each subsection he is evaluated, given remedial help,
or recycled through the specific phase of his training in which
he is deficient. There is extensive emphasis on education by
an apprentice system, where instruction is given during the
actual performance of the exercise or task.

Project 100,000 is a striking example of the operation of
basic training in the military establishment. In August 1966,
100,000 men who according to the standards existing then
ordinarily would have been screened out, were inducted in an
experimental program. Included were young men with limited
educational background or low educational achievement
(Category IV). Project 100,000 ensured that a group of "deprived" young men would be taken into the armed forces both

because of the pressure of military manpower needs and as an experiment in basic education. If the task had been assigned to a civilian educational system, the system most likely would have segregated these men, devised a special curriculum, and engendered in them the feeling that they were clearly inferior manpower resources. The armed forces, however, merely included them in its regular training cycle.

As of 1967 more than 49,000 men had entered the armed forces under Project 100,000's new standards. Previously only a small proportion of men who scored between 10 and 30 on the Armed Forces Qualifying Test were accepted, and then only after they had scored 90 or more on two or more aptitude tests. The revised standards permitted the acceptance of all high school graduates in Category IV without additional testing. Those who were not high school graduates with AFQT scores between 16 and 30 were accepted if they scored 90 or higher on at least one test; those with scores between 10 and 15 were required to pass two aptitude tests. Over one-third of the men who entered the program were voluntary enlistees. Their average age was twenty-one. They had completed an average of 10.5 grades of school. About 32 percent had failed at least one grade of school, and 17 percent two grades. More than 29 percent were unemployed and an additional 27 percent earned less than $60 a week.

After one year of the project we found sufficient evidence to demonstrate the wastage of human resources that had occurred previously because of rigid entry requirements. More than 96 percent successfully completed basic training, although the discharge rate ranged from a low of 3 percent in the army to 9.5 percent in the air force. (The defensewide discharge rate for all other men is about 2 percent. These rates include medical discharges for conditions other than lack of aptitude.) Equally remarkable is their achievement in advanced training, where the attrition rate was 12.3 percent, compared to the average army attrition rate for all men of 8 percent. Their success in some highly complex fields is especially notable: 74 percent in communications and intelligence and medical and dental specialists; 87 percent in administration and clerical schools; 78 percent in electrical and mechanical equipment repair; and 88 percent in crafts. Over half of those in training for electronic equipment repair successfully completed their courses (55 percent). It should be noted that these success rates were not achieved in special courses designed for the "intellectually disadvantaged" but were made under the same requirements as those established for men with higher entry attributes.[1]

After training the men were assigned not only to "infantry, gun crews, and allied specialties" (33 percent), but, further, their success in advanced training had increased their versatility so that relatively more were ultimately assigned to tasks which will provide useful civilian skills: electrical and mechanical equipment repair, 20 percent; service and supply handlers, 18 percent; and administrative and clerical workers, 10 percent.

Success in basic training, which involves an opportunity for developing a sense of self-esteem and a feeling of group participation, became the basis in part for further education and advanced training. Of special importance because it represents the newly emerging approach of the military to technical training, are the experiences of Project Transition. As a response to the task of preparing its members for transition back to civilian life and as a contribution to larger societal goals, the armed forces have instituted a program of technical training for enlisted personnel who are completing their service and who did not have an opportunity for technical training. The training is especially important for recruits from lower socioeconomic backgrounds who served in combat units and have acquired only skills which are not transferable to civilian employment.

It is important to emphasize that the skill training in Project Transition comes after the soldier has been accepted and socialized into military life. This is just the reverse of civilian society, where educational success is demanded first as a criterion for institutional involvement. The Israeli army is an example of a military force which strongly emphasizes the education function. All citizens are eligible to serve in the Israeli armed forces except a small group of severely handicapped. There are no social nor educational barriers. After mastering basic training and the rudiments of soldiering and not before, the recruits receive basic literacy education. Project Transition also attempts this type of education.

Third, the organizational climate of the military supplies an appropriate context for its basic education and socialization function, especially for recruits from lower socioeconomic backgrounds. In contrast to the material conditions of the slum, life in the military is organized and relatively satisfactory. Food is available in large amounts. The uniform is significant in two ways, in its intrinsic quality and in the fascination that develops from being conspicuously dressed. The physically active and athletic-like character of basic training also should be mentioned. Of equal or greater importance is the fact that the culture of the enlisted man is a direct outgrowth of civilian working class life. The standards of language and physical contact, of indulgences such as beer drinking, do not require the recruit suddenly to renounce earlier patterns of gratification.

The one dramatic difference is that the military is a single-sex society. This might be viewed as a serious deprivation for males who have had extensive sexual intercourse in civilian life, but there is reason to believe that the reverse is true. Most of the young men are satisfied to be relieved of demonstrating their manly character through unsatisfactory and disrupted sexual relations. Instead, the military offers a wide variety of alternatives which are in effect more compatible with the psychosexual needs of late adolescence. The all-male society of the military supplies the basis for the rapid development of dyadic friendship pairs which are among the most stable the young men have had.

Fourth, the basic social context is important. It is not political indoctrination but the realities of the military establishment that link the young men to the larger society. The military is a racially integrated society, and this has profound impact for both blacks and whites, since it represents the reality of the federal government. The recruit soon discovers that it is a society operated under a judicial system which, despite its particular features, offers him a greater sense of protection than he had in civilian life. His medical needs, his welfare and insurance, his personal protection are directly available as a matter of right and not as the result of exchange relations in which he feels he is being exploited. We do not mean to underestimate the resentment that develops toward authority that potentially is always present, but we want to emphasize the importance for the recruit of being in a stable environment.

Evaluation of basic education in the military establishment must include a consideration of the impact of weapons training on aggressive behavior of the recruits. We are dealing with at least two different levels of analysis. On the one hand, participation in the armed forces teaches an individual the mechanics of warfare and the use of force which can find organized application in conscious criminal behavior or in parliamentary activities in civilian life. On the other hand, there is the question of what the handling of firearms, and particularly the use of the bayonet, can do to a person's conscious and unconscious impulses. We are dealing not only with aggressive impulses which are directed outwardly but also with those directed inwardly.

While the evidence presented above included data on the development of stronger personal controls as a result of military experience, there are no simple answers to the effects of weapons training. Possibly for particular individuals the military training experience exacerbates aggressive impulses. We offer the hypothesis, and it is no more than an hypothesis, that the type of firearms training that a typical recruit receives in military training contributes to the control of his aggressive impulses by sublimation and by socialization in a regulated context. It would appear that military arms training is more desirable than experiences with weapons in a semi-criminal gang. We do not contend that the present training system is fully satisfactory; there is still needless exposure to the bayonet.

Fifth, the information and control systems of the military enhance the position of the recruit from a deprived and disorganized background. The military accepts responsibility for his well-being. Specific persons are responsible for observing and monitoring the recruits' experiences and the results. The machinery is elaborate, cumbersome, and at times inefficient. But there is a peculiar sensitivity to the needs of a particular individual. The sensitivity derives in part from the professional ethic that the officer—both commissioned and noncommissioned—has prestige among other officers to the extent that he takes care of his men. It is also a result of the information system, which makes it possible to follow up on a particular recommendation or a particular action. The recruit is living in a residential setting, and it is therefore more difficult for his community to avoid confrontation with his problems or needs. If a recruit has a medical problem, or needs remedial education, the circumstances are different from civilian life, where intervention often means referral to a particular agency without followup. In the military the outcome must be reported.

But the system of controls in the military is not based on formal and official channels exclusively. The recruit is removed from his home community and is made part of a more heterogeneous group. He knows that at some point he will or can return to his home community. He does not completely break his social and emotional ties, so guilt and disruption are minimized. The presence of other young men who have grown up outside his home community is a basic ingredient of his military socialization. He comes to deal with, to work with, and to become the comrade of men with diverse styles and aspirations. He comes to recognize the existence of a larger world. In contrast to a social agency, or the community settlement house, the military is not based on the notion that the young man must accept himself. The military is a school for fashioning new self-conceptions and a system in which informal communications serve to explore and test out these alternatives.

The overriding conclusion of this examination of the armed forces as an agency of basic education and socialization is not that the military can serve as an alternative to defective civilian institutions, but rather that relevant recommendations or lessons for the reconstruction of civilian institutions can be drawn from the military experience.

Even if one seeks use of the available data to argue for a positive role for the military in basic education and socialization, then at best the military would be able to supply a second chance only to a proportion of individuals with these needs. Of course, this is a vitally important point; the military has succeeded in basic education and youth socialization precisely because it has limited the number which it will handle. The armed forces operate effectively because those who have failed in civilian life are not segregated into special units but are incorporated into larger groups made up mainly of young men with adequate education and social background. Strangely enough, the armed forces are operating in a format suggested in the Coleman report, which emphasizes the importance of heterogeneous student populations.[2] The Coleman report concentrates on racial segregation, but its principles have broader implications.

Perhaps about 20 percent of the male youth who have been failed by existing educational practices could have a second opportunity in the armed forces. Such an estimate is based on a return of the military to its size before the build-up in 1965 for the Vietnam war. It would involve about 40,000 young men each year out of a potential 200,000.[3]

While there are specific lessons to be learned from the military experience, the military itself cannot supply a model for a civilian institution in a democratic society, nor can the military have the exclusive or even major responsibility for a civilian function. Only a limited number of societies have been able to control their military by democratic political institutions. To assure democratic control the military cannot be isolated from civilian society. Granting the military limited involvements and specific responsibilities in basic education is one means for preventing such isolation, but it would be incompatible with the requirements of a democratic society for the military to become a major national school.

But in a sense the issue runs deeper. The military is in a process of reconstruction, and it requires reconstruction just as the civilian educational system does. The lessons for basic education that can be drawn from the military are limited to specifics aspects of its operations during the period after World War II and before the current Vietnam expansion. The old fashioned army of 1939 had much less capacity for basic education because of its limited size and its repressive authority structure, and it is very difficult to estimate the probable characteristics of the post-Vietnam military. The military establishment will have to be made compatible with the demands of a world community. Movement toward a world community requires that military organizations abandon earlier concepts of victory and move toward international law and social change. A world without illness would still have doctors, although they would be called illness-prevention specialists. Likewise, a world without war would still have specialists in violence, although they might not have much of a basic education function.

In one sense the military as an agency of basic education and youth socialization bears a striking structural resemblance to the residential treatment center. The military establishment is often described as having an anti-introspective nature, but the residential treatment center is also designed to reduce reliance on introspection as a basis for personality change. The similarity within the two institutions derives from their concern with organizational climate. Both institutions take persons from the larger society for periods of time and create a special educational community. Both are based on the assumption that human material can be changed after infant and childhood experiences. Both seek to create a consistent and integrated setting to achieve their goals. The military has the special character of a generational cycle, of inducting a new group each year which will in turn be "graduated." As a result, in the military, as compared with most residential treatment institutions, the danger of oversocialization into the organizational environment is reduced. The special character of the military means that lower class youths can assimilate new values, because for a time they are on a more equal footing with the more privileged members of society. The underutilization of the middle class groups supplies an important ingredient for change. What civilian institutions and agencies are prepared to reproduce this environment?

The fundamental lesson is that a second chance for the culturally deprived and those who have failed in educational settings involves entrance into some sort of comprehensive institutional setting. The social work and educational professions have fiercely and successfully resisted such developments. The boarding school, which has always been an institution for the affluent, now emerges as an important supplementary agency for the lower classes. Military basic training includes a variety of specific devices for managing such residential agencies, but the basic issue remains the development of programs in which educational and vocational standards are imposed after or along with the development of self-esteem.

NOTES

1. Summary Statistics on Project One Hundred Thousand, Office of the Assistant Secretary of Defense (Manpower), Washington, 1967.
2. James Coleman, *et al*, *Equality of Educational Opportunity* (Washington: U.S. Government Printing Office, 1966).
3. Morris Janowitz, "The Logic of National Service," in *The Draft: A Handbook of Facts and Alternatives*, ed. Sol Tax (Chicago: University of Chicago Press, 1967).

Basic Education and Youth Socialization Anywhere Else: a reply to Roger Little

MARC PILISUK

If I understand the essence of Roger Little's paper correctly, it is that there is an important lesson to be learned, particularly by educators, from the "second chance" function that the military, through its Project 100,000, has been able to provide for members of disadvantaged minority groups. With this conclusion I could not agree more completely. The practices of military socialization and the acceptance of these practices by persons like Roger Little indicate, in fact, that the lesson must be learned quickly, for the hour is quite late.

In assessing the efficacy of rehabilitative functions of Project 100,000 we should not lose sight of the fact that this "experiment in basic education" was not conducted for purely altruistic reasons—or even as an attempt to dissipate the imminent specter of civil disorder—but primarily, as Little implies, to reduce a military manpower shortage. The most important question to be raised then is not whether Project 100,000 was successful; rather the question is what should be taken as an acceptable indicator of success on the part of educators and mental health practitioners.

A vast amount of knowledge and skill regarding education and vocational training has indeed been acquired within military institutions. This parallels its vast amount of technical knowledge and skill mastery in almost every phase of organized human endeavor, since the military has been active in numerous fields. Not only is it the largest vocational training institution in the United States, as Little points out; it is also the largest contractor of both hardware (manufactures) and software (research) and the largest employer of health personnel. Besides operating the third largest supermarket chain in the United States, it is, considering the number of its employees and the size of its landholdings, the third largest socialist state. Each of its functions, including the educational and vocational training function, has been a natural outgrowth of an organization intended to fulfill one basic purpose: the defense of American interests by means of violence and the threat of violence.

Through the vast financial resources available to the military (more than 60 percent of the national budget), through its highly centralized and authoritarian decision structure, and through its ability to remove people from the legal, judicial, and social institutions which affect other citizens, the military has been able to produce some truly remarkable results in particular areas of human endeavor. Each result, however, bears in some way the markings of the official and actual purposes of the larger organization.

One cannot deny the important rehabilitative effects of some of the practices of the armed services' Project 10,000. Certainly the ability of the armed services as an institution to take on these disadvantaged people without regard to their prior history and to ignore their previous records of delinquency and failing academic grades works to the advantage of the recruit. The assumption on the part of the institution that each recruit is capable of making the grade in the program is very important in building the recruit's confidence. Also, the heterogeneous grouping of individuals—mixing people from different backgrounds, different ability levels, and different races—can itself be very useful and has been shown to be of value in Project 100,000. There is something unusual, however, in the assumption of any rehabilitative agency that it can apply a particular technique to everyone in the same way and still be effective. There are certainly cases where this approach is not feasible, and belief in its universal efficacy might be construed as another form of therapeutic dogmatism. Still, one should not deny the positive effects of the confident attitude of the therapeutic agent, be he master psychoanalyst or master sergeant.

Doubtless also, as Little points out, people from disadvantaged backgrounds who were previously unable to qualify for admission are getting better food, more equitable justice, and better medical care in the military than they were able to get anyplace else in society. Certainly, these services are of value in the rehabilitation of almost everyone, and it reflects sadly upon our society that some of its people must be underfed, ill-housed, uneducated, or without medical care unless they are in the military.

The sense of meaningful participation in a larger purpose, or of having a role to fulfill in a larger organization, the expectation by others that one can fulfill that role adequately—all are techniques which bear further study and application in the rehabilitation of young men. The concept of residential treatment—of taking people out of their ordinary disadvantaged communities, of obliging them to become part of a total institution—can also have certain positive as well perhaps as certain negative effects, and I would certainly concur with the positive effects that Little has mentioned. But Little does not touch upon the negative effects of participation in military service in his article.

Little speaks positively of the basic training in a set of skills which all members of the institution can and must know. He considers this a form of assimilation into the system, which helps to deemphasize prior social characteristics and create a pattern of personal growth. Most of the soldiers I have known look upon basic training as a destructive experience in which their superior officers' concern for spit-and-polish is regarded as an attempt to maximize the recruits' ability to accept authoritarian discipline even in matters of trivia. It is a time of dehumanizing masking of personal identity through enforced acceptance of a uniform, a crewcut, and a regimen of ungodly hours, harsh physical rituals, and irrelevant and purposeless tasks.

I believe that Little forgets that the function of basic training is not to rehabilitate youth but rather to render them effective parts of an organization which is incapable of tolerating discussion and dissent within its ranks, particularly because its main function of inflicting extreme malevolence on a national foe is one which requires an equally extreme form of discipline.

Little speaks positively of the fact that once admitted to the armed services, the recruit will be incorporated into the organization's existing functioning roles without question. Similarly he points out that having become part of the organization, the soldier "recognizes that he has real work to perform and that he has a real capacity to assist or retard the function of his immediate group." Is it out of place for us to ask "to assist his group to what end"? Is it out of place for us to ask that a "rehabilitated" human being be able to ask the same question for himself? But the essence of military service is that the end is not to be brought into question; only the adequacy of ability in its pursuit is to be considered.

Little summarily dismisses the loss of sexual expression among the recruits: presumably their previous mode of sexual expression was a false and misleading way of asserting their masculinity. However, he seems to feel differently about the recruit's sense of positive identification with his rifle. Here, the "power of his weapon" combines with the modern military concept of teamwork to help "make him rapidly aware of his individuality." This point is reiterated in Little's discussion of the uniform, its intrinsic quality, and the fascination that develops from being conspicuously dressed. I would not wish to contest my own value-laden images of masculinity with those of Little, but I feel that many people in the mental health field would esteem different characteristics of the human male. Unlike the bantam rooster, the human male is sometimes esteemed by a function other than the ability to strut and claw.

What Little considers to be positive features of the climate of the military are shared by other total institutions, such as the state mental hospital and the prison. There, too, the working class culture and vulgar language predominate. There, too, the regularity of food and other services provides a dramatic difference from the ghettos from which the occupants come.

It is certainly a telling fact about our society that Little is able to argue that the disadvantaged and incompetent youth can gain fairer justice in the military than anyplace else in society. It is equally telling that the military should be providing the largest, and possibly the best, example in the country of a vocational rehabilitation program for disadvantaged youth when there has been an educational system in the country for many years. Resources for educational experimentation and staffing have not been equal to the military's, and it goes without saying that the scope of military-related experimentation and staffing (occupying more than one half of American scientific personnel) is largely to blame for the squeeze in other areas. Yet with all its advantages, the function of the military organization is not lost in the provision of services it gives to its members. It provides an adequate and effective socialization into a society of paid killers. Little's argument that 100,000 members of disadvantaged backgrounds could be effectively rehabilitated into the mainstreams of society is unconvincing when we consider that during the same period another (perhaps some of the same) 25,000 Americans, disproportionately representative of similar backgrounds, were killed while performing their rehabilitated roles in Vietnam—while killing 100,000 Vietnamese.

The sense of performing a role in an organization with a larger purpose is nowhere better illustrated than in the military services and at times of warfare. It functions as well, unfortunately, on both sides of the battleground and operates independently on the value of the cause for which that military organization was brought into existence in the first place. Goebbels is said to have been a most reasonable-sounding man. I could picture his defense of the Hitler Youth Corps and can find nothing in Little's arguments for military education that would be unsuited to such a defense.

Little does speak briefly about the functions of modern military organizations, about the needs of such organizations to abandon earlier concepts of victory, to move toward notions of international law and social change. What he gives too little attention to are the reasons that the United States does not move toward accommodation of such a world. Hearings by the House Armed Services Subcommittee in 1959 disclosed that over 1,400 retired officers with the rank of major or higher, including 261 of general or flag rank, were in the employ of the top one hundred defense contractors. A study in 1964 showed seventy-four senators and representatives with continuing status in the armed forces.[1] In 1957 one study showed 200 active (not reserve) generals or admirals on assignment to "nonmilitary departments of the government or to international or interservice agencies." An added 1,300 colonels or naval officers of comparable rank and 6,000 lower grade officers were similarly assigned. Indeed, Little's point that the modern military cannot be isolated from civilian society is well taken. The evidence would seem to show that we no longer have a set of distinctly civilian institutions in American society, and the burgeoning military bureaucracy can in no way be counted upon to correct this important deficiency. The notion that people are no longer being trained, exclusively, to bayonet other people—there has been a transition from the role of the soldier as butcher to the role of the soldier as a silent, unquestioning technician—does not reduce the validity of this point. If all military supported contracts were to end suddenly, then we would have unemployed engineers and IBM punchcard operators, all in need of basic rehabilitation.

Little speaks with pride of the relatively high proportions of successful entrants in complex and advanced programs. But what does success in an intelligence unit produce? To beam over the miracle that "intellectually disadvantaged" youths succeed in these programs "under the same requirements as those established for men with higher entry attributes" is to forget that the successes in such programs may prove far more disastrous to American society than the failures. At a time when we are field testing our arsenal of techniques for military control and pacification through firepower, chemicals, bribery, and education of many foreign and domestic peoples, is it not more fitting to ask whether the military establishment is obsolete and contradictory to priorities for human needs? Rather than seek justifications for its new uses—either as a model or as an agency for nonmilitary functions—perhaps it is time to terminate a mode of military dependency which is fostered by the periodic induction of major portions of society. Whatever the intellectual advantage or handicap, there would certainly be a moral advantage in utilizing agencies for rehabilitation which function under a basic premise that it is wrong to kill. The long-term advantages of such an education may be felt by all of us when the 100,000 riflemen return to find the conditions in the ghettos and rural slums slower to change than they were in the army.

There is absolutely no doubt that an organization equipped with the resources of the American military, and with its power, can involuntarily extricate young men from their social environments and bring them into a homogenizing low level training program, which can in fact build up the self-confidence and the skills many people have not had opportunities to develop in their home communities. It can transform these people into components of an effective and mindless machine imbued with dedication to the task of organizing itself for the infliction of extreme malevolence. In our efforts to rehabilitate the American youth who have suffered because of deprivations in their home communities we can afford to be humble and must be willing to take lessons from whatever source available. But as any therapist knows, if he has hope to be permanently effective, he must be able to learn from his clients as well.

The military is the example par excellence of the assumption that its values and its practices are correct and all that remains to be done is to bring people into the organization and make them operate more effectively within it. This has been the failing philosophy of the war on poverty—the assumption that the background culture of the people the program is trying to help need not be respected, that that culture has nothing to offer either for the people themselves or the society which is trying to assimilate them. I believe that the military could learn much from a program which would send all of its high ranking officers involuntarily for a period of service to some black militant organization in the ghettos. It is not, however, a lesson that I feel they should be forced to undertake but rather one which those who are more informed might select voluntarily. The same choices for rehabilitation should be available to disadvantaged youth in our urban ghettos. The availability of choice and the assumption that institutions must respect the life and dignity of the individual are basic to education in a free society.

NOTE

1. *Journal of the Social Sciences,* 3:86 (July 1965).

War and Violence: the consequences of domestic institutional failure

HERBERT I. SCHILLER

A common, though curious, tendency in this country has been the inclination to look very far from home for the origin of national ills and popular anxieties. Reduced to an extreme formulation, the rule might be that the greater the physical distance separating the perceived hostile host from American shores, the larger the threat to domestic well-being and security. As a case in point, the 6,000-miles-distant Russians for twenty years were made responsible for our fears and our various misfortunes. Of late the still more remote Chinese have been the object of our increasing concern.

Even in the exceptional instance when a problem is acknowledged to be domestic, its existence frequently is explained by the presence of mischief-making representatives from far-off places. In those situations in which the invocation of extracontinental forces as the inspiration of local difficulties is totally unconvincing, distant regions within the United States itself have been accused by some as the seat of outside troublemaking: "Northern agitators" or "Eastern radicals."

Almost as if in preparation for the eventual disappearance

of specific national, state, and regional menaces, a developing demon that is receiving increasingly serious attention is the population explosion—not in America, of course, which recently celebrated the birth of its 200 millionth inhabitant—but everywhere else around the world.

What then (if anything) besides our active imagination is threatening us? If not Russians, Chinese? If not Chinese, people in general? If not people in general, black people in particular? Putting aside for the moment the well-known intractability of these various groupings, we must consider a few questions. Who, we may ask, is filling our skies with pollutants and our sons and daughters with frustration and resentment? Who has ordered the rural migration of uprooted farmers and the urban decay attendant upon the mass inflow of impoverished agricultural workers? What drives us to intervene on every continent and to station a million of our young men around the globe? What makes so many of our schools so poor and so many of our aged so miserable? Why have our information media been reduced to their present banality? And, finally, what makes the national mood so insecure at the time when national arsenals possess megatonnage promising overkill annihilation of would-be aggressors? Are we perhaps already observing the consequences of our not yet totally fluoridated water supplies? Or are there more prosaic clues to these numerous mysteries?

Let us begin with the simple facts of production and distribution. The United States, to be sure, is a very special case, but its condition spotlights the global predicament. Nowhere else are the technical capabilities and resources so developed and the returns so meager and blighted.

The annual value of America's output—the so-called Gross National Product—is now approaching $900 billion, and personal income constitutes almost $750 billion. One way of understanding what these staggering sums represent is to imagine an entirely unlikely situation. If the national income pie were divided equally this year, 200 million Americans would each receive exactly $3,750. A family of four would get $15,000, a family of five $18,750, and so on.

Now we know at once this is unrealistic, because it does not take into account many things we hold dear. It overlooks the freedom to accumulate as well as the freedom to do without. It leaves no room for "incentives," and any responsible economist will vouch for their indispensability. No one knows what would happen to automatic systems of production if incentives were unavailable. Could computers, for example, be expected to perform satisfactorily if their individual worth were denied and an IBM machine treated indistinguishably from an RCA unit?

Then too in all other ages and at all other times, it has been clear that if the few were expropriated, the many would benefit scarcely at all, except for the momentary exultation derived from a little leveling. Still, $3,750 per man, woman, and child seems to weaken this particular argument.

No one seriously could claim that the deferral of egalitarianism is producing a massive underground disaffection in American life. Yet Senator J. W. Fulbright does believe, and I am in agreement, that "poverty, which is a tragedy in a poor country, blights our affluent society with something more than tragedy: being unnecessary, it is deeply immoral as well."[1]

When the canvas is enlarged to take into account the international community, the incongruities become overwhelming. In 1968 total personal income in the United States increased $57 billion over the preceding year, or almost $285 per person. One year's incremental advance in America, on a per capita basis, exceeds for its individual citizens the total annual income of one and one-half billion people in the "have-not" world.

While these gaps widen, the efforts of the weak and less developed nations to improve their positions through economic bargaining are invariably rebuffed by the few well-off Western nations and by the United States in particular. Even more to the point, the growing arsenals of American superpower are openly deployed in hundreds of overseas bases against potential insurgencies that promise radical transformations in desperate lands. The cumulated military expenditures of the United States alone since the end of World War II now exceed a thousand billion dollars—a claim on resources that, if differently applied, could have remodeled a good part of the face of the earth. And each year the military budget continues its assault on global and domestic living standards. No less a cause for anguish is the fact that these expenditures have created an international climate of terror and pathology and a domestic atmosphere of nihilism and profligacy. We are now beginning to understand the wider meaning of these outlays. We are discovering in our own community the aims of the garrison economy.

Not long ago, on the same day that a government-appointed Commission on Civil Disorders reported that "the condition of the Negro in big city slums was deteriorating and that his hopes of escaping were dwindling,"[2] the Pentagon announced that "special army teams are fanning out across the United States to coordinate anti-riot planning with state and city officials. . . . The data [they will make available] will include street maps, aerial photos, and details on communications nets and proposed command posts and emergency camp sites."[3]

In short, the intervention that America has been practicing globally for twenty years, with expertise derived from dozens of far-flung campaigns, is being readied for domestic application. What is unfolding in back streets and alleys across the country is a local version of the international cold and sometimes hot war. One element has changed. The carefully created mystique of operations in far-off places is missing. Also, the objective is more visible. The battleground against social change has suddenly appeared inside the country itself. The police and the national guard battalions in Newark, Detroit, Watts, and Harlem are domestic equivalents of the pacification troops and our forces of law and order in the Dominican Republic, Lebanon, Vietnam, Panama, Cuba, Thailand, and dozens of other places where American soldiers have been concentrated.

Why is social change, abroad or at home, so bitterly contested by America, a country where the margin for experimentation is so huge as to make risks, if not negligible, at least tolerable? This is the question with which we must grapple. In my judgment the answer will explain more than anything else the course we have been pursuing and the likelihood of a new direction.

To my mind a large part of the explanation rests in the total acceptance of privatism in American life. The educational system, the mass media, and other organs of opinion-making, and especially the business community reinforce tirelessly the sense of self and privatism that permeates our society. Accordingly, the American life style, from its most insignificant detail to its most deeply felt beliefs and practices, reflects an essentially self-centered outlook which in turn is a fair image of the structure of the economy itself. The personal system of transportation, the single-owner home, the private business, and the competitive health system are obvious if not natural features of the privately oriented economy.

In this setting we can expect that those changes which do occur will be effected through individualistic and private organizational means. In the face of the disintegration of urban life, land use remains private. When space communications were developed in the 1960s, offering the potential instrumentation of international social intercourse, a private corporation (Comsat) was entrusted with this global responsibility. The elimination of hardcore urban unemployment, it is suggested, should be made the responsibility of successful, large-scale business companies. When blacks press for a change in their status, it is a matter, they are informed, of personal talent and ability, demonstrated through individual performance.

It can be argued with some justification that individualism and privatism were constructive modes of behavior and organization earlier in American history. Today this claim cannot be pressed rationally. The multitude of connected activities which bind together a modern economy have entirely changed the environment of decision-making. The character of contemporary urban-industrial society, as well as the global interdependencies, alter the perspective in which the question of individual initiative and private prerogative has to be examined.

The question of individual freedom is bound up not so much with control and restriction as with an attempt to set decision-making at a level which can anticipate, comprehend, and provide for the needs of the individuals and groups who may be affected by the actions proposed. It involves selecting certain combinations of elements in a complex community that offer larger opportunities for the bulk of the population.

The only agency in society able to apply social yardsticks to decision-making and also able to look beyond next year's budget is the national government. To quote Senator Fulbright again, "At the heart of the problem [poverty, race, jobs, and schools] is the absence of sufficient funds and political authority strong enough to control the anarchy of private interest and to act for the benefit of the community."[4] America's impasse arises because the citizens from their earliest conscious state have been led to regard social decision-making as a menace. Experiences with federal authority have deepened these suspicions; it has, more often than not, represented the interests and the objectives of the strongest private elements rather than the needs of the commonweal. Not surprisingly the popular taste has been soured by such national initiatives.

Yet localism, privatism, and the ascendancy of the self are entirely unsuited to the socioeconomic tasks which should have been undertaken long ago and which are now becoming violence-flecked emergencies. The centers of dozens of our cities urgently require renovation and reconstruction. Were meaningful activity to be initiated, expenditures could feasibly exceed hundreds of billions of dollars. The pathetic insufficiency of what passes for action is highlighted by the ecstasy with which some national administrators hail an offer by a few private insurance companies to raise a billion dollars at some unstated point in the future for some unstated urban construction.

The migration of destitute rural workers, black and white, to the urban cores—a classic illustration of the unregulated market in operation—inevitably results in the swelling welfare statistics of our major cities: In New York alone more than one million inhabitants receive assistance. "Realists" are quick to offer moral codes for governing the behavior of this helpless tide of Americans who have been dispossessed by technology and impersonal forces beyond their control from their ancestral conditions of impoverished but isolated existence.

Another striking example of the vacuum in national responsibility, with attendant domestic and international consequences, is the privatist approach to health and medical care. Our wealthy society participates in an almost incredible doctor drain, in which, according to one observer, "poorly developed countries are today subsidizing [the American] medical manpower pool."[5] While it is not surprising to discover that significant numbers of United States doctors are serving in poor countries throughout the world, it is startling to learn that the nation is "relying heavily on some 40,000 foreign-trained physicians who currently comprise 14 percent of the active physicians in this country."[6]

The international situation is no less grim. Former Secretary of Defense Robert McNamara noted before he left office that "there can then be no question but that there is an irrefutable relationship between violence and economic backwardness. And that trend is up, not down." Furthermore, he added, "it would perhaps be somewhat reassuring if the gap between the rich nations and the poor nations were closing and economic backwardness were significantly receding. But it is not. The economic gap is widening."[7] How has this country reacted to the developing crisis? For a variety of reasons, not all of them mean or without merit, it has cut back its overseas assistance in 1968 to the lowest level in two decades, and at the same time it has done nothing to assist the efforts of the "have-not" states to expand their exports into American markets.

On all sides, domestic institutional structures and attitudes act as barriers to renovation and creation at home and abroad. In less rapidly changing times there was much to be said for proceeding slowly and carefully with adjustments in the social process. Now, in the midst of a vast human awakening across the world and a torrent of technological advances, flexibility and a broad scale of action are minimal requirements for avoidance of social disaster. Writing about the still-to-be-experienced effects of cybernation, one observer declares that "even the job of simply preserving a *going* society will take a level of planning far exceeding any of our previous experiences with centralized control."[8]

Yet the willingness to play and to subordinate self to group are barely perceptible. The inability of American society to adapt its institutions to meet the enlarged social tasks that confront the nation is producing domestic chaos and international violence. Seen in this perspective, the effort to hold back sweeping social change across two-thirds of the globe on the grounds that it interferes with the private interest of a tiny but powerful sector of the American community is producing local wars which threaten to become global nuclear encounters. The mobilization of the American economy to wage these wars serves to intensify the domestic inequities separating the affluent from the destitute, and it also erodes the confidence of all strata of the population in the ordinary processes of politics and group bargaining. Until the American production machine can be brought under *social* control, further Vietnams are inevitable, and rising conflict in the nation's streets and cities is unavoidable. If one must feel saddened and grim by these prospects, the events themselves may be producing their own antidote. This would be the rise of domestic political groupings that will and can secure a fundamental shift in what Senator Fulbright calls our "grotesque inversion of priorities." Yet even now it is questionable whether it is still possible to turn the powerful American industrial machine away from waste and destruction toward human improvement and social justice.

NOTES

1. U.S., *Congressional Record*, vol. 113 Part 27, Dec. 13, 1967, p. 36182.
2. Robert Semple, Jr., "Hope for Negroes Found Dwindling," *The New York Times*, Nov. 23, 1967, p. 47.

3. William Beecher, "Army Helps City Plan Riot Control," *The New York Times*, May 19, 1966, p. 47.

4. Donald M. Michael, "Cybernation: The Silent Conquest" (Santa Barbara: report to the Center for the Study of Democratic Institutions, 1962), p. 28.

5. *The New York Times*, Nov. 18, 1967, p. 12.

6. *Ibid.*

7. Philip M. Boffey, "Health Crisis: LBJ Calls for Re-shaping of American Medicine," *Science*, 158: 1160-62.

8. Beecher, *op. cit.*, pp. 1, 49.

Social Change and Abortion Law Reform

ALICE S. ROSSI

Free associations to the word "abortion" would probably yield a fantastic array of emotion-laden responses: pain, relief, murder, crime, fear, freedom, genocide, guilt, sin. Which of these associations people have no doubt reflects their age, marital status, religion, or nationality: to a forty-four-year-old Japanese or Hungarian women the primary response might be "freedom" and "relief"; to an unmarried American college girl, "fear" and "pain"; to a Catholic priest, "murder" and "sin"; to many black militants, "genocide."

These responses underline the complexity of individual emotion and social cleavage in the United States on the question of abortion. It may be many years before Americans use the more neutral expression of "pregnancy termination" as the British did in naming the abortion bill that became effective in England in 1968. Some of the affective sting of the word may be neutralized by placing abortion in a wider historical context. To do so forces the realization that abortion is only one of many devices man has used to control human fertility. It has only been a few centuries since many European cathedrals had revolving doors with a basket attached in which a woman deposited her unwanted newborn infant. In contemporary times such child abandonment largely has been transformed into a more humane system of infant adoption. Infanticide also has declined as a means of controlling fertility. Compared to either infanticide or child abandonment, abortion of a fetus during the first trimester of pregnancy is clearly a far milder form of fertility control.

In the world today abortion is used either as an alternative to other, primarily contraceptive methods of fertility control, or as a backstop method of control when other contraceptives fail. Abortion continues to be a major method in numerous countries in the world: in Catholic countries where the distribution of birth control devices has been prevented or kept to a minimum, and in underdeveloped countries which as yet have had no widespread exposure to modern contraceptives. In France the annual number of abortions equals the number of live births. In Latin American countries there is an average of one abortion for every two live births, although in some countries, like Uruguay, the ratio is estimated to be as high as three abortions for every live birth. For many years to come a high abortion rate will continue to be the major brake on the dangerous population growth now taking place in Latin American and Asian countries, far overriding the effects of family planning programs which distribute pills and loops. If there was ever any question about the fact that abortion remains the single best strategy to effect changes in the birth rate, it must surely have been answered by the dramatic doubling of the Rumanian birth rate in the course of one year, from 1966 to 1967, after legislative restrictions on abortion were instituted in December 1966.[1]

Compared to underdeveloped and Catholic countries, the United States abortion rate is a far less dominant element in the fertility control picture. Medical statistician Christopher Tietze estimates that between one-fifth and one-fourth of all pregnancies in the United States are terminated by induced abortion.[2] The estimates have been 8,000 to 10,000 legal hospital abortions annually and from 250,000 to well over a million illegal abortions.

There is no way to tell what proportion of the abortions in the United States represent the only method of fertility control used by some persons and what proportion represent a backstop measure when contraceptives fail. It is reasonable to assume, however, that women who want to control their fertility but lack money, knowledge, or a partner agreeable to contraceptive usage constitute one large category who rely primarily on abortion. Undoubtedly a large proportion of the poor women who enter municipal hospitals every day with post-abortion complications use the only cheap but the most dangerous method, self-induced abortion. Any social or religious group relying on inefficient contraceptive procedures, such as the rhythm method, is similarly likely to be overrepresented among those who resort to illegal abortion. In addition, even if all women of childbearing age in the United States used the pill, a one percent failure rate would yield as many as one-quarter of a million unwanted pregnancies annually.

At any point in time there are several million women in the American population who have personally undergone an abortion as a solution to an unwanted pregnancy, yet public attitudes continue to show sharp distinctions between contraception, which is approved by an overwhelming majority, and abortion, which is viewed in largely negative terms. The widespread acceptance of contraception is in part a tribute to the ideological appeal of the birth control movement itself. The guiding ideology has been family planning, which projects a positive, socially desirable image of married couples spacing their children and timing their births in a rational manner. Contraceptive devices are used to regulate the births a couple desires and the emphasis remains on the welfare of the child, the mother, and family stability. The ideology is in part public relations sugar to coat the pill with the concept of birth control, which projects a less traditional image and suggests that some births are not wanted, and that contraceptives can enhance the sexual pleasure of men and women independent of maternal health and family stability.

Unfortunately euphemistic terminology can affect the actual programs and the target groups contacted. Until very recent years family planners have studiously avoided assistance to unmarried women, and they have totally ignored the problem of unwanted pregnancies. In short, abortion has been kept clearly separate from the whole family planning movement, and family planners have contributed relatively little to the public dialogue about the incidence of abortion, the danger of illegal abortion for women's health, the role that abortion has played historically in restricting population growth rates, or the critical examination of whether abortion has any place in a criminal code.

There is, however, no longer any clearcut distinction, even on technical grounds, between conception prevention and pregnancy termination. The intrauterine loop is more accurately described as an abortive device than a contraceptive device. The loop does not prevent conception as condoms, diaphragms, and pills do; it either prevents the implantation of a fertile ovum in the wall of the uterus, or produces a spontaneous abortion within a few weeks after uterine implantation (medical authorities are not sure which of these two processes is actually at work). Yet the family planners define the loop as a contraceptive device and have actively engaged in its distribution in underdeveloped countries with explosive population growth, and it is being prescribed by American physicians who have begun to worry about the side effects of the pill. The refusal to consider abortion as part of the fertility control picture is a serious limitation on the American effort abroad to assist countries belatedly confronting their population problems.[3]

As evaluation studies reach publication, it becomes clear that loop insertions and sterilization procedures are having "some" effect on Asian birth rates, but Kingsley Davis has argued strongly that underdeveloped countries will not avert major economic and political crises brought on by overpopulation unless demographic practitioners mount a far more rigorous campaign of birth restriction, including widespread facilities for simple, inexpensive abortions.[4] Like American physicians on the domestic scene, public health officials often merely react with shock to the proposal that family planning clinics should be total fertility clinics, serving both married and unmarried women and providing abortion facilities for clients whose prescribed contraceptives fail them.

Mounting interest and political activity concerning abortion have developed during the past five years. Abortion reform and study associations have mushroomed in many communities across the nation, and a first international meeting in 1968, under American sponsorship, drew representatives of more than a dozen countries. Reform bills were introduced in thirty state legislatures during 1967, with Colorado, North Carolina, California, and Maryland being the first states to actually pass slightly liberalized bills. Vigorous attempts at legal reform in New York State failed in 1967 and started again slowly in 1968. In February 1969 Lawrence Lader, Lonny Myers, and Garrett Hardin spearheaded the first nationally coordinated association calling for total repeal of penal code coverage of abortion.

The bills passed in the last few years, and those under consideration in state legislatures, have been modeled after the 1959 recommendations for revision of state penal code of the American Law Institute (ALI). What liberalization has meant, therefore, was an enlargement of the grounds for exemption from liability to criminal prosecution under the penal code, from danger to the "life" of the mother, the most prevalent state clause, to the grounds of grave risk to the physical and mental health of the mother, chance of deformity in the child, or pregnancy as a result of rape.

What is particularly important to note about the liberalized code is that it exempts from prosecution predominantly women who want to be pregnant. The law keeps the whole issue firmly in the context of maternal and child health: it is not a woman's rejection of maternity, but the unfortunate condition of her heart or liver or other organ, or an unfortunate exposure to rubella that justifies the granting of a legal abortion. Clearly the protection of the health of a woman or the avoidance of a high risk of a deformed fetus are health reasons hard to object to. Almost as many people want healthy mothers and babies as favor motherhood itself. Except for emotional traditionalists or Catholics who adhere to strict doctrinal positions on abortion, there is widespread support for legal change that would permit abortion on grounds of health or deformity. But such reform does nothing to solve the basic problem and postpones the coming to grips with the majority of the cases of women who for a variety of personal and social reasons do not want a child they accidentally conceived.

Here is the heart of the abortion problem: what should an individual woman do who finds she is pregnant against her wishes and what should professional and public policy be toward such a woman? It is perhaps understandable that Americans find this a disconcerting question. We resist the image of a woman not wanting a child because it violates what we would prefer to keep intact, a sentimental reverence for a nurturant, loving mother. To accept the idea that not all women want the child they conceive raises the threatening possibility that one's own mother might not have wanted him.

Yet the confronting of the reality of exactly such circumstances in family life is a daily occurrence in the professional lives of social workers, psychiatrists, and physicians. Despite their intimate knowledge of such problems, practitioners in these fields have not informed us concerning the probability of emotional damage to children born to mothers who unwillingly accepted an unwanted pregnancy, although the same professionals espouse the theoretical and clinical view that the most fundamental headstart a child can have is to be born into a loving environment as a wanted child. A probability of fetal deformity of one in three births when the mother has been exposed to rubella has been considered sufficient ground for recommending an abortion. Would psychiatrists claim any different probability of emotional difficulty in an unwanted child born to an unwilling mother? If not, then the mental health fields should be among the first to support a legal change that would reduce the incidence of unwanted pregnancies brought to term, but this they clearly have not done.

But an even more controversial and difficult question must

be confronted. Demographic research on family size shows increasing evidence that both in desires and in actual fertility, as evaluations of current family planning programs abroad emphasize, the most difficult problem facing the world is the reducing of the rate of wanted pregnancies. Kingsley Davis pointed out recently that in the very countries which family planners cite as showplaces of family planning success (Korea and Taiwan), the programs are aimed at women who do not want any more children because they already have at least four; the programs largely ignore girls not yet married or married women early in their childbearing years.[5] Judith Blake analyzed fluctuations in family size desires and compared them with actual fertility rates, showing that family size desires have remained relatively constant and high over long periods of time, suggesting a gap between desired and attained family size that she calls "latent child hunger" and concluding that nowhere in the world has modernization alone had an abiding and drastically downward effect on family size desires.[6]

Both Blake and Davis have urged the view that no significant stabilization of the population growth rate in either underdeveloped or industrialized nations can be expected as long as attention is focused narrowly on family planning programs. Reliance on the value position that all persons should have the number of children they desire, the key idea in the ideology of family planning, is inadequate because people desire too many children. In the United States in 1966 white women aged twenty-one and over considered as ideal an average of 3.4 children. My own research, has shown that college graduates had a desired mean family size of 3.2; 38 percent wanted four or more children. What must be changed to reduce these desires is the basic motivational structure for having children, and such an approach must necessarily involve changes in the structure of the family, in the position of women, in sexual mores, and in opportunities for legitimate alternative satisfactions and activities apart from family roles. Only in this way can future reduction of family size be attained.

What women do with their lives is a central issue in fertility control and population growth. Maternity cannot continue to be an exclusive goal of women, for this encourages views that the more children the better and that no marriage is complete without a child. Praise and social approval for women with large numbers of children are no longer functionally appropriate to an urban, crowded society. This applies to economically well-to-do women as well as to poor women, to American women as well as Latin American women, to white women as well as black women. This is a delicate and pressing issue in American politics in 1970, for there is mounting pressure on Congress to pass legislation providing vastly expanded subsidization of family planning. This is being urged under the guise of a mandate for help from the poor for more birth control devices. However, an increasing number of us fear that this is really a poorly concealed mandate from the well-to-do in American society who wish to see fewer and smaller families on welfare and a halt to any increase in the proportion of blacks in America. Class-directed efforts by the federal government toward contraception unnecessarily politicizes the population problem, and is in addition self-defeating, since the solution of excessive population growth must come through encouraging the vast majority of the American population, not the small minority represented by the very poor, to reduce the number of children they want. In this context legal change to permit women to abort unwanted pregnancies would seem to be the easiest step to take in coping with the population problem, for it involves the removal of present barriers that women do not want, rather than the more difficult task of changing deep-lying motivations.

Let me turn finally to the tactical question of how our punitive abortion laws can be changed. We should consider first the reasons for the growing concern and political activity during the 1960s aimed at even moderate revision of existing abortion laws. There is no reason to believe that the incidence of illegal abortion has changed in any drastic way during the past thirty years. If anything, there has probably been a reduction in illegal abortions as more effective contraceptives have been developed. Of course this may be more than compensated for by the large increase in the number of young people reaching the sexually active years as the babies born in the postwar boom reach adulthood.

An important development has been the trend toward more open discussion of all aspects of human sexuality. Venereal disease was more openly discussed during World War II than ever before. The postwar publication of the Kinsey reports sparked widespread discussion of sex and contraception. Since the birth control pill was marketed a decade ago, there has been continual debate about its effect upon the sex lives and reproductive behavior of Americans. Of special importance was the wide dissemination of the findings of demographic research, showing that despite what the church has said, the majority of American Catholics were using mechanical and chemical contraceptives. This had very special political consequences, because it neutralized the issue of birth control in politics, paving the way for the gradual introduction of sex education in public schools, and for increasing federal appropriations of large sums for birth control education and distribution of equipment in domestic programs among the poor and in aid to underdeveloped countries. Significantly perhaps, abortion did not become a widely discussed problem until the "reproductive renaissance" of the 1946-1960 era had ended. High-order births that had been welcomed by American couples for the preceding two decades were no longer desired in the 1960s.

The step from open discussion of contraception to open discussion of abortion was speeded up by the thalidomide cases a few years ago, strengthened and reinforced by the German measles epidemic at about the same time, when increasing numbers of people learned what medicine had known for twenty years—that such exposures risked serious deformity in the fetus. No progress occurred in revision of the abortion clause in penal codes between 1959, when the ALI proposed its revised model code, and 1964, but concern for maternal and child health stimulated by the thalidomide and rubella cases has provided the impetus for a concerted attempt at legal reform since 1964. Unfortunate from a broad historical perspective, perhaps, is the fact that the ALI model code, drafted during the conservative 1950s, was the one readily available in the more liberal mood of the mid-1960s. Many abortion law reformers have hoped that the ALI mental and physical health exemption would be broad enough to permit a wide range of interpretation. Surveys of physicians, however, indicate overwhelming support for the ALI exemptions, but a good deal less support for medically approved abortions for women with personal or economic reasons for not wanting a child.[7] In other words, physicians seemingly will not help the majority of women who now resort to illegal abortions to obtain medically safe abortions, where and when the abortion laws are revised. Preliminary data from Colorado and California suggest that this expectation is being confirmed. A clue to why the legal abortion rate increases only slightly in these states can be seen in the procedures for screening applicants, usually hospital abortion committees. Such committees place a group buffer between patient and physician that may reduce the anxiety level of physicians by shifting responsibility for denial of an abortion from him to an impersonal collective, but this increases anxiety for the patient and makes her lose precious time if she is determined not to carry the pregnancy to term.[8]

I think a good case could be made that the hospital abortion committee procedure is very like the "needs tests" in the welfare field, with the same insensitivity to the indignities heaped upon applicants. Under the terms of the New York bill defeated in 1967, a woman with an unwanted pregnancy would have had to apply for an abortion, pass the functional equivalent of a welfare "needs" test by permitting herself to be examined by not one but several physicians, have her psyche probed for signs of distress, and then wait out the slow moving machinery of the hospital bureaucracy for a decision that would affect in deeply personal ways what her responsibilities would be for the next fifteen years. The psychology of the situation facing the abortion applicant is exactly like that facing the welfare applicant, with an expectation of compliance and humility on the part of the applicant. A woman is forced to show her weaknesses, her inability to cope under stress, to secure the help of the profession; if she shows her strengths, the profession will refuse its services.

This committee procedure carries the added risk of increasing the probability of surgical complications or death when a woman later obtains an illegal abortion, after hospital denial, since the abortion will be performed at a later stage of pregnancy. The mortality rate in pregnancy termination cases in Sweden, where the committee procedure is followed, for this reason is higher than in eastern European countries, where the committee procedure is not used. This consideration was a factor for British reformers, who in writing their Medical Termination of Pregnancy Bill specified that a decision could be accepted from any two registered general practitioners. After a preliminary attempt by the medical establishment's Medical Defense Union and Medical Protection Society to require that one of the doctors be a specialist, the society prepared a pamphlet advising their members that general practitioners should be considered specialists in cases of social abortion, because they are more capable of assessing a patient's emotional and environmental situation than the specialists, who do not have personal knowledge of the patient.

In the U.S., discussion of abortion during the past five years has been kept almost exclusively in a medical, legal, and theological framework, and the framework has determined the direction of attempts to analyze and solve the problem. If abortion is considered within the context of fertility control, and in light of the place of pregnancy in the life of women, we can no longer determine so clearly who is the appropriate expert to speak, and much of the medical and legal literature has only limited relevance. A new cluster of issues become the more relevant ones: sex and the relations between the sexes, the determinants of reproduction motivation, the role of maternity and the life goals of women, the question of a woman's right to control so private an area of her life.

Women themselves have played a minor role in public and professional discussions of abortion, precisely because the problem has been dealt with in the narrow legal-medical framework. At the Washington conference in 1967 women figured more as actresses in the dramatic skits presented than they did as speakers and discussants. Of all the professions in American society law, medicine, and theology are the ones in which women constitute a small minority, well under 10 percent. Those few women lawyers, doctors, and psychiatrists who have been active in abortion reform or participated in professional analyses of the problem have by and large taken positions that go far beyond the conservative reform proposed by the ALI, and they are more likely than their male colleagues to view abortion within the context of personal rights.

Other women, deeply concerned with this issue, do not yet feel free to speak up publicly. The fields in which women have been represented in significant proportions, and occupy high status positions, are nursing, social work, and education, very often as local, state, or federal employees. Subtle as well as overt pressures censor the tongues of many of these women who believe no woman should have to choose between such undesirable alternatives as carrying an unwanted pregnancy to term or seeking an illegal abortion. One high ranking woman in the federal government wrote on her personal stationery to ask me for a reprint of an abortion article, explaining that although she was very interested in the problem, she could not express such interest on official stationery.

This instance neatly illustrates the political fact that abortion is at the stage of public awareness that contraception was a few decades ago. The government did not enter the family planning field until it was very clear that numerous Catholics were using contraceptives, so that it was apparent that the church position did not represent the views of Catholic voters. Needing far more extensive circulation than they yet have received are results of surveys which show only very slight variations in views of abortion law reform by religious groups. In a 1965 survey conducted by the National Opinion Research Center, which I analyzed, Catholics were only slightly less in favor of reform than were Protestants.[10] Most importantly, they imposed the same qualifications that members of other religions did. They did not reject abortion on doctrinal grounds as church spokesmen do. As on the birth control issue, there is a vast discrepancy between the beliefs and practices of the Catholic population and the doctrinal position taken by the church. This 1965 survey was taken just at the point when public discussion of abortion was on the rise. The Association for the Study of Abortion conducted another survey in 1967,[11] and a comparison of the two surveys gives a crude measure of attitude change in two years.[12] In 1967, 75 percent of the sample endorsed reform. More importantly, 72 percent of the Catholic adults, as compared to 83 percent of the Protestant and 98 percent of the Jewish adults, favored reform. The comparison revealed a 20 percent increase in support for abortion law reform, from 55 percent in 1965 to 75 percent in 1967.[13]

Why, then, since Catholic voters in the state clearly favored the reformers, did the New York bill fail? For one reason legislators are in contact not with the average public, but with articulate spokesmen of the organizations and institutions concerned about a given issue. In this case, they faced conflicting testimony of legal and medical experts, and uniform opposition from Catholic church spokesmen.

A second important point involves an acute problem always encountered in seeking change through state legislative action. American political groups have cut across nondivisible group cleavages, such as religion, ethnicity, and race, and have sought alignments along economic lines within political party structures. Economic alignments can in one sense be divisible ("half" a budget request, for example) in ways that religious or racial cleavages cannot. Thus, the Democratic party has been able to use a nonideological appeal to economic interests to weld support among groups which otherwise would have been arch antagonists: white, fundamentalist Southerners and urban working class Catholics and Jews. In the American experience, ideological issues that cannot be translated into

economic terms have usually been resolved by the Supreme
Court, a body outside the established party alignment. In both
great constitutional issues of recent times—civil rights and
apportionment of voting districts—Supreme Court decisions
took the place of political action within the party system.[14]

The inevitable compromising that produces unenforceable,
inadequate revisions of abortion statutes stems from the fact
that this is an ideological issue which does not follow political
party lines but often divides the parties along religious lines.
A political reform requires either defining the problem in
terms agreeable to all religious groups, or persuading legislators that religious cleavage is not as deep as their exposure
to self-appointed lobbyists would indicate.

With the momentum already established by the passage of
the ALI recommendations into the statutes of several states,
the most likely development in the future will be the passage
of similar laws in the remaining states, unless widespread
discussion helps to redirect efforts in a new, more fundamental
direction.

Such a redirection may be possible if reformers can shift
debate on abortion from the narrow legal and medical dimensions of the problem to the question of population excess, the
consequences of unwanted births for the lives of women, the
potential emotional damage to children born unwanted, and
the basic human right of women to control their own reproductive lives. Finally, the routes followed in solving related
problems offer some lessons. Legal restrictions on medical advice about contraceptive methods were removed not by state
legislatures but by challenges of the constitutionality of the law.
Justice William O. Douglas argued in one Supreme Court
case that a California statute against contraception violated
constitutional amendments that created "zones of privacy" in
which the government is constitutionally prohibited from
entering. The same legal argument applies to abortion: statutes which define abortion as a crime may be contested as
unconstitutional because they violate the right of a woman to
control her own reproductive life according to her own con-

science. The effect of such a decision under constitutional protection would be to remove abortion from the criminal code, leaving legal control to the provisions of laws governing the licensing of physicians and hospitals, as it is in every other medical procedure.

This is less a utopian goal than it might have seemed a few years ago. For one thing, there is a growing sentiment in this country that any law which is not enforced, and is in fact unenforceable, and which in no way reduces the incidence of behavior the law is designed to restrict, should be repealed.[15] This was the American experience with prohibition laws, and the same point applies to abortion statutes.[16] Few would claim that the million American women who obtain abortions every year are immoral or feel disrespect for human life; most have other children to care for. That abortion rates are higher in Catholic than non-Catholic countries should itself be sufficient evidence that having an abortion is not an index of immorality or lack of respect for life. Experience in other countries also is instructive here: abortion in the Soviet Union has had an erratic history, shifting several times from legal to illegal and back to legal again. Each time abortion was defined as illegal, mounting concern for the health of women led to its repeal. All the law affects in the Soviet Union, and all it affects in the United States, is whether women have medically safe or unsafe abortions.

Secondly, those who take a strictly doctrinal position that any abortion is a sin because it involves the killing of human life cannot in conscience support a modification of the abortion statute to cover special cases of any kind, since the law therefore is judging some abortions to be morally permissible. Dean Robert F. Drinan argued this point at the Washington abortion conference in 1967: "A system of permitting abortion on request has the undeniable virtue of neutralizing the law, so that, while the law does not forbid abortion, it does not on the other hand sanction it, even on a presumably restricted basis." The question of when a fertilized ovum become a human being cannot be resolved on embryological grounds, and theological judgment has varied with time and advances in scientific knowledge. Individuals vary widely in these definitions. We can perhaps hope to gain consensus on a judgment that a person who is born and alive is indeed a human being. For a fetus that cannot exist outside the mother's body only individual values and conscience can govern the definition. Hence the human being to whom we must give priority is the woman, not the fertile ovum.

The views expressed by Dean Drinan are also echoed in the testimonies of many doctors and psychiatrists at legislative hearings on ALI-modeled bills, and they are implicit in the objections some civil rights workers have to government-sponsored family planning programs. Drinan's suggestions answer the objections raised by all these groups by lifting the problem of designing laws which define some abortions as legally permissible and others as criminal (which satisfies few people) to an entirely different basis: the defense of the right of women to control their own reproductive life in light of their own intelligence, values, and conscience. This basis would avoid the religious and racial cleavages that have marked the issue for so long. From the political point of view, the view that individuals in a free society should be guided by their own intelligence and conscience, with no pressure or control from government or profession to either have or not have an abortion, and with no legal restriction on access to competent medical help, is a position that could eventually gain the support of all groups in our society, for there is no coercion beyond the dictates of individual conscience.

The fact that there has been a dramatic increase in public support of abortion reform during the short span of two years gives reason to hope that further debate may contribute to a growing consensus on the basis of personal rights, and hence to testing the constitutionality of the penal statutes on abortion or a direct repeal of state statutes. Both Americans for Democratic Action and the National Organization for Women have already passed resolutions for abortion law repeal on precisely these grounds of personal rights, and this is the strategy

Drucker has shown to be most successful in our political history: court decisions on constitutional grounds for the resolution of issues that tap cleavages cutting within party alignments. Lucas has recently reviewed constitutional limitations on enforcement and administration of abortion statutes and suggests that there are ample legal grounds for contesting the statutes as violations of constitutional rights.[17] He suggests also that the argument applies with equal force to state restrictions upon the use of chemical abortifacients when medical research has produced reliable ones.

In addition to the removal of abortion from the penal code the problem of cooperation between the medical field and the women who seek abortions will remain. This will be no less difficult to achieve, but perhaps physicians and hospital administrators will be stimulated by continued public and professional debate to rethink their resistance to extending such aid to women and will accept their responsibility as a profession to contribute to rather than hinder the rights of women to control their own lives.

NOTES

1. Malcolm Potts, "Legal Abortion in Eastern Europe," *The Eugenics Review,* 59:232-50 (Dec. 1967).
2. "Foetal Deaths, Spontaneous and Induced, in the Urban White Population of the United States," *Population Studies,* 11:170-76 (1957).
3. VanNort points out that demographers in Western countries have so accepted the dominant values of their society that they have failed to deal in any thoroughgoing way with either abortion or infanticide as alternatives to approved methods of birth control, and suggests demography must operate with a wider variety of assumptions. Leighton VanNort, "On Values in Population Theory," *Milbank Memorial Fund Quarterly,* 38:387-95 (1960).
4. "Population Policy: Will Current Programs Succeed?", *Science, 158:* 730-39 (1968).
5. *Ibid.*
6. "Demographic Science and the Redirection of Population Policy, *Journal of Chronic Diseases 18:*1181-1200 (1965); *Parental Control, Delayed Marriage and Population Policy,* Population Reprint Series No. 238,

(Berkeley: University of California, 1967); and "Reproductive Ideals and Educational Attainment among White Americans, 1943-1960," *Population Studies*, 21:159-74 (1967).

7. Robert Hall, "Therapeutic Abortion, Sterilization and Contraception," *American Journal of Obstetrics and Gynecology*, 91:518-32 (1965).

8. Packer and Gampell are among those critical of the hospital abortion committee procedure as a device to rationalize physicians' denial of help to patients. Cf. "Therapeutic Abortion: A Problem in Law and Medicine," *Stanford Law Review*, 11:417-55 (1959).

9. Jane McKerron, "Abortion: Can Doctors Cope?", *The New Statemen*, Feb. 9, 1968, p. 166.

10. Alice S. Rossi, "Abortion Laws and their Victims," *Trans-Action*, 3:7-12 (Sept./Oct., 1966).

11. Results of this survey are not available in published form. Mimeographed summaries have been released by the American Orthopsychiatry Association, however.

12. It should be noted that the two surveys are not strictly comparable. The 1965 survey was based on a national probability sample, whereas the 1967 survey was confined to residents of New York state. Secondly, the 1965 survey asked separate questions for each of six situations, whereas the 1967 survey asked one question covering all three ALI recommended exemptions, maternal health, fetal deformity, and rape. To make these as closely comparable as possible, the least endorsed of the three situations covered in both surveys is used as the base figure for 1965.

13. The New York state survey also indicated that even among Catholics who characterized themselves as "very religious," 63 percent favored the ALI reform.

14. Peter Drucker, "On the Economic Basis of American Politics," *The Public Interest*, 10:30-42 (Winter issue, 1968).

15. This view that the law should not govern morality is elegantly argued by the British legal scholar Granville Williams, *The Sanctity of Life and the Criminal Law* (New York: Knopf, 1955).

16. Robert F. Drinan, Dean of Boston Law School, presented this argument at the Kennedy Foundation conference on abortion in Washington in 1967. He argued that when a law is not enforced and is unenforceable, it is wise "for the law to withdraw it rather than have the majesty of the law brought into disrespect by open disobedience and unpunished defiance." (mimeo).

17. Roy Lucas, "Federal Constitutional Limitations on the Enforcement and Administration of State Abortion Statutes," *The North Carolina Law Review*, 46:730-78 (June 1968).

The Ideology of Mental Health

LEONARD J. DUHL

The change in psychiatry and mental health, as well as a shift in my professional life from the National Institute of Mental Health to the Department of Housing and Urban Development, have determined what I think about the field and how I perceive it as a new kind of ideology for myself. Not so long ago when I first began to see the national problems of service and manpower in community after community, I found myself very angry at those persons sitting in an office or clinic who were preoccupied with the particular problems they faced every day. At that time I felt they were blind to the overwhelming pressures urging changes that were being brought to bear on the professions. I have lost that anger because no matter where I stand, whether at the National Institute of Mental Health or the Department of Housing and Urban Development, the perception has changed radically. Because of the necessities of the job I find that I have to live in a very different world.

I shall attempt to explore both vantage points. In addition, I will discuss a third vantage point, that of someone who began his training with a medical model of the perception of problems and of illness, who later was exposed to psychoanalysis (which I feel is an ecological view of individual behavior), and then had experiences with the broader problems of the social sciences. My own exposure very quickly took me into public health, and I found that exposure to this new profession began to modify and change my thinking. The kind of training that I had originally received has been modified in time by experience, by exposure to planners, to public health people, to economists, to lawyers, and to politicians, and, more recently, to the poor, the Negro, the Peace Corps, and the alienated adolescents.

One of the first things that concerned me was the breadth of our mental health needs in the United States. Even considering only the problem of repairing those people who break down from emotional disorder, we have been doing an inadequate job. It became obvious in looking at the problems in the field and our perceptions of them, that the kinds of programs and the ways in which we have been trained, and even the research, have been inadequate. Fifteen years ago we knew very little about where people turned for help, who besides the psychiatrists and the mental health profession gave that help, what pathways into care were available for the mentally ill, and how we should deal with the repair system. The responses to these questions revealed that no system of mental health care was available for those who needed to be repaired when they broke down. I believe that if the system was to work or to be developed, it could not develop out of our profession alone, but out of a whole host of other professions in tandem. Nicholas Hobbs and I discovered the work of the educateurs in France who were treating emotionally disturbed children with a minimum amount of psychiatric intervention. After that we returned to the military and private schools in the States who were treating the mentally ill without their being so labeled. Consequently, I felt that a more complete systematic view of who is involved in the repair process was needed. I then began to inquire where people who were ill and could not get well were contained. Originally I investigated mental hospitals, and then homes for the aged. I discovered that some of our biggest containing institutions were our public housing projects, our ghettos, our slums, and indeed some of the developments for senior citizens in the communities around America.

What then of normal development? How do people learn how to be well or how to be sick? How do they learn how to cope with the kinds of problems that they face? In institution after institution psychiatrists had absolutely no contact with, or the mental health profession barely impinged upon, that which played a very important role in mental health. As the institutions in the repair system were added up, both the containment system and the normal development system, we found that the arena we were working in was that of the open society of America—the arenas of the city, politics, and of power. If one accepts that primary goals of our profession are the lowering of the incidence and prevalence of disturbance, mental illness and emotional disorder and the increasing of the ability to cope with the kinds of problems which people face, we must seriously question whether or not the various institutions that impinge upon the lives of individuals are aiding and assisting in this process. Although the mental health profession may be at the end of an assembly line at Pruitt-Igoe Housing Project in St. Louis, trying desperately to assist people who have broken down under strain, the housing project itself is serving as an illness factory, turning patients out at a rate more rapid than could be cured at the end of the line. The mental health profession plays a relatively small role in all systems having to do with repair, containment, or normal development, and therefore I cannot as yet say whether this is directly the responsibility of the mental health profession. We have a very small part of the action. Basic decisions on the allocation of resources in the urban world—the amount of money that goes into mental health, the amount of manpower assigned into it, the way that we view the rules and the regulations of housing, of welfare, and the way we look at the law—are relatively unimportant.

The organization I am currently associated with is concerned mainly with bricks and mortar and financing and insurance, and it is gradually turning into a federal institution concerned with the problems of cities. As I watch the decision-making take place around land and power and money, the comment comes back to me: "But Doc, the things that you stand for are really the icing on the cake, the gravy, and if the other issues are dealt with, the kinds of things that you are concerned with will be taken care of."

Nevertheless, something very important has happened in the last few years to change our ideology, and we have no control over it. This has been the impact of the confrontation that started with the civil rights movement and is better understood as the poor of the cities begin to press for new kinds of services, programs, and allocations of power.

More interesting than the civil rights movement is the fact that each of our professions, whether mental health professionals, city planners, or lawyers, is beginning to reach out from where it once stood to broaden its base into the parameters of its field. These parameters have increasingly begun to overlap so that the concerns of the neighborhood legal workers are almost identical with the community mental health workers. The increasing competition and confrontation among the professions, coupled with the pressure from the poor and the young, are beginning to raise the issues of how power will be allocated and how decisions will be made. The way decisions were made, until very recently, could be summarized by a statement of about five years ago: "If you want to build a highway, you just bulldoze right through." I could never get professionals from our field to be concerned with the fact that those highways were breaking up communities, affecting the way services were rendered, and indeed impinging on all aspects of the development of individuals in the community.

But what has happened? A new and strange alliance has developed, at this moment a tenuous one because the level of communication between the parties is still not very good, between the professional mental health worker, concerned with problems of the community, and the confronters from the poor, the adolescent. Whether there should be a shift in the hierarchy of values by which decisions are made is being considered. What is the more important question: the bulldozing a highway through, or the relationship of that highway to the people—what it will do to them, and whether they have to be involved somehow in the decision-making about that road.

Recently David L. Bazelon, known as a mental health judge, decided a case before him in the Circuit Court of Appeals in Washington about the highway construction in the cities. Under petition by the citizens he stopped construction because there had been no involvement of the community in the processes that led to the decision-making about the path of the highway. He did not use the language of mental health; he was talking about new allocations of power in the total community.

The following case will reveal some of the kinds of problems that must be faced if we are concerned with mental health and the community in the way I have outlined. Rutgers, the only medical school in New Jersey, was once a private institution. Now in the state system, it was to be moved to the center of Newark in the midst of the slums—indeed just where the riots took place last summer. The medical school, interested in its own development, decided after looking at all the latest medical schools that a medical school is appropriately concerned with research, with good cases, and with being somewhat like Harvard. The decisions were made to design the school on 160 acres in central Newark and to equip it with no outpatient facilities, with the school instead using the Newark city hospital—known in the local trade as "the slaughterhouse." Administrators applied to Public Health Service for funds to build the school.

The ideology evident in the planning of that school is one that I think is long out-of-date. The decision-makers were not concerned with the community. They did not consider the fact that especially if there is only one medical school in the state, it has a responsibility to be involved with the com-

munity, as well as to produce researchers. The pressure began
to build from the people of Newark, who opposed the medical
school. Indeed, they said if such a school went up, it would go
down brick by brick. The black population confronting the
issue was opposed to anything developing in the area. Then
an accident occurred. The land that the school and the city
were interested in was land under urban renewal. Urban
renewal is very important to people who run universities and
cities because it is free land, or relatively free, and the medical
school applied for this land. Their request for 160 acres eventually came to the Department of Housing and Urban Development. The question was how should the Department respond? Should we decide by the rationale of what is the best
economic use of this land in purely financial terms? Probably
the best thing would be to put in industries, businesses, or
office buildings. Should we also respond to the new goals of
putting up housing, which is what the citizens really wanted?
Should we worry about the relocation of the people living in
the community? The answer was yes, because this was the
direction that HUD was taking in the cities. The medical
school found out that it not only had to plan a medical school,
but it had to worry about relocation of people, housing, and
jobs for the people of the community. They felt their business
was simply to run a medical school, but the people in the
community felt otherwise.

Another interesting accident occurred at that point. The proposed medical school site happened to be in the Model Cities
area. The Model Cities program attempts to pull all programs
in the community together and to achieve a new kind of com-
prehensiveness. All the overlapping parameters of programs
had to be looked at carefully. Interestingly enough, there was
no mental health provision in the planning of the Model Cities
program, except that a consultant had written into the application that the medical school would play an integral part in the
community and would start training workers in the community
in the health fields. As happens in many communities, consultants had been called in to write applications that were never

seen by the persons who submit them and, subsequently, I do not believe the dean saw the application. Nevertheless, the department began to hold them to those criteria.

The Public Health Service (PHS) learned that HUD was concerned with the quality of medical care and the delivery of health services in the community and that the medical school must be designed to meet those needs or else it would not be given the land. The PHS stated that the medical school had to be concerned about housing, jobs, and relocation. The state agreed to set up a high school program for the training of health manpower personnel to work in the community. The program at Lincoln Hospital in South Bronx was reviewed, and it was determined that this type of mental health program had to be brought to Newark as part of the medical school program. The program came because the black community and its advocates began to specify what they thought a health program should be in the community.

A whole series of trade-offs occurred. The medical school land went down to 57.9 acres, a local housing corporation in which the local community participated was set up, and an agreement was made that one-third of all the jobs would go to local residents, despite the unions. The PHS secured agreements from the school about jobs and medical care delivery systems. Some very interesting things occurred within the black community, which suddenly found that the interchange in the processes of negotiation was a learning experience, and they realized they did not have to completely confront and negate the system, but through negotiation and trade-off there could be a gain-gain situation all around.

This was a mental health process in many ways. That the poor could confront the system and command the events that affect their lives meant that there was an important change in them. A sad part of the story I heard indirectly: that the mental health clinic which sat next to this hospital through the riots, through the negotiations, and through the Model Cities application felt no need to participate in any of the events and was simply doing its business of delivery of service, in spite of occasional appointment cancellations. They felt that mental health was still the delivery of service in a clinic. I should like to suggest, then, that the kinds of things that I am talking about, which have to do with politics, with decision-making, with the relations of institutions to each other, and with values, are really part of our new ideology, which can no longer be confined to a clinic.

In this new world the psychiatrists and the mental health personnel are playing a very interesting role. On one level we are protestors; on another we seem to have collaborated with other protesters. In another role we become advocates that the community can hire to aid and assist the protesters against the system, but in many instances we are becoming what somebody called an inspector-general for human values in the decision-making of the city. I am suggesting that whether you are talking about the national level and the need to participate in the political action, if you happen to be responsible on the local level in community mental health programs, if indeed your goal is to lower the level of pathology in the community and to maximize the ability to cope, then you too have to get into that kind of decision-making in your local community. We have been accused many times of diluting our skills with these kinds of concerns; these we are told really are responsibilities of the citizen, and that the psychiatrist and the mental health worker should just continue to do what they know best, and to do it well. I am not sure that I can abide by that kind of criticism. Certainly I feel that as a citizen I have a right to intervene in matters concerning what happens to my life and how the society is making decisions in general. When the critical issue is as specific as the care for people who break down, it is our *professional* responsibility to intervene. It has been suggested that our training is inadequate to do some of these things. There are eternal battles in psychiatry itself about whether you have to be a good clinical psychiatrist first and then you can go on into the mental health world in this broad way that I am talking about. This may not be necessary, and indeed we may have to recapitulate the whole history of psychiatry as we teach it. A new kind of teaching may be evolving.

I should like to comment on what I think is beginning to happen in the United States and what I think the role of the mental health practitioners will be. The medical school for a long time was the only institution in the university concerned with the developmental training of people who intervene in the behavior and life of others, and its primary concern was with action. I suggest now that we are entering a period when we must develop an analog to the medical school, a new institution concerned with intervening in social and individual behavior, with institutional change as well as individual change, with the development of research concerned primarily with action. Every time I look at cities, whether it is Newark or any other city, the kind of data that I can get either from the community or from the academicians is inadequate to understand the problems of intervention and change. We have to train new kinds of specialists, generalists in change in the community, as well as specialists in the mental health law, and other professions. We must begin to develop a common core curriculum for all those concerned with change in our urban systems, whether they be in health, education, welfare, transportation, planning, law, or the courts. The language of the mental health worker, of the people trying to set up health systems, is foreign to people dealing with housing development and transportation. Those concerned with a new kind of mental health activity will be trained in new kinds of curriculums in a new kind of institution whose primary concern is the total community.

This means that some of the lessons that we have learned in our field can be applicable and can be translated into a new language. The concerns with change, with process, with decision-making, with intervention, and with defense can be reapplied to the new world. We have a lot to learn, because if what I have suggested is correct, we must add to our knowledge in many fields, especially in the utilization of power. This is beginning. It is going to happen not because of us, not just because Negroes are making demands, but also because events are leading to the point at which the society we have created must be changed and modified. In the America of the past if we did not like what we had, we could move on; we could fight the natural environment, the natural ecology. Now we have created an ecology which we cannot handle and must modify. I think the problem also involves the reconstruction of our own internal ecological environment so that some of the current concerns in the mental health field can go into decision-making.

One final word about the clinician. Throughout my work in the broad field of community mental health I have continued to see patients. I now perceive patients in a different way. Even the process of intervention with individuals, with families, and with groups has become modified. I have also become aware that the concerns of the clinician can often give us important clues that can be fed into the system on a much broader basis. When Robert Leopold, Gerald Caplan, and I worked in the Peace Corps, we were fascinated by how often the psychiatric clues that we had about changes in behavior, about psychiatric breakdown throughout the organization, told us as much about the organization as about the individual patient. The psychiatrists working in some colleges and universities have had the same experience. So I think there is a need for interchange, a need for input from the clinician. I think, too, that all clinicians should not be required to become concerned with the issues I have outlined. I gave up my original anger about their not looking at the world the same way I do, but I believe it is critically important to understand that a clinician plays an important role in a much larger system, that other people play significant roles on different levels, and that the relationship between a clinician or a worker in a clinic or a hospital to this much larger system is very important. The clinician must communicate. I think the problems of communication between the levels of concern are very, very difficult. The minute a clinician hears me, he feels that I am protesting against the way he is doing business. Though one may be excited about some of the things that are happening in the world, many people tend to be extremely defensive. The same is true of the community psychiatrist who sees the clinician doing the psychiatrist's job. Communication with the politician and the planner is probably worse.

I have said that the mental health people in Newark did not participate in the Model Cities program or anything else, but I have learned something. I have learned that nobody asks mental health professionals into the decision-making, because doing so means in part that others are going to have to give up power, and nobody gives up power voluntarily. Only if practitioners begin to insert themselves and are present when the decisions are made about how the city operates, how the mental health center relates to a total community center, how resources are allocated politically, will mental health specialists have some power. But I do not think specialists can have a piece of the action only by protesting that the system is wrong. It is critically important that although one sees the system as wrong, one understands how to intervene and play the game of decision-making, which is presently ongoing.

Ideology really refers to any systematically related sets of beliefs held by a group of people, provided that a system of beliefs are sufficiently basic to the group's functioning. The word "ideology" was originally coined in the eighteenth century to refer to political beliefs, but its usage has been broadened. Now the ideology of mental health has become the ideology of society, and we must reconnect the professions to the ideology on which a democratic society is based.

Resistance to Change in Mental Health Professionals*

IRVING N. BERLIN

Personal satisfactions, contributions to the welfare of others, status, and money have all been suggested as reasons that individuals enter, remain in, and contribute to the mental health professions. I suspect that these are also the primary reasons for resistance to change and for the kinds of anxieties manifested by many when our rapidly changing society requires that we become more responsive to community needs and find more effective, innovative, and responsive models of theory and practice.

From time to time I have examined my own resistance to trying some new method of psychotherapeutic intervention, to considering some new factors in the etiology of childhood mental disorders, or to investing myself more fully in developing the theory and practice of mental health consultation. Mostly I recall pervasive feelings of uneasiness. When recently I was again challenged to teach in a different way and to dem-

---

*This paper appeared in slightly revised form in the *American Journal of Orthopsychiatry*, *39*:109-15 (January 1969).

onstrate crisis intervention, these old feelings returned. Trying to dissect some of the component parts as I experienced them, I became aware of a feeling that I would be exposed and unsure in these new efforts, that my contributions might not be seen as unique. As I became more involved with the community and with other mental health professionals, I found that the feelings of constant challenge to my ideas or efforts required me to affirm my efficacy, knowledge, or capacity to resolve problems better than anyone else. Such feelings and behaviors often stood in the way of collaboration. I noted also that my most frequently employed defense was one of all-knowing omnipotence, which by implication indicated that a new method or idea was old hat, had been tried before, and had not been effective. Under these personal circumstances I began to understand my own and my mental health colleagues' resistance to change in viewpoint and practice.

One's personal satisfactions in the mental health professions depend upon his having learned a certain body of theory and practice and having become fairly proficient in its use. We recognize that with continued use we can become more proficient and comfortable as experts. Most of the current models of interpersonal therapeutic engagement provide a fairly neutral, safe, and uninvolved haven for the therapist. Except perhaps in work with psychotic adults and children, the therapeutic position is one of relative uninvolvement, personal safety, and power. It is interesting that the recent increase of adolescent patients has resulted in many problems for therapists, because sick adolescents usually will not permit others to remain unengaged. Their demands and harassment for honest and direct expression of feelings is quite threatening to many on the therapeutic team who are trained in another model.

Personal satisfaction in the work also depends very much upon a sense of effectiveness and accomplishment. In many instances, in both private practice and agency work, we have some control over the psychopathologic problems or social class of individuals with whom we will work. Thus we can often select to preserve our feelings of effectiveness. In some settings relatively brief diagnostic contacts without follow-through give us a sense of helping individuals and families to accept the existence of problems and the need for help. We can then make a referral without being involved in further assessment of the effectiveness of the referral procedure or subsequent help to the family. In individual work with children and parents we can, with practice, select the workable families which will give us a sense of satisfaction. We can then designate the others as unworkable or hopeless and refer them to agencies or younger colleagues just beginning practice.

In all our work we are intimately involved in relieving suffering and helping others to live with less pain and turmoil. That we reach only a few people may be troubling, but since we are obviously providing some surcease from pain and disability, we can feel personally gratified that we are contributing in the best sense to human welfare.

How status and money affect our resistance to change is a very touchy area. There can be no question about the importance of status in our society as a whole and the mental health professions in particular. That status is frequently linked to income is also evident.

The paradigm of status in the mental health professions is the psychoanalyst. For a number of historical reasons having to do with the development of the most comprehensive, meaningful, and transmittable body of theory and practice, psychoanalysts have in one way or another been our most influential and effective teachers and models. Therefore, the model of individual work with patients for a fifty-minute hour, the couch, and high hourly fees has become the zenith in mental health practice. It is little wonder that individual work with patients in private practice has become the symbol of status in psychiatry, psychology, social work, and even psychiatric nursing. Licensing acts in various states which permit nonmedical private practice with the mentally ill have the psychoanalytic model in mind.

Money is clearly most easily come by in private practice, where one can be his own boss and can be adequately recompensed for long years of training. There can be no quarrel with the human need for a good income and the comforts and status that come with it.

The body of theory with which we work and the assumptions upon which it is based are usually not made explicit or tested carefully in practice. However, pragmatically the theories seem to work because patients keep coming and many appear to improve. Thus, a kind of certainty and security about one's theoretical and practice models occurs without much challenge, except with individual patients with whom we are not very effective or who disrupt our complacency by refusing to fit into our particular formulations. With such patients we can usually talk about resistances, and then find someone else we can work with more easily without needing to reexamine any basic premises of our theory or practice.

For most of us uncertainty is anxiety-provoking, questioning of our basic premises is threatening, and evaluating of our work so we can continue to learn and grow is frightening. Interestingly, the psychoanalytic model of the analyst's ongoing self-examination to ensure that he stays attuned to his own internal unconscious interferences in his work with patients, as well as his continual assessment of the effect of his interpretations on the progress of the patient, are basically the scientific model. In the scientific model close scrutiny and testing of all possible variables are essential, in addition to frequent reassessment of the basic hypotheses as the evaluations of actual practice or experiment shed light or raise questions about underlying premises. It is unfortunate that this model, while in theory an excellent one, is infrequently adhered to in practice. Its practitioners are the most open to new evidence in all the behavioral sciences which might shed light on their basic hypotheses. They also tend not to be doctrinaire and therefore lead the way to new formulations in theory and practice. For most of us it is easier to find a niche and stay there; the anxiety, wear, and tear are less, and the security is greater.

I also suspect from some recent investigations in a variety of professions that one major obstacle to change and the use of new methods is a fear of discovery that one is not as competent or effective as he had hoped. All new learning is hazardous, as well as anxiety-provoking, when it involves unlearning old methods and developing new skills. The teaching of new methods and procedures to trainees finds teachers trained in old models resistant. To look anew at our methods and basic hypotheses, to begin to evaluate what is true and helpful in the old, what can be translated to new situations, what are the immediate and long-term results of both old and new methods, of necessity engenders anxiety. In education, engineering, medicine, the mental health professions, resistance to change sometimes takes the form of acknowledging the relevance of new ideas and methods but not accepting them in practice or trying them out fully in new training and practice areas. A case in point would be the concepts of community mental health centers—continuity of care, responsiveness to the community's need and priorities as well as involvement with the community, the development of new treatment modalities and personnel—which are often officially subscribed to but rarely carried out fully.

One of our most serious internal team problems as mental health professionals is now reflected in new mental health programming. Leadership devolves automatically upon the high status psychiatrist, by tradition and because of the issue of medical responsibility, despite the fact that other team members may be more effective administrators or more skilled community mental health workers and that consulting physicians could carry the medical responsibility. In community mental health centers competence and effectiveness in doing the job should be the issue.

In new mental health programming a variety of professions as well as nonprofessional community representatives all want their say. Since nonprofessionals may be more aware of the needs, priorities, and methods by which a particular community could be served, many mental health professionals view involvement of others as a threat to their status as experts. In one community setting, as an example, the mental health professionals were experts in providing one-to-one psychotherapy to children and their families. In this poverty area the community representatives, local residents, church leaders, school personnel, and juvenile court workers expressed the need for more effective and widespread interventions in the first years of school. They felt that school failure which continued into the third or fourth grade usually resulted in total school and job failure for the children. The community representatives and professionals asked the mental health workers to address themselves to these concerns. The mental health professionals had first to resolve their feeling of threat at "being told what to do." After prolonged discussion they came to accept their area of expertise as "how the tasks should be done." But only after the resolution of threat to their status were they able to become engaged with the community toward a mutual goal of more effective educational and mental health services for a high-risk population.

Another example: In the face of the acute shortage of mental health professionals in a school system, it was suggested that individual services be kept at a minimum. Instead, it was proposed, the mental health workers might learn to use consultative techniques to enhance the capacities of counselors, teachers, and administrators to work more effectively with an ever-growing population of disturbed students.

Resistance to learning such mental health consultative techniques became evident when many of the workers began to raise the question of who was going to provide such services—social workers, psychologists, or school nurses. Each professional group wanted to have an exclusive franchise in exchange for giving up their already well developed and sought-after skills in individual services. Learning to be a consultant meant parting with the role of advice-giver and dispenser of favors (ridding the educator of a disturbed child). It meant involving the educator as a collaborator and withstanding his anger when, instead of removing his problem, the consultant engaged him still further in the problem. Consultants had to work with educators in securing the necessary data to understand a child's learning and behavior problems and in evolving a method of working with the child and family which might enhance the child's effectiveness as a student and reduce disturbing behavior. Only over a period of several years, when the consultative methods were acknowledged to be effective by school personnel and the special skills of each profession were utilized and recognized, did the status problems diminish.

In the area of training and use of nonprofessionals innumerable status problems occur. Despite the acute shortage of professionals which can never be overcome, stresses appear as aides are trained to do part of a particular mental health job and begin to do it well. We are all threatened with loss of status when our job function is no longer unique and we fear that someone can replace us. It becomes difficult to accept a coordinating function, a consultative and teaching role, as we note that a meaningful therapeutic relationship can be established and maintained by indigenous workers and case aides. Our role of supervisor, consultant, and emergency troubleshooter, which makes the nonprofessionals' work effective, seems less gratifying, since it is removed from a direct sense of effectiveness with the client or patient.

Perhaps most striking is the resistance to consideration of totally new models and concepts of therapeutic intervention. The public health model, which considers population problems and seeks methods for alleviating them, is threatening to those of us trained in individual work. The request that we translate some of the concepts we have learned in individual, family, and group therapy to deal with a wider range of problems and for more people evokes anger in many of us. When asked to concern themselves with primary and secondary prevention rather than with refining treatment methods, mental health professionals often contend that this is not within their province. To become competent in these areas requires a new conceptual framework which utilizes dynamic mental health concepts garnered from psychoanalysis, dynamic psychiatry, social work, and clinical psychology.

As a member of a new team, the mental health professional collaboration with a wide variety of health, education, and may need to relinquish his autonomy and learn a new kind of welfare allies. Many of us are poorly prepared for such a role and require considerable encouragement and role models in our professions to make a new role appear worthwhile and acceptable, despite our convictions that it may serve more people more effectively.

In one school district, to illustrate, it was possible to get all the mental health personnel involved in developing consultative and other interventions in the school and community because the crisis in the community would not permit them to deny the failure of the traditional methods in the face of overwhelming problems. But the transition from effective individual practice to effective mental health consultation with teachers, counselors, and administrators, to group work with children and parents to involvement with Head Start, kindergarten, and primary teachers, aides, and parents in a prevention program, required development of pilot models. As these models became viable and effective, other mental health and school personnel were able to learn from them. Weekly process seminars helped to explore uses of these methods and helped to test new ideas. Not only were successes shared, but all the problems, doubts, and anger about feelings of inadequacy and helplessness in the face of community pressure could be talked about early. We came to understand our turmoil as we sought to learn new methods and to find our satisfactions in new and different indicators of personal effectiveness.

For example, teachers' and school administrators' realistic concerns and feelings of being overwhelmed by the continuous confrontations with angry, disgruntled Negro and Mexican-American students in several junior and senior high schools led to ongoing discussions about these issues. It became clear that the mental health professionals were uneasy about the anger and confrontations presented to them by teachers, counselors, and administrators but were reluctant to voice such uneasiness. As the seminar members became able to discuss their feelings openly, they began to look at the data presented by school personnel and by students. The issue of how one could avoid confrontation and its threat to his position of authority and how one could begin to turn confrontations into collaboration bore fruit.

In one school the worker, who had excellent relationships with both administrators and teachers, was able to open discussion of how they could gather data about how best to serve their students, since they were aware of student dissatisfaction and needs. This led to dialogue among teachers, students, and administrators about making the curriculum and the school experience most meaningful. The actual efforts to change both methods and curriculum reduced tensions in the school and led to the development of a method for continued, regular dialogue at all levels and provided a model for other faculties and consultants to strive toward.

An evaluation program to determine the effectiveness of consultative methods finally convinced some mental health professionals that they were having some impact. Apparently the subjective impressions of the educators and community representatives who believed more children were staying in school and learning were not sufficient. It was as if, having given up their traditional methods of work, the mental health specialists had also temporarily lost any way of validating their usefulness. The reassurance which they had previously found adequate, such as statements from clients, patients, or colleagues, in this instance no longer sufficed. Evaluation, with clear controls and mutual engagement of all concerned in developing criteria for effectiveness, resulted in a much greater sense of involvement and personal satisfaction.

Several part-time workers gave up or reduced their more lucrative private practices as they began to feel effective in using new methods. Comments were often made about the feeling of strength, satisfaction, and sense of involvement resulting from participation in a community effort. There also seemed to be an overriding sense of purpose in the joint efforts to reduce disability and enhance the capacity for more effective living by children and parents in the community.

The Changing Posture of the Mental Health Consortium*

HOWARD E. FREEMAN AND ROSALIND S. GERTNER

Not much more than half a century ago a man and his ideas provoked the development of a new health specialty—one that emphasized different concepts and expanded the vocabularies of health practitioners to include such terms as "adjustment"; one that has concerned itself intensely with problems of communication and the patient-practitioner relationship; one that has shifted the search for the causes of illness at least somewhat away from the germ; one that has excited large numbers of persons about the prospects of manipulation leading to changes in the individual; and one that has been attacked by some as a totally charlatan activity and embraced by others as an essential component previously absent in health care.[1] The specialty under discussion is essentially a social invention. Probably, like other inventions, it was discovered many times before but remained obscure and dormant because of the community's lack of structural readiness to adopt it.[2]

*This paper appeared in slightly revised form in the *American Journal of Orthopsychiatry*, 39:116-24 (January 1969).

At the beginning of the century there was a man and an idea, but also a style and organization to community life that converged to make viable this new specialty. Daniel David Palmer and chiropractic therapeutics came along at a time when the small town and rural Midwest community members with their Protestant-ethic orientation were ripe for a new mode of health care. Its acceptance and development stems from structural circumstances: like the wheel, the airplane, and the bagel knife, it is an idea that may have been thought up many times but never, in one sense at least, really invented before. The same almost certainly is true of psychiatry and all the little psychiatries that go by other names.

The field of mental health, and the development and growth of the consortium of professional groups involved in it, is rooted in the attractiveness of ideas and practices compatible with a period of marked technological change, of expanded emphasis on educational and intellectual attainment, and of intense concern with economic achievement, material objects, and a bourgeois style of life. It also was a period when concepts of philanthropy were changing.[3] The sweet little old ladies in their black straw hats were being replaced by paid do-gooders. These neophyte professionals with unashamed aggressiveness sought a body of knowledge that could be transmitted to new recruits, if only so that they might enjoy a modicum of respectability and a small degree of riches. Then too in the academic world the subject matter of the social studies was rapidly changing, and disciplines were realigning themselves. Psychology received explicit recognition as a legitimate subject in higher education, eventually with the prerogative of training persons to practice as clinicians.

Perhaps the structural-functional perspective is less than an adequate explanation for the development of new health specialties. Certainly, however, the persistence and robustness of health specialties stem from their remaining in harmony with the social order, in the same way that modifications and adaptations are provoked elsewhere by structural changes. The revision in name, for example, of the American Board of

Dermatology and Syphilology to the American Board of Dermatology that occurred in 1955 represents an emphasis on skin condition and appearance among a wider segment of the community. Likewise the growth of the practice of orthodontics can be reasonably interpreted in this way. The proposition that all of health care, particularly mental health care, represents an expression of the structural character of community life is not an original one. Iago Galdstone has observed that since antiquity the organization of medical care and the provision of health services, whatever they may be, have reflected the social, political, cultural, and economic character of the community.[4]

In all of medical practice the current pressures of the social order are provoking intense concern about existing modes of delivery of service and task allocation among medical personnel. The growing radical left among physicians is committed to challenging both the way health care is conceived and the way it is undertaken. They have proposed major alterations in present programs. Within these ranks it is held, for example, that the organization and coordination of medical care services cannot focus on illness alone, but on health and illness in the community, the hospital, the home, and the agency. Moreover, it is deemed critical that comprehensive program development include and encourage the participation of the recipients of service. As one of the leaders in community medicine has noted: "We are faced not with the task of teaching techniques we have not yet mastered to thousands of subprofessionals we have not identified to meet needs we do not fully yet understand in a pattern of organization we have not yet invented."[5] Furthermore, there are some special considerations in the prevention and treatment of mental illness that link the stance of the field to social, political, and ideological factors.[6] First, there is a long-term awareness of the association between characteristics of the social order and the mental health of community members. It is not only recent work such as that of Leighton and his associates that emphasizes this view.[7] As George Rosen has brought to our attention, Benjamin Rush in the eighteenth century informed us that mental health required a stable and ordered society which would provide the proper stimuli and the necessary conditions of well-being.[8]

Second, the mental health field is particularly conspicuous for the absence of scientific investigations that demonstrate persistently and convincingly the efficacy of its existing preventive and treatment programs. As a consequence, the field is unusually vulnerable to social change.[9] Ullmann puts the matter quite sharply in an analysis of institutional treatment in a number of psychiatric hospitals:

The effectiveness of the treatment staff might be improved in much the same way as a monkey pounding on a typewriter can be helped to locate the works of Shakespeare. That is, we can increase the hours the monkey types (i.e. reinforced time with patients and decreased administrative ventures), or increase the number of monkeys engaged in typing (i.e. increase treatment staff through increased or more selective expenditures). However, even as with monkeys, someone would be required to separate the poetry from the meaningless letters. While there is some value to "more of the same," the addition of something new seems to be called for.[10]

Third, the concept of mental health itself continues to be challenged in many quarters. At best it is viewed as a vague and ambiguous one, at worst as meaningless and without any real reference to conditions in the "outside" world.[11] And if the fragile constitution of this concept were not enough, it is also strikingly susceptible to a variety of usages and interpretations when differential weights are attached to various dimensions, depending upon the social characteristics of the community members involved.[12] Myers and Bean for example, in their recently published ten-year follow-up study of former mental patients, identify social class differences in the relationship between the manifestation of psychiatric symptoms and the individual's overall performance in work and other instrumental tasks.[13] Upper and upper middle class patients over a

ten year period apparently do not experience either greater
social isolation or employment and financial problems than
others of similar class status who have not undergone a period
of hospitalization or outpatient treatment. But among those
of low social economic status mental illness apparently is
catastrophic for both the patient and his family; among the
poor the impact of the illness is maximally related to serious
employment and financial problems and a high degree of
social isolation.

Finally, whether the underlying reason is one of the selection process, who chooses a career in mental health, or of the
socialization experience during the early stages of professional
development, a significant number of individuals within the
consortium of practitioners are strongly oriented toward immediate and if necessary unconvential social action to ameliorate undesirable inequities and disorganization in the American urban community. The value orientation being described
is illustrated well in the writings of Robert Coles,[14] for
example.

It is not the "mental health movement" that is responsible
for the state of affairs in the field, but the current outlines of
the social order.[15] In many ways the characteristics of contemporary mental health practices and the roles taken by practitioners are inconsistent with new and projected needs, and
this has led to what may be politely described as a field in
a state of flux.

Given the current demands—concern with the poor, the
growing aged population, the drug-using adolescent group—
the traditional lines of demarcation between the various practicing professions have blurred; reliance on a particular mode
of therapy is regarded as futile; role assignments of individuals are no longer sharp; and status relationships within the
consortium are unclear. A portrait of the mental health consortium would resemble pop art in the extreme. On the one
hand, there are medically trained persons who share long
years of relatively similar training and extremely rigid certification requirements. On the other hand, there are innovative
groups, such as aides recruited from among the poor to meet

the needs of persons in poverty areas, who have little in common with each other or with their professionally certified practitioner colleagues. At the same time that psychodynamically oriented social workers are reviewing the relevance of sociological theories for mental health programs, psychometricians are occupied with the stresses of administrative positions in new appointments as directors of mental health centers and catchment areas, formerly open only to physicians. And child psychiatrists are learning about cost-effectiveness analysis and systems design so that they may prove competent as social planners.

The changes have been phenomenal. At an organizational level, the distinguished British expert Richard Titmuss noted: "this blurring of the hitherto sharp lines of demarcation between home care and institutional care, between physical disability and mental disability, between educationally backward children and so-called 'delinquent' children, and between health needs and welfare needs, is all part of a general movement toward more effective service to the public and toward a more wholistic interpretation and operational definition of the principles of primary, secondary, and tertiary prevention."[16]

The picture emerges sharply when the specific functions of mental health personnel are considered. It is now possible to legitimately act as a psychotherapist without participating in the long training traditionally required;[17] the person formerly regarded as a nonprofessional or limited practitioner not only may assume therapeutic roles and responsibilities, but as he does the distinctions between ranks are further obscured. In some cases the nonprofessional worker has become so much a part of the therapeutic team that he ends up by teaching the professionals charged with training him.[18] Furthermore, the urgency with which some mental health professionals are engaged in rethinking and redesigning their current role assignments in search of more distinctive professional niches provides additional testimony to the increasingly flimsy role definitions which currently characterize the field.[19]

It seems clear that we are approaching, at least to some

degree, a situation in which all organizations are multi-service ones, in which all categories of personnel offer and undertake a variety of prevention and treatment activities, and in which all people are welcomed and encouraged to participate in the spectrum of programs. At first glance perhaps it may seem that the changes that have occurred signify the arrival of the millennium. It would seem that what is developing is a system of health care in which democracy is being expressed at an organizational level, both in relationships among treatment personnel and in participation of community members. But before one embraces the current scheme of things with enthusiastic abandon, we should speculate on the consequences of the current posture and on the course of future events.

A debate among three esteemed sociologists in one of the sociological journals some years back has considerable relevance for our views on future arrangements in the field.[20] Melvin Tumin discussed the possibility of a social system's being completely structured along a horizontal axis. He argued quite forcefully that theoretically there is no reason that this type of social order cannot be realized. His point of view that vertical stratification is not endemic to social life was challenged by both Davis and Moore. They are at least equally persuasive that while it is possible for a society, community, or organization to conduct its affairs with all men being equal, inevitably it will be necessary for some to be more equal than others.

It is not critical to settle the debate here, for even if Tumin were correct in the abstract, the concept of a flat, horizontal system within an organizational entity is extremely difficult to imagine within the context of contemporary American life. Yet apparently this is the direction of development within the consortium of mental health professionals.

Is there a basis for concern, given the proposition that all may be equal but some must be more equal than others? To the extent that a horizontal arrangement is both a feasible and an appropriate way to organize relationships within the mental health field, a reformulation of role relationships and task assignments must necessarily be within an overall plan. But this is not so in the case of the consortium of mental health practitioners. Indeed, if one wishes to be either cynical or snide, he can argue that the present arrangements and the direction of relationships within the consortium stem from the inability of the parties involved either to do their own jobs better than other people, or other people's jobs better than their own.

The increasingly vigorous argument that medical training is a dispensable component in the psychotherapist's toolkit demonstrates the extent to which functional monopolies of therapeutic tasks and activities are becoming problematic.[21] Professional attributes formerly used to separate the various roles and functions within the consortium seem to be losing their sanctity as the boundaries between the professions become more permeable and the tasks of each one less rigidly defined. The cry is heard that jobs be assigned according to competence rather than professional identification.[22] But the formulation of criteria by which therapeutic competence may be ascertained continues to be vague. This seems especially apparent in the organization of therapeutic communities, where it is held that "every team member is encouraged to use whatever therapeutic skills he possesses in any situation."[23] If individuals who traditionally have occupied the superordinate roles were in fact distinctively qualified for special positions—psychiatrists in comparison with everyone else, and degree-holding professionals of various ilks as opposed to attendants, aides, and intelligent laymen—it would have been difficult if not impossible to wrest these persons from their niches. The trend toward "equality" and task disbursement within the consortium of mental health practitioners may be looked upon as a most brilliant ad hoc strategy, albeit unwittingly arrived at, which literally may function to prevent a revolution within the ranks of the disadvantaged among the consortium: a victory, indeed, if one thinks about the possibility of the gatekeeper recruited from the poor snuggled on the clinical director's couch by popular vote.

One means by which persons in high status occupations

protect their positions is to monopolize certain functions, and to maintain this monopoly by a series of legal and formal mechanisms of certification. A consequence of successfully developing such certification procedures is a built-in inability to be flexible and to move rapidly in reorganizing educational and training programs. Despite the obvious successes of the Martin Luther Kings, Stokeley Carmichaels, and the like, psychiatrists, even today, are telling us that "clinical training, with continued clinical work, not only sensitizes one to transference and countertransference problems of individuals and group psychotherapeutic work vital to self-awareness in all personal situations, but it also keeps one focused on the individual human being and his needs and reactions to programs and process. It also makes it possible to utilize clinical acumen in all of one's interpersonal relations at all levels."[24] While training in the entrenched mental health professions like psychiatry apparently resists change of significant proportion, practice in the field seems to be demanding considerable role versatility. The successful mental health professional may soon be distinguished from the unsuccessful one primarily by his virtuosity as a quick-change artist. It is simply foolish to hold that the astute clinician makes the best community organizer, that lengthy practice experience with neurotic middle-class housewives is useful in the development of comprehensive health and welfare programs for the poor, or that success in treating the school-phobia problems of suburban grammar school children gives a purchase on dealing with school dropout and drug problems among core-city teenagers.

Of course, there have been modifications in the educational and training programs of those who are or at least were high up within the consortium of health professionals. But it is fair to state, by and large, that most of the educational innovations have occurred within the less respectable professional groups or in disciplines based on almost entirely new academic programs. In simplest terms the trend toward egalitarianism and the sharing of roles and tasks may be viewed as a means of avoiding possibly even more marked rearrangements in patterns of relationships within the consortium.

The trend toward equality and the sharing of tasks may, of course, be defended on the grounds that the reduction of status differentials and a lack of rigidity in the therapeutic contributions of the various parties involved is desirable in keeping with the holistic philosophy of treatment.[25] The basis for this position has been challenged by Perrow, who argues that the claims made of the accomplishments of therapeutic-community type organizations are without substantial empirical support and at the very least are inconsistent with knowledge about the functioning of organizations.[26] This need not mean that existing bureaucratic arrangements, such as those in institutional settings and in the developing community mental health centers, represent a necessarily effective and efficent set of arrangements. It may well be, as Ullmann observed in extending Etzioni's views, that staff and line concepts in professional organizations have to be reversed.[27] Under these reversed conditions the major treatment activities would tend even more to be carried out by experts rather than being undertaken by almost anybody, as occurs under the generic solution of everyone's doing everything.[28]

Even if the concept of equality and sharing of tasks could be accomplished, it represents a temporary solution, given the congruence between the world of the practicing profession and that of the business community. Although William Whyte's analysis of participation in the social structure is certainly not above criticism, it is difficult to deny the relevance of some of his observations regarding the motivations and dispositions of individuals in their occupational roles.[29] Reserved parking spaces if not rugs on the floor, a new dictaphone if not keys to the executive washroom, and travel money to attend conventions if not country club membership are often present in the bargaining encounters of persons in the field. Like executive training programs, a variety of different types of educational adventures in the health and welfare fields are predicated on producing new leaders, even if we do not know who and what they should be. Students at an undergraduate level in places like Wesleyan University are being trained as policy makers; new schools of policy science

are in the offing; several of the large systems-oriented planning
and development corporations are in the business of human resource curricula development; and some professional schools
concerned about their relatively low reputations are turning
to innovative leadership programs in hopes of instantly up-
lifting their status.

The continued trend toward equality and diffusion of the
roles of the various subsets within the consortium of mental
health practitioners, until there is one indivisible ball of wax,
is a remote possibility. Rather, a better guess is that new
groups within the consortium will begin to dominate and control, and the field will return once again to a more vertical
sorting of individuals and to an increased specialization in
task allotment. The ideology of American social life, as well
as the dynamics within the consortium, will lead to the gradual assumption of increased power by professions now regarded as marginal in status and competence and denied the
opportunity to participate fully. As they legitimize their place
and tighten requirements to obtain their credentials, they will
render the traditionally superordinate groups illegitimate and,
like the carpetbaggers of the Civil War era, will first infiltrate
high society and then capture it.

Whether or not this is entirely desirable cannot be assessed.
It depends in part on whether the structural influences on the
provision of health care services continue in the same direction as they currently are moving. If not, one may suppose that
again some kind of strategy will be used to hold the loosely
knit consortium of mental health professions together, until
another restructuring takes place.

A postscript is called for. In developing this paper our
original intent was to examine future manpower needs in the
mental health field. This is not entirely a topic without research, as anyone who has read Albee's volume, or critiques of
it, and other studies is aware.[30] In these times, however, to
approach the problem of manpower in the mental health field
one must confront the matters discussed in this paper.

The complex links among the social structure, program development, and arrangements within the consortium render impossible any estimates on either the quantity or quality of people required in terms of a table of organization. The question that must be answered is beyond the scope of present knowledge; one must be concerned with the issue of the nature of the inputs required to develop an orderly but flexible set of arrangements within the consortium to respond to the shifting demands of the social structure.

Even if he would not agree with our analysis, Robert Rieff has observed: "The mental health professions' posture is not that of a group of people with a successful product harassed by a clamoring demand, it is more like a group of desperate men struggling to hold back a flood and who cannot find the hole in the dike. This kind of manpower crisis is totally different from the usual shortage, for while it is true more bodies are needed to stem the tide, unless the hole is found and repaired or the water redirected, it will be a losing battle."[31]

NOTES

1. J. Dintenfass, *Chiropractic: A Modern Way to Health* (New York: Pyramid, 1960).
2. R. Merton, *On the Shoulders of Giants* (New York: Harcourt, Brace and World, 1965).
3. R. Bremner, *From the Depths: The Discovery of Poverty in America* (New York: New York University Press, 1956).
4. "Doctor and Patient in Medical History," *Journal of American Education*, 37:222-32 (1962).
5. H. Geiger, *Challenge to the Professions—Catastrophic Illness: Impact on Families* (New York, National Cancer Foundation: 65, 1967).
6. Howard Freeman, "Social Change in the Organization of Mental Health Care," *American Journal of Orthopsychiatry*, 35:717-22 (1965).
7. C. Hughes *et al.*, *The People of Cove and Woodlot* (New York: Basic Books, 1960).
8. "Emotion and Sensibility in Ages of Anxiety: A Comparative Historical Review," *American Journal of Psychiatry*, 124:771-84 (1967).
9. Howard Freeman, and O. Simmons, *The Mental Patient Comes Home* (New York: John Wiley, 1963).

10. L. Ullmann, *Institutional and Outcome: A Comparative Study of Psychiatric Hospitals* (New York: Pergamon, 1967).

11. Thomas Szasz, *The Myth of Mental Illness* (New York: Harper and Row, 1961).

12. Howard Freeman, and Joseph Giovianni, "Social Psychiatry of Mental Health," *Handbook of Social Psychology* ed. Gardner Lindzey and Elliot Aronson (Boston: Addison-Wesley, 1969), pp. 660-719.

13. J. Myers, and L. Bean, *A Decade Later* (New York: John Wiley and Sons, 1968).

14. "It's the Same but It's Different," *Daedalus, 94*:1107-32 (1965).

15. J. Stretch, "Community Mental Health: The Evolution of a Concept in Social Policy," *Community Mental Health Journal, 3*:5-12 (1967).

16. "The Welfare Complex in a Changing Society," *Milbank Memorial Fund Quarterly 45*:11 (1967).

17. B. Glover, "Psychiatric Nurses: Technicians or Cotherapists?" *Psychiatric Opinions, 4*:11-13. (1967).

18. G. Reding, and E. Goldsmith, "The Nonprofessional Hospital Volunteer as a Member of the Psychiatric Consultation Team," *Community Mental Health Journal, 3*:267-72, (1967).

19. S. Garfield, "Clinical Psychology and the Search for Identity," *American Psychologist, 21*:353-62 (1966). Also A. Bendman, "Problems Associated with Community Mental Health Programs," *CMHJ, 2*:333-38 (1966).

20. "Some Principles of Stratification: a Critical Analysis," *American Sociological Review, 18*:387-94 (1953). K. Davis, "Reply to 'Some Principles of Stratification,' " *ASR, 18*:394-97 (1953). W. Moore, "Comment on 'Some Principles of Stratification,' " *ASR, 18*:397 (1953.

21. A. Mariner, "A Critical Look at Professional Education in the Mental Health Field," *AP, 22*:271-81 (1967).

22. M. Smith, and N. Hobbs, "The Community and the Community Mental Health Center," *AP, 21*:499-509 (1966).

23. P. Jarvis, and S. Nelson, "The therapeutic community and new calls for clinical psychologists," *AP, 21*:526 (1966).

24. Irving Berlin, "Training in Community Psychiatry: Its Relationship to Clinical Psychiatry," *CMHJ, 4*:357 (1965).

25. R. Vinter, "The structure of service," *Behavioral Science for Social Workers*, ed. E. Thomas (New York: The Free Press, 1967).

26. *Handbook of Organizations* (Chicago: Rand-McNally, 1966).

27. L. Ullman, *Institution and Outcome*. See footnote 10.

28. B. Wooton, *Social Science and Social Pathology* (London: George, Allen and Unwin, 1959), Chap. 9.

29. *The Organization Man* (New York: Simon and Schuster, 1956).

30. G. Albee, *Mental Health Manpower* (New York: Basic Books, 1959).

31. "Mental Health Manpower and Institutional Change," *AP, 21*:544 (1966).

The Nonprofessional: promise or primrose path?

DIANA TENDLER

Approximately four years have elapsed since the passage of the Economic Opportunity Act, which, building on the experiences of earlier demonstration community action programs, set into motion a kaleidescopic, far-ranging, not always well defined series of efforts aimed at many segments of the American population that live in poverty. The motivations were probably mixed. The temper of the times, a sense of urgency to do something for a long-neglected portion of our citizenry, for some the growing fears of "long hot summers," the needs of financially burdened municipalities for new resources, the contention of professionals that new programs and activities were required all combined to create a climate of exciting, often-frantic activity, not seen perhaps since the early days of the New Deal. What started with promise and enthusiasm has increasingly become a grave responsibility for planners and professionals, particularly in the human services.

One of the major areas that has expanded as a result of the impetus and support of federal funding has been the engagement of more nonprofessionals in a wide variety of human services. (OEO programs, Title 1 of the Elementary and Secondary Education Act, and the Scheuer-Nelson Subprofessional Career Act are examples of legislative empowering of funds for the development of personnel in education, health, and welfare.) Increasing numbers of persons are involved; organizations in public service-education departments, health and mental health, municipal civil services, as well as voluntary community agencies have announced programs in which nonprofessionals are currently engaged or proposed as employes.[1] Higher education institutions have participated as resources in a number of "training programs." Without the wide-ranging federal programming resulting from President Johnson's declaration in January 1964 of "an unconditional war on poverty," it is doubtful that we would need to consider some of the specific issues that are presented here—the dilemmas, problems, and alternatives posed by the introduction of nonprofessionals into the helping services.

We shall examine the use of nonprofessionals in the context of current programs for the solution of problems of poverty in the United States. Poverty in America in the 1960s is identified as structural rather than attributable to cyclical economic processes; that is, "Poverty in modern America tends to be a permanent state, concentrated among certain disadvantaged groups and in many cases continuing generation after generation."[2] Many social scientists also see it as more technically susceptible to amelioration than at any other time in the nation's history, although they believe that philosophical readiness to accept important social changes is impeded by the highly individualistic traditions and concepts that derive from the Puritan ethic.[3] There is an identifiable sector of the population which constitutes "the poor," approximately one-fifth of the total. This one-fifth live below the conventional poverty line of $3,000 for family income, and many show additional susceptibilities and vulnerability by being old, nonwhite, from broken families, poorly educated, or unskilled, with difficulties in fitting into the labor force.[4]

The description of our poverty population is familiar. It is cited here because it has some bearing upon the development of anti-poverty programs in which such persons become not only the objects of social planning but also potential personnel, especially in the nonprofessional ranks. Among the solutions proposed for dealing with the problems of a technologically advancing "automating" society are incentive plans in which shifts and changes in the utilization of manpower are important. Indeed this is a basic part of the rationale for the employment of nonprofessionals, well stated by Herbert Gans, who suggests the creation of "subprofessional" categories as the start of "an entirely new occupational stratum,"[5] a viable way to deal with issues of professional shortages and employment needs of the poor.

> By calling them technicians or subprofessionals, opposition from the established professions would be reduced, and new curricula could be developed which would avoid some of the lengthy instruction which has become entrenched in these professions.
> The greatest need is for technicians of working and lower class origin who could help the low income population attain the social and cognitive skills required to become a part of the larger society.
>
> . . . .
>
> [Proposals such as recruitment into unfilled jobs and the creation of a subprofessional stratum] encourage the kind of work that will be important in the society of the future, as well as dignified and rewarding for the job holder. In addition these proposals could reduce the workload which is rapidly becoming an overload in the existing professions, thereby halting the stratification of American society into an overworked professional minority and an underemployed majority, a trend that has many undesirable social and political consequences.[6]

Riessman and Pearl offer a similar rationale in their development of the new careers concept, which carries the ideas further by suggesting a "ladder" for the achievement of occupational mobility.

The New Careers theory proposes that all the human service occupations (health, education, recreation, welfare, etc.)
can be broken down and reorganized to provide a much more
efficient service-product while simultaneously allowing people
who have little or no training to play a productive role in
entry service positions. These untrained individuals will have
the opportunity of learning on the job and rising in the service hierarchy with the ultimate option of becoming professionals.

The theory requires a reorganization and redefinition of
jobs for both the professional and the nonprofessional . . . .
First the theory proposes that untrained nonprofessionals can
perform a great many of the tasks now performed unnecessarily by professionals. . . . Second it proposes that a hierarchy
of these jobs can be developed requiring different degrees of
training. Third, it proposes that this training can be acquired
on the job itself and through systematic in-service training
and job-based college courses, with the idea of providing
people with employment first and diplomas later. Fourth, it
proposes that this reorganization will free professionals to
perform a much higher level of specialized services that require advanced training and experience.[7]

Although there has been a great increase in the use of nonprofessionals in many human service areas, apart from the new
careers concept few experiences have been reported in the professional literature reflecting alternative theoretical orientations or reporting on findings from other approaches.

The general orientation presented here has considerable appeal to many practitioners in the helping professions. The approach recognizes the pressures under which help is given—
with a reduction of certain services because of manpower
shortages. It also takes account of the considerable time for activities other than the unique contributions of the professional's skill, along with the time-consuming supportive activities that might be shared with technicians, volunteers, and
nonprofessionals. Despite some bureaucratic modes and pro-
tectionist notions about the sanctity of professionals' functions,
the value system of the helping professions encompasses con-

cern with the development of large-scale social programs, as well as commitments to producing more desirable outcomes from treatment and to attempting changes in practice and staffing that will benefit those they serve. If professionals concerned with social improvement are to make effective use of new proposals for personnel resources, it is important to identify the issues involved in such proposals.

Those of us who have had some role either in the employment and training of nonprofessionals are often excited by the possibilities we perceive. Many professionals have been deeply moved and emotionally affected by the confrontations and revelations experienced. One is impressed with the quality of communication that is achieved, by the strong desire for participation that many nonprofessionals show, by the evidence of persons with real talent and ability who are afforded an opportunity to make a contribution. Indeed, these experiences are a reminder that the stakes are high but that the indications of possible success of some of our early efforts must not prevent a full examination of the questions that emerge. We must now make this examination, lest programs and plans born in new hope should find themselves a part of disillusioning, inadequately planned efforts that might serve to further alienate, and may end in attributions of failure to the very groups toward whom directed. Professional imperatives for diagnosis, evaluation, and prediction seem applicable to the situation at hand. Lincoln's words: "If we could first know where we are and whither we are tending, we could better judge what to do and how to do it," reflect the spirit of this examination.

The following issues seem of significance: the conditions under which the involvement of nonprofessionals has taken place; the identity of the nonprofessional; the tasks we ask the nonprofessional to perform; the recruitment of the nonprofessional; and the training of the nonprofessional.

In most programs which have used nonprofessionals, whether new programs such as Headstart or community psychiatry or already established organizations with nonprofessionals added to fit into already existing structures, the exigencies of funding have severely affected the ability to plan. Even where some preliminary planning has been done, changes in budgetary allotments, dates when funds are available, and the uncertainty about their duration has seriously affected an organization's view of a program. Professionals thus have been concerned with funding, time, and circumstance and have not been able to give sufficient attention to relationships between activity and outcomes. For those of us involved in some of the early new efforts some compromises had to be made between the more usual concepts of advance study and planning and the need to seize new opportunities. Perhaps to the credit of the professionals involved, the choices that were made emphasized action.

However, now that we can examine some of the consequences of what was often precipitate action, we are in a better position to weigh assets and liabilities, to avoid getting set into institutional modes which accommodate such problems and which bureaucratize the inadequacies. We would be less than honest if we did not admit that some of our pet ideas simply do not work and should be abandoned and that others need further study and identification of conditions under which achievement is greater. Demands on our professional "objectivity" are in effect greater, by virtue of our attraction to the positive social aims and objectives of programs for nonprofessionals, to which many of us emotionally subscribe.

Subprofessional, paraprofessional, indigenous worker, staff aide, expediter, case manager, technician, informal leader, intervenor, community worker, facilitator, ancillary person, neighborhood worker; these are but a few of the terms that identify the new nonprofessional. He has come into the human services mainly through federally funded programs, either in demonstration projects, or as a result of Office of Economic Opportunity guidelines that have stressed "the maximum feasible participation of the poor." The terms used for his description are occupational, functional, and geographical and reflect social class identifications as well as distinctions which relate to positions held in the occupational heirarchy.

The nonprofessionals we talk about most often are persons who reside in poverty or target areas, individuals with presumed knowledge about neighborhood and/or client groups and who appear to have some skills in interpersonal relations and an ability to interact with the populations to be served. The vague definition hints at some of the difficulties that have emerged in identifying these persons. It has been easier, Frank Riessman indicates, to describe "what he is not . . . not simply a citizen volunteer, [nor] . . . the traditional kind of employee . . . not a professional . . . not a political action organizer [but] . . . an amalgam of all these various roles . . . the new marginal man."[9] Similar difficulties in individualization occur in relation to the often-used phrase "the indigenous worker," to which many meanings have been ascribed. Apart from its dictionary meaning of "native," the phrase has been interpreted by some as equivalent to subprofessional, or a person who has all other qualities but professional training; in other instances it refers to residency in specific areas, or membership in the client and patient population.[10] To some it has begun to assume a somewhat negative, class-bound connotation, and Martin Rein's comment that suburban P.T.A. groups are rarely refered to as "indigenous" seems appropriate.[11]

Descriptions of the nonprofessional often convey the sense of an anonymous, conglomerate being, a member of "the poor," who is alternately seen as apathetic, unresponsive, and in need of motivation, affected by the stigmata attached to poverty, or as uniquely suited, by virtue of his exposure to the life style of the slum, to be a major resource in our contacts with clients with whom we have heretofore been unsuccessful. A new romanticism, possibly influenced by a sense of guilt about our past failures as well as our real concern with past injustices, has posed the danger of stereotyping the poor. The new nonprofessional is many people and represents a considerable range of characteristics.

The new nonprofessional may be the older single woman who has been self-supporting in factory or menial jobs, the young, or not so young, male adult school dropout, the ADC

mother, the older person from a residual neighborhood population, the predelinquent adolescent, the young mother of
children whose family is intact but is affected by her unskilled
husband's limited wages, the imigrant newcomer. In many
instances, he is a member of a minority group, particularly in
urban areas. This list can probably be expanded, but my purpose is not an exhaustive listing, but rather a stimulus to
thoughts about the implications of personal and social characteristics, the capacities and competencies they may reflect, the
somewhat different personal and vocational aims that they
may seek in their employment.

On the basis of already accumulated experience we can begin to identify characteristics of some of our nonprofessional
personnel. The data from community demonstration projects
as well as OEO programs does not bear out the picture of nonprofessional workers as the apathetic poor.[12] At least these are
not the persons who have worked in programs that are in effect. Rather, it would seem that the applicants attracted are
often quite highly motivated, as well as equipped with communication and other useful skills. Whether this is due to organizational decisions or to self-selection processes among
poverty groups is not very clear, but it does suggest that certain types of persons are more commonly found among nonprofessionals, or at least are most frequently characterized in
the literature. Riessman comments: "It should always be remembered that we are probably not selecting a representative
"lower class" population but in all likelihood are selecting
"bridge" people who can communicate with both class groups
(low income and our own middle-class population). This nonprofessional population has considerably more ambition,
drive, envy, and less identification with the poor."[13]

If, in fact, such persons represent the major resources for
nonprofessional personnel, such trends will possibly affect
their performance and may also have implications for their
continuing commitment to nonprofessional jobs. The observed
tendency for persons who are upwardly mobile to reject their
past origins, to establish social distance, may well affect the

nonprofessional's special virtues—his ability to communicate with the poor. Judgmental attitudes, the responses of "moral indignation, punitiveness, or suspicion" in responding to clients, and the observation of some expressions of competition, "think they're different from the poor and would be more effective than professionals if they had the chance," are phenomena noted by many workers in the field.[14] Granted that recruitment processes attempt to select with these hazards in mind, to find the true "bridge" person (an admittedly difficult screening job), what are the effects of continued employment as a nonprofessional, particularly as it changes or influences the nonprofessional's concept of self, affects the sense of esteem, status, and self-realization? For those of us who have followed the career patterns of nonprofessionals whom we have trained and encouraged in their movement upward, it does appear as though the process may produce new aspects of role conflict, not so much in the initial stages, but increasingly stressful with the increasing assumption of responsibility. Certain responses of nonprofessionals, quite understandable as adaptations to their life circumstances and personal mobility, may not be always functional for their contributions to human service programs.

We have discussed some characteristics of nonprofessionals as they may be dysfunctional for their job performance. An equal hazard would be to confuse service aims and the personnel implementation required to accomplish them. In the interest of giving employment opportunities, we should not overlook the primary aims of the helping service.

As has been stressed elsewhere, work must be meaningful, and its contribution to larger organizational and social purposes must be perceived. If we conceive of task or job definitions as making the viable connection between the use of manpower and the organizational aims of the human services, then adequate task definitions must be set, and the professionals within the organization must take the responsibility for their formulation. Despite the professionals' possible disadvantages as captive members of organizational structures, they seem the most likely persons to do such planning. In assuming the most active role in task difinition they would need to envision the total context of professional and nonprofessional activities in relation to the helping resource's service purposes and objectives. They cannot afford to be affected by sentimental considerations or pressures of time, or seduced by unique and unusual experiences of initial success; their professional competencies must be engaged in consideration of what is to be achieved, what are the organization's objectives and consequent policy, and what kinds of personnel can accomplish these aims.

A major observation, readily available in initial work with nonprofessionals, is the frequent request for a clear and explicit definition of what they are to do, what will be expected of them in their job performance, a challenge which we have not met sufficiently. What seem like simple requests often cannot be so easily answered. Some of the responses developed seem to be oversimple in descriptions of the characteristics of the nonprofessional that make him eligible for consideration for employment, while others sound like somewhat obfuscated titles designed to provide status rather than activity. Some examples in a recent government monograph will illustrate the former type in definitions developed at the Center for Youth and Community Studies.[15]

Position	*Qualifications*
Foster Home Aides	Must be able to read, write, and count, be responsible enough to be left alone with children.
School Classroom Aide	Must be able to read, write, and count. Like children. Be dexterous.
Probation Aide	Should be able to get along with offenders without being conned by them.

Job titles attempting to differentiate levels of competence by "assistant" and "associate" sometimes are misunderstood; the "family worker" and "family assistant" titles among Headstart trainees tended to suggest that the higher level position of "family assistant" reflected a lower status, and the meaningful differentiation was finally understood on the basis of pay rates. While it may be quite difficult to translate the elements into accurately descriptive brief titles, the combination of skill and expected competency along with personal characteristics seems necessary.[16] Additionally, consideration and related links between professional and nonprofessional levels and definitions are often lacking. Apart from the New Careers literature there has been little study of such efforts. This has implications not only for individual placement, but for the consequences of comparisons made by new employees. It seems important to reflect the whole range of skills and unique differentiations in conjunction with each other, if one is to avoid the misunderstandings of his own and other functions that can lead to an anti-professional stance.

In the development of such definitions we should use as the underlying base the professional model of helping, perhaps with some modifications that relate to changed service aims. Such a model reflects our most important experiences to date and has influenced our views regarding judgmental attitudes and the ability of the nonprofessional to understand the meaning of confidentiality—two of the many concepts and principles that professionals consider important to significant interaction in helping processes.

Within this same framework concepts like "the poor can talk better to the poor," the act of helping as part of a "helper therapy" principle, have been suggested as unique contributions of nonprofessionals. While these points represent some creative observations about the effects of nonprofessional involvement, they need further elaboration. Under what conditions are they applicable? Desirable? What relationship do they bear to basic service goals of the organization? What is the relationship to appropriate task differentiation among all agency personnel?

The present dependence on a rather hit-or-miss system of recruitment has sometimes yielded the gifted persons who seem to make something work—but is this success always transferable, so that workers who will prove valuable can be more positively identified on a regular basis? What about the casualties—what do they represent in numbers or proportions of a nonprofessional staff? What identifiable factors can explain the degree to which either the person and the situation may have been responsible for failures or successes? In short, can we develop a more systematic description of the new nonprofessional and the functional competencies that may be demanded by the job.

The questions of task definition raised here, as well as other related issues, at present should be concerned less with the implications of an extension of categories, until we have learned from our present programs. Perhaps only certain groups among the potential reservoir of manpower can be involved in nonprofessional jobs in the human services. As we learn more from operating and planned programs we may also be able to view the utilization of nonprofessionals as a part of an incentive plan, which would take its place among a range of anti-poverty measures.

An important question is recruitment of nonprofessionals. Our main experiences thus far have been with entry positions, although we can anticipate more data on individuals moving up in job levels as programs continue. The tendency in such programs has been to recruit from already identified client groups or from a "client community." Because of starting pressures and imperatives for action these programs have often approached recruitment less systematically than efforts such as task definition and training.

Finding applicants has generally been a lesser problem than deciding about their selection. Often hiring practices have tended to stress nonqualifications, factors which might be presumed to result in noneffective functioning. This orientation again is strongly derived from the professional models of criteria for appropriate helping behavior. Also clear task definitions or job demands and qualifications apparently have resulted in the recruitees' responses being more positive. Many training programs report high levels of initial anxiety among professionals and nonprofessionals resulting from vague specifications for jobs. Records need to be kept of the basis on which recruitment takes place and the later job performance and outcome. We must consider how much responsibility the recruitment process itself may have for rejects. Firstly, who are rejects and how many are they, and what are the bases for rejection? Should we look more carefully at the impact of rejection on the individual as well as on the community? To what degree does careful selection, granted one has established criteria, affect the community's view? Is careful selection perceived as a limitation and denial of opportunity?

In terms of interest, effort, and investment, the training of nonprofessional may well be the most significant matter. We can observe both considerable imagination in developing training patterns and tendencies to offer rather stereotyped models. Training has taken place under a variety of conditions and settings; it has been in the form of orientation prior to service, in-service, and on-the-job training, in various combinations. It has taken place within the hiring organizations at formal educational institutions such as universities; it has been paid for by program funds, or by contractual arrangements with institutions, or by private management corporations as a part of competitive bidding for government awards. Sources of support have clearly influenced the structure, time, and content of these programs, but we need more systematic information to judge the advantages and disadvantages of the various methods. Have the specifications of certain limits in time and funding affected training processes? Have the persons responsible for training accepted these limits too readily, against their better educational judgment? There are some indications that with continuing experience some of the training setups are beginning to utilize some of their experiences with training programs more systematically, but evidence for an overall trend in this direction is needed.

We need also to evaluate the various sources of difficulties encountered in training processes. Do they derive from the characteristics of the nonprofessional, from deficiencies and problems within the organizational structure, or from the inadequate specifications or confusion created by job definitions? We have tended to stress the characteristics of the nonprofessional and to see problems with authority, over or underidentification with the institution and/or client groups, unrealistic optimism or cynicism, or combinations of these characteristics without reference to special effects or possible interrelationships. While these observations of factors to be taken into account in planning training efforts have been helpful, they may have led to a perhaps unwarranted emphasis upon change in personal attitudes rather than attention to changing structural elements, which may be harder to alter, but at the same time may be a major source of role ambiguity.

The same issues affecting recruitment and job performance, issues concerned with how much identification with professional models of conduct and recognition of the particular competencies of professionals can be communicated, again assume importance. Some of these features need to be taught in the training process. The nonprofessional, according to our view, would not get very far in using his style and inherent capacities if other content were not added. Problems in learning to perform on the job are not those of the nonprofessional per se, and professionals must make a careful analysis of job content and weave this into nonprofessional training. Educational objectives should be tied more closely to what the job calls for, and the temptations to more clinically-oriented exploration (frequent characteristics of trainers) need to be controlled.

Training programs emphasized the special style of learning that characterizes low income people and the need for trainers to consider these patterns. We have been strongly influenced by writings on the effects of early educational disadvantage and the need for special techniques in teaching adults with inadequate prior education. Granted the importance of techniques, there is something disturbing in outlining learners' needs and trainers' performance in terms of the "mental style" of low income persons. While qualities such as "content-centered rather than form-centered," "problem-centered rather than abstract-centered," and "physical and visual rather than aural" may characterize general attributes of low income individuals,[17] too ready incorporation of such ideas by the trainer may produce attitudes and expectations that limit his responsiveness to the demands of the teaching process. It has been suggested that the "success of a training program depends primarily on the attitude of the trainer towards the trainee. The trainer must convey a feeling of respect, acceptance, and support. He must create an atmosphere that allows the trainee to develop his own particular style, the method of operation with which he feels most comfortable, and the trainer must support the strengths, abilities, and sense of idealism the trainee possesses. It is not so important that the trainee understand the dynamics of his motivation or behavior, but only that he recognizes what works and what does not work."[18]

Perhaps a major difficulty is the tendency to talk about "training," which has a technical and mechanical implication, rather than to view the situation as an educational process, which demands that the educator function with responsibility and autonomous judgment in providing meaningful educational experiences, in this instance helping nonprofessionals to become successful practitioners. The implications of what we have called training—which facilitates important changes for the nonprofessionals involved, enhances the contribution they can make to the activities and goals of the helping professions, and affects as well their own destinies—requires a hard look at present and emerging questions.

Our greatest responsibility is the carrying out of our professional imperatives, in conjunction with the advantages and disadvantages that nonprofessionals introduce. We have a double commitment to greater realization of human potential and achievement of social progress of which it is a part. Which way will we go?

NOTES

1. Frank Riessman, "Issues in Training the New Nonprofessional" (unpublished manuscript, 19xx).

2. Robert Bendiner, "Poverty is a Tougher Problem Than Ever," *The New York Times Magazine*, February 4, 1968.

3. *Ibid.*

4. Wilbur J. Cohen, and Eugenia Sullivan, "Poverty in the United States," *HEW Indicators*, (Washington: U. S. Department of Health, Education, and Welfare, Spring 1965).

5. *Some Proposals for Government.*

6. Chicago: Rand-McNally, 1967, pp. 152-62.

7. Frank Riessman, "The New Careers Concept," *The American Child, 49*: 4. (Winter 1967).

8. Frank Riessman and Arthur Pearl, *New Careers for the Poor* (New York: Free Press, 1965).

9. Frank Riessman, "Strategies and Suggestions for Training Nonprofessionals," 1965, pp. 4-5.

10. Norma Panaro Dietz, "Who's Who Among the Nonprofessionals" (Washington: paper for administrative use of the Office of Juvenile Delinquency and Youth Development, December 1966).

11. "Problems of Community Planning and Social Change," *New Careers: Ways Out of Poverty for Disadvantaged Youth* (Washington: Center for Youth and Community Studies, Howard University, March 1965), p. 50.

12. Peter Marris and Martin Rein, *Dilemmas of Social Reform* (New York: Atherton Press, 1967), p. 225; Frank Reissman, "Strategies and Suggestions for Training Non Professionals," Gertrude Goldberg, "Untrained Neighborhood Workers In a Social Work Program," *New Careers for the Poor* (New York: The Free Press, 1965), pp. 125-33.

13. Frank Riessman, *New Careers*, p. 3.

14. *Ibid.*

15. Dietz, pp. 14-15.

16. Freeda Taran, paper for the Howard University Conference on New Careers, March 1965.

17. Frank Reissman, "Some Characteristics of the Disadvantaged," *Creative Adaptation to Change* (New York: Report of Seminars, Metropolitan Critical Areas Project, Camp Fire Girls, July 1965), p. 33.

18. Dietz, p. 18.

The Mental Health Professions: who, what, and whither?

RICHARD H. WILLIAMS

Howard Freeman and Rosalind Gertner have given a broad perspective, in structural functional terms, of the rise of the mental health consortium. They have also emphasized certain aspects of social dynamics which keep the mental health field in a state of flux. And they have looked with a questioning eye at changes of roles and tendencies toward diffusion of roles.

The broad issues they have raised are important. It is clear, sometimes in rather specific ways, that sociopolitical changes and innovations have a profound impact on the positions—roles, statuses, and authorities,—of mental health specialists and other professionals. A current major example is the passage of the mental health centers act, and the provision of large sums of money for the construction and staffing of centers. This innovation has already had an impact on training programs and career patterns.

There is another element on the American scene which may be equally important, and certainly more frightening, in shaping the roles of the mental health professions. I refer to mass violence, and the problems of the ghetto, poverty, and racism

which it expresses. What are the role boundaries, or degrees
and kinds of responsibilities of these professions in relation to
these phenomena, which many regard as a serious threat to the
democratic social order? I shall return to this issue.

Thus, I am aware of these broad issues and, in particular the
last one which I was made painfully cognizant of during a recent meeting on mental health in metropolitan areas. Even so,
I am optimistic about some of the specifics of changing positions in our field, and I believe one can see at least the glim-
merings of an emerging valid structure.

The pivotal profession, psychiatry, is in many ways going
through the throes of changing roles and orientations in ways
more traumatic than the other mental health professions. To
a considerable extent the others have for some time either
been jockeying for position on the mental health team or justi-
fying themselves in private practice and are somewhat more
accustomed to the struggle for identity.

Two facts are clear. First, each year there are more psychiatrists, although it is generally alleged that they are in woefully
short supply. In testimony to Congress in 1968 it was stated
that "between 1960 and 1965 membership in the American Psychiatric Association grew from 11,600 to 14,300. A National
Institute of Mental Health sponsored manpower survey conducted in 1965 by the American Psychological Association
located 18,750 psychiatrists (including residents) of whom
15,200 were estimated to be in active practice. The number of
psychiatric residencies offered has increased from 3,838 in
1960 to 5,000 in 1965."[1] I believe Franklin N. Arnhoff will
agree that this trend has continued. Second, the position of
many psychiatrists is changing. This same testimony states that
"in the past decade, the role and function of the psychiatrist
has expanded due to a number of trends in mental health programs, primarily away from custodial care, and toward the
closer interrelation of mental health programs with community
general health services."

The forward thrust in this process of change is symbolized
by the term "community psychiatry." Although some still re-

gard it as a minor subspecialty of psychiatry, I sense a change in some influential places that may lead it to become an integral part of all psychiatry. And it is more than just a symbol, term, or rubric. I believe there are valid training programs being developed and careers being carved out.

One of the best ways of grasping and understanding this change is to view it through the eyes of psychiatrists who are experiencing it. Fortunately, a most poignant expression of the process involved has been developed by Mathew R. Dumont, a young psychiatrist with the National Institute of Mental Health's Center for Metropolitan Studies, a position from which he must come to grips with all of community psychiatry.[2] I should like to share the impressions I have gained, as someone charged with looking at and putting into perspective the whole field of mental health, from looking at Mathew Dumont and a significant part of his generation.

Dumont, like many of his fellows, had worked very hard to become first a doctor and then a psychiatrist. But he was not satisfied, probably because of a particularly acute social conscience. So he became a community psychiatrist. His first impression was that he found himself, as he puts it, "in an undefined role, catering to undefined needs of an undefined clientele." And he asks, "Am I still a psychiatrist, still a physician, or have I become an inadequately trained social scientist or some kind of a revolutionary?"

Apart from the initial bewilderment, what are some of the salient orientations which emerge? One, which is frequently heard, is that psychiatrists who practice psychotherapy alone devote attention to mental illness, and for the most part only the mildly neurotic. He feels this approach to be grossly inadequate, not only for the frequently stated reasons that the "one to one" will not do in the face of manpower shortages, or that certain classes of grossly disturbed people cannot be reached by traditional psychotherapy, but also, and primarily "in the face of a picture of overwhelming individual, family and social disintegration among the poor."

He is impressed by the accumulation of evidence that mental illness does not reside entirely within the individual. For example, the illness may be between, not within, family members.

He is convinced that if the psychiatrist is going to talk about the community, he must be fully exposed to it. Since he deeply believes that the greatest needs are to be found in the slums, he did a study of homeless men by spending time in a tavern. In so doing he was able to discern important patterns governing their behavior.

Perhaps the most important perspective emerging from his experience is that he does not discard the medical model. He insists that it is important, too, as a corrective to the social science approach, because the medical model is "unremittingly devoted to the well being of individuals." He defines mental health as freedom. He arrives at a view of community psychiatry as "psycho-dynamic psychiatry with an interchangeable focus on individuals, families, institutions and communities." It also includes an awareness that man's physical environment has a major impact on mental illness and health. It can give insight into behavioral responses which can contribute new perspectives for social policies.

The psychiatrist is becoming, and is viewing himself, as one of the behavioral scientists. He does acquire special knowledge of some aspects of the dynamics of action systems through his clinical training and experience. Dumont states, "It is the well being, the happiness, the freedom or mental health of individuals, but more of them than can be treated as his own patients, which are his ultimate motivation." And he wisely recommends that the community psychiatrist never lose his clinical base and always spend some of his time treating patients.

An examination of what can happen in another slightly different culture will help answer the question: Are the developments we are seeing in the mental health professions a response to sociocultural conditions peculiar to the United States, or are they in significant part inherent in the evolution of these professions? I take the latter point of view and will briefly describe one instance, which will not prove my point, but the book *Community Mental Health: An International Perspective* will give many more examples.[3]

The example with which I am most familiar is the Mental Health Center in the thirteenth arrondissement in Paris.[4] This center evolved around 1958 with a small group of French psychiatrists who had become dissatisfied with the traditional, primarily custodial, pattern of serving the mentally ill. They were also interested in prevention and the promotion of mental health. This development occurred before the centers idea had crystallized in the United States. The key persons do not speak or read English, and until I arrived in 1963, they were unaware of our centers program. This does not necessarily deny that some cultural diffusion has been involved, but it does suggest a significant amount of independent parallelism.

This center is a private corporation which performs public function and serves a geographic catchment area of about 180,000 persons. The idea has subsequently caught on in France, and the *politique de secteurs*, or policy of organizing a variety of mental health services by geographic sectors with continuity of care within has taken hold and is now the official policy of the Ministry of Health. The program in this district is considered a pilot.

The program includes out-patient services, in-patient services in a new hospital located south of Orly Airport but within easy reach of Paris, and, serving only the thirteenth arrondissement, a day hospital, emergency service, consultation to community agencies service, two kinds of workshops, a beginning home treatment and home placement service, and several activities labeled as "mental hygiene," including an ex-patient's club and mental health education in various forms. The center also has taken leadership in a geriatrics program for persons not defined as patients, and there are services for adults and for children.

The catchment area is divided into six geographic sectors. In each there is a team of a psychiatrist, a social worker, and a visiting nurse (the only visiting nurses in France). These teams are divided into two groups of three, and certain specialists, such as psychologists, vocational counselors, or relaxation and physiotherapists, are assigned to one or the other group. The team is responsible for the patient, no matter where he is in the system of services—out-patient, in-patient, day hospital, workshop. Thus continuity of care is strongly emphasized.

And what is the position of the psychiatrist? A striking feature in the program is that all the psychiatrists must be psychoanalytically trained. This requirement, I believe, reflects a concern so strongly felt by Matthew Dumont, that the psychiatrist must have vast clinical experience. But the psychiatrists function essentially as community psychiatrists. Structurally, they have a dual role. On the one hand, they are the leaders of a treatment team in a geographic sector and are responsible for the treatment program of their patients. On the other hand, they administer one of the institutions in the program, such as the hospital, the day hospital, or the workshops. Thus, they combine both treatment and administrative roles, but within a clearly differentiated structure, so that the two roles are not confused. They see patients frequently in the presence of other members of the team, especially in the out-patient clinic, or they may see them individually, wherever they are in the system. Much of the psychiatrists' time is spent in seeing that a system of comprehensive community mental health services works, both in relation to the particular institution for which they are directly responsible and for the program as a whole. They spend considerable time in indirect services through consultation, especially in the children's program. They make use of group therapy and psychodrama, and occasionally take individual patients in deep, psychoanalytically-oriented psychotherapy, or in brief analytically-oriented therapy. But these modalities of treatment are quite frankly regarded as a way of maintaining their clinical skills and insights, which they believe to be useful in all that they do, and not feasible as a widespread public health measure. For example, in psychodrama there may be one patient and several therapists playing.

The number of psychologists also continues to increase. For example, the membership of the American Psychological Association was 18,215 in 1960 and 23,561 in 1965. The relationships of psychologists to the field of mental health are more diversified and less clearcut than in the case of psychiatrists or psychiatric nurses. Some psychologists are engaged in direct clinical work, but many do research and teach and have at least an indirect bearing on the field. The Congressional testimony cited previously indicates that "the 1964 National Science Foundation Register survey of psychologists revealed that 69 percent of the 16,800 responding considered their work to be relevant to mental health."[5] This response undoubtedly reflects the influence of the NIMH. Since the beginning of the program, the NIMH has sponsored a very broad base of research in the behavioral sciences, in which psychologists have participated extensively. In recent years there has been a broadened base of support for training beyond the clinical field.

In the case of psychologists, perhaps more so than for the other mental health professions, a broad historical view is important in understanding the present position. Forrest Tyler and Joseph Speisman of the staff of the Division of Manpower and Training Programs at the National Institute of Mental Health have done an excellent analysis.[6] In studying their material, I see essentially six main periods in the evolution of the psychological profession since the early 1900s. In the period prior to World War I psychologists followed the traditions of Wundt and James in the model of the university-based scholar-scientist. World War I generated needs for selection, training, and placement of military personnel, and, immediately after the war, for counseling and guidance which gave impetus to "mental measurements" and other forms of applied psychology, the second stage. The model suggested by Tyler and Speisman is "scientist-teacher-tester." Third, a major war again influenced the role of the psychologist, and in World War II there was heavy demand for therapists. Fourth, the Mental

Health Act of 1946 gave further impetus to this trend. It was expressed particularly in the Boulder Conference of 1949 and emphasized the "scientist-practitioner" model, in which the claim to a therapeutic role was established, in addition to the traditional role of "scientist-teacher." Fifth, there was some pressure in the mid 1950s for psychologists to give more emphasis to social processes in the community.

In the sixth stage this ferment continued, and in 1965 a conference in Boston emphasized a field called "community psychology." This model has many of the characteristics of community psychiatry. It shows dissatisfaction with the "medical model," more so than in community psychiatry, and with exclusive concern with mental illness. The model views psychologists as change agents, "participant conceptualizers, and scientist-professionals." As Tyler and Speisman put it, "conceptually and factually this role focuses on bridging many formal gaps in psychology, so the community-oriented psychologist may be a measurement and research psychologist, but he may also be a social and/or developmental psychologist, and to some extent a counselor and clinician."

There is an important, and complementary, difference in the evolution of community psychiatry and community psychology. Although psychology has laid claim to a therapeutic role, and although research and research training is increasingly emphasized in psychiatry, the psychiatrist remains anchored in medical clinical experience in depth, and the psychologist is more apt to concentrate on research experience in depth, thus continuing the earlier scholar-scientist emphasis within the field.

In France psychology has not gone through the full-scale evolution just described. But the experience there does serve to bring into bold relief an aspect of this evolution which has been experienced in this country as well, the potential conflict of roles in relation to therapy within the core of mental health service programs. The training of psychologists in France has tended to be much more exclusively "academic" than in this country. The graduate student gets much less clinical experience or practical experience of any kind. Applied psychology usually has taken the form of psychometrics, with a modicum of development of consulting psychology, mainly with a few industrial consulting firms. There are psychologists in the program in the thirteenth arrondissement, but what do they do? The question was the subject of frequent debate by the team. There are two distinct kinds of psychologists. First, there are those who have been analyzed and analytically trained. They are specifically labeled "psychotherapists." They work part-time, and they do psychotherapy only, except for meeting among themselves and with psychiatrists from the geographic teams, who come sometimes to discuss referrals for psychotherapy. There are two major problems for the psychotherapists, both relating to their position in a community mental health center and to their relations to other members of the team. As far as neurotic patients are concerned, the psychotherapists maintain that there is no difference in their role in the center and their role in private practice, which they also do, except in how they are paid and how they get referrals. But in relation to psychotic patients, they admitted that because of the massive "taking in charge" necessary, if they are to deal at all with psychotics (and they want to), they would have to relate somehow to the team, and there would have to be two-way communication, in spite of threats to the sacred confidentiality of the therapeutic hour. The director of the adult program wanted the psychotherapists to be "sectorized," or identified with a particular geographic team. The psychotherapists did not wish to be so assigned, mainly because of a sensed threat to their independence and a reduction in the choice of patients.

A second group of psychologists referred to itself as "psychologist-psychologists." They had not been analyzed but had the traditional role of psychological testing, which no one questioned, in principle. But this was not a very satisfying role to the psychologists, and not a prestigious role from the point of view of the psychiatrists and other members of the team. These psychologists did participate in what little research there was undertaken and were given a few administrative duties. One did a little teaching. The crux of the matter was that these psychologists were desperately seeking a therapeutic role. The psychologists could see that the hospital nurses were being given a special course to develop their therapeutic role. There were *ergo-therapists* (occupational therapists) and *kines-therapists* (physical therapists) where the name of the role admitted therapy, although they had not been analyzed. Essentially, the psychologists were in a semantic bind. If they did therapy it would be regarded as psychotherapy, and that was considered taboo, whether or not they were medical doctors, unless they had been analyzed.

The Congressional testimony states that "in social work, as in psychology, it is difficult to confine the mental health contribution to the psychiatric social worker as it is to the clinical psychologist alone. A recent change in the graduate school curriculum to a single generic approach makes the distinction between psychiatric social work and the rest of social work even less clear than in the past."[7] The National Institute of Mental Health made a survey of professional personnel in clearly identifiable mental health establishments, and about 7,500 social workers were estimated to be employed in the 2,000 institutions surveyed.[8] This group is primarily professionally trained, with 74 percent having master's degrees, 13 percent with graduate study but no graduate degree, and only 11 percent with a bachelor's degrees or less. These figures can be compared with the general data gathered by the Department of Labor for the same period, which indicated "there were not less than 125,000 persons providing social work services in voluntary and public agencies, of whom approximately 25 percent were graduates of schools of social work and 75 percent were trained in agency inservice programs."[9] Currently, the New Schools project represents a major push in the development of training facilities in social work. It is estimated that there will be twenty new schools in the next three to five years. The project also affects the career patterns for the profession as a whole, and since many of the faculty in the new schools will be new to teaching, they are taking special preparatory courses. Social work is also now involved with undergraduate training. There are many similar elements in the evolution of social work and developments in psychiatry and psychology. The conception of the role of social work is being broadened. Richard Brotman and Martin Livenstein refer to the "educator-organizer" as a new role model for social workers in community mental health practice. The organizer-educator is a practitioner-at-large whose performance covers all or most of those duties which up to now might have been handled exclusively as specialties.[10]

There is a tendency within social work to wish to broaden the units of treatment, shifting the emphasis from case work and individual counseling to group work. Some go as far as to claim that "case work and individual counselling is increasingly giving way to the group work method, thus launching new opportunities for social group work."[11]

Social workers are beginning to think "comprehensively," as, for example, with the concept of comprehensive health centers, and the breaking down of what appear to many as artificial barriers between health and welfare services and between physical health and mental health. Similarly, the field shows a growing identification with community psychiatry, with some social workers believing their profession contains specialists in community organization as a backup for community psychiatrists.

Some of the traditional methods, such as case work, are shifting in content and emphasis, as: "The community psychiatrist's parallel is the community organizer, whose casework has the following characteristics: avoidance of waiting periods, quick diagnostic assessment, immediate engagement of the client's ego capacities, direct confrontation and examination of the key emotional issues, an awareness of the type of learning possible during periods of high emotional tensions, and disciplined variety of therapeutic optimism."[12]

This general trend toward community mental health programs and greater efforts to manipulate social factors presents a special challenge to social work, partly for semantic reasons. Its label suggests an expertise in social environment. Jerome Cohen, for example, states that "social work is in a position to make an important contribution to the development of knowledge and practice skill related to the social basis and consequences of mental illness in all its forms."[13] In fact, there is great enthusiasm in some quarters. Winborn Davis claims that "Social work has an unparalleled opportunity to assume leadership in comprehensive mental health centers where traditionalism must be set aside. . . . A variety of skills is required of social workers in the comprehensive mental health center: therapy of various types, supervision, administration, consultation, community education, planning, social action and community organization, training research, and so on."[14]

For a balanced view, however, we must recognize a trend, parallel in time but quite divergent in direction, for social workers to go into private practice. It is an attractive road for some, as it seems to involve greater autonomy, higher incomes, and relief from the strains of bureaucratic restrictions.

I refer briefly to the situation in France in this instance. The trends there are similar, but less pronounced. The amount and level of training for social workers is generally less than in this country. Case work has only recently been introduced in France, and it currently carries considerable prestige for the handful of social workers who have been trained for it. In the thirteenth arrondissement the social workers have a natural, settled, and secure position on the team, which is much less problematic than the psychologist-psychologist. A social worker has been clearly assigned the role of chief administrator in the out-patient clinic, just as social workers have increasingly taken on administrative tasks in this country. In general, the range of patients' needs which social workers are expected to meet is clearly understood by all, and they fit in nicely with the geographic teams. Since this is a single pilot program, and the social workers who have found their way into it have clearly defined and generally satisfying roles, the situation does not encourage the degree of ferment that we see here.

The Congressional testimony cited previously indicates that nursing is the largest health profession, with an estimated 621,000 active professional nurses practicing in the United States in 1966. This large number is important in assessing the field of mental health as a whole because of the recent tendency to emphasize training in mental health for all nurses. As with the other mental health professionals, the shift away from custodial care, and the emphasis on community mental health are having a profound impact on the nursing profession, especially psychiatric nursing. This impact is not without its strains, ambiguities, and ambivalences. As Gershen Rosenblum and Leonard Hassol indicate, the nurse "is confronted with complexity. Here she must define a non-existent role in an agency devoid of nursing structure and nursing tradition . . . . The nurse's role is still ambiguous, incompletely defined and, to a certain degree, indifferently accepted by other mental health disciplines."[15]

A particularly salient aspect of the problem can be seen in settings which consciously attempt to be therapeutic communities. This matter has been well formulated by Marguerite Holmes and Jean Werner, who comment:

> Basically, psychiatric nursing is the same in all settings. But a therapeutic community has distinct characteristics: vanishing traditional nursing roles; indefinite roles of all disciplines concerned; added responsibility for therapy shared by patient and staff; intensified staff-patient relationships; and a series of problems for nursing, now just in the exploratory stage. There is no definitive description of the role of the psychiatric nurse who performs therapeutic functions along with other professions. They are all committed to understand emotional development and encourage emotional growth.[16]

In a number of places conscious attempts are being made to define this new role for the nurse in settings which are community-oriented and which emphasize diffusion of therapeutic roles, such as in the Fort Logan Mental Health Center in Colorado. But even there the structure had not at first been clearcut, and, as Helen Huber points out, "Ft. Logan's absence of guidelines and clear-cut structure brought out the nurse's traditional conflict over whom to please, the patient, the physician, hospital administration, the nursing profession or herself."[17]

On the other hand, as such nurses as Dr. Gertrude Isaacs, June Mellow, Gwen Tudor Will, and others have been pointing out, nursing has long been accustomed to interdisciplinary settings, and the nurse has always been regarded as a "helping person." Nurses can function well in crisis intervention, as well as in more sustained, supportive therapeutic relationships. Many are also able to take over a role parallel to the community psychiatrist and community psychologist, in the form of the psychiatric nurse consultant.

A most significant trend in training, which relates to the nursing professional as a whole, is the increased emphasis on mental health and human behavior in undergraduate training. Nurses, traditionally defined by the public as helping persons, are in a strategic position to help with the mental and emotional problems involved with all aspects of health and disease.

Two aspects of the nursing role in the thirteenth arrondissement center again illustrate important characteristics of the evolution of the mental health professions. First, at the center there is a determined effort to develop a therapeutic role for the nurse, and a special training program, one of two in all of France, has been established. Its goal is to train the nurse "to take patients in charge" in whatever institution they are working.[18] The term *prise en charge* in French mental health programs refers to a therapeutic relationship, not to custodial care.

Most of the nurses in this program have state diplomas in general nursing. There are a few psychiatric nurses, but in France this is a lower status title acquired only through experience and minimal in-service training in a mental hospital, a position about equivalent to our psychiatric aide. They are employed full-time, mostly in the hospital, and spend eight to ten hours a week for sixteen months in sessions specifically devoted to training.

The training is based on the premise that the role of the nurse is to help the patient care for himself. She is a helping person in relation to rather specific contents of self-care: medications, personal hygiene, dress, sleep habits, and the general rhythm of daily life, such as maintaining a reasonable level of activity. This role inevitably creates a relational experience with therapeutic consequences. The training is analytically oriented, but it definitely does not intend to turn the nurses into analysts or psychotherapists. I sensed no questioning by other members of the team that nurses develop relationships with patients, or that these relationships can have therapeutic value which are improved through training. There were, however, some differences of opinion about how to draw the line between this type of relationship and psychotherapy, especially among the psychotherapists (psychotherapists in this case are part-time personnel, somewhat apart from the geographical teams, and they are concerned about their status in various respects).

Much of the emphasis in the nurses' training is on helping them to become fully conscious of their role and especially of their own feelings and feelings about patients. It is analogous to sensitivity training, but with specific emphasis on nursing. Nurses attempt to develop a part of the understandings that doctors and psychotherapists acquire during their analytic training. Most of the nurses' training is done by group discussion. As in T-groups used here, the discussions bring to light difficulties of communication and differences of perception, attitudes, and judgments. These experiences can at times be painful, and individual support through consultation with a psychiatrist is also provided. Also, the nurses are supervised in their relations with patients, partly through the group discussions and partly in individual supervision. Before the end of the training each nurse completes a special study of some aspect of her activities and documents a range of problems, supplemented by visits to other places and reading. A psychiatrist supervises this work.

Second the program in the thirteenth has developed what for France is an entirely new role in the mental health field, the visiting nurse. As is likely with new roles, tensions arose, particularly in relation to the social workers. Early in my study of this program I was waiting in the hall of the dispensary, or outpatient clinic, expecting to attend a joint meeting of the social workers and visiting nurses. I sensed considerable tension and actual commotion in the room where the meeting was to be held. The chief social worker, who is also the administrative head of the dispensary, came out and asked if I would mind not attending the meeting, as the anxiety level was too high. This was the only instance during my study of this and one other program in France where anyone objected to my attending any sort of meetings, including meetings between a doctor and an individual patient.

During the next two months the visiting nurses and the social workers were able to sort out their respective roles very well. The nurses became more clearly conscious of themselves as nurses. They wore white uniforms and dispensed medications; the social workers did not. But beyond that the nurses took on a more maternalizing role. They became helping persons in relation to the intimate problems of everyday living. The social workers were more reality-oriented and concerned themselves with such matters as housing, social security, or public assistance payments within the rubric of case work. Thus, both had therapeutic roles which were considered to be complementary. With the psychoanalytic orientation of the establishment, the nurses and social workers sometimes made home visits together, with the nurse in the role of the good mother, and the social worker in the role of the stern older sister.

Although I am concerned mainly with the evolution of the mental health professionals, the work of the nonprofessional and indigenous worker is significant. Their increasing involvement in the mental health field will, I believe, have a very important impact on the evolution of the mental health professions as such.

One of the reasons that the nonprofessional has been

brought into the orbit of mental health service programs is the shortage of manpower; another aspect is in some ways more important. It involves the problem of getting the intended users of services—particularly the poor—to make use of them: bridging the gap between them and the professionals who want to help. A recent report on the indigenous nonprofessional proposes a strategy of "a created unity between the skilled specialists from the helping professions and trained workers from the groups being helped. Indigenous nonprofessionals can greatly increase manpower resources; they can serve in ways which are significantly more appropriate and which can effectively increase utilization."[19] The traditional approach of using only very highly skilled professionals has not only limited the supply of helpers, but has also produced gaps in communications with individuals who need help.

In addition to increasing manpower somewhat and reducing poverty somewhat by employing a few of the poor, this development has two other consequences. These workers are receiving training so that they may remain indigenous but become increasingly less nonprofessional. I believe that the New Careers concept is a potentially important one, whereby indigenous workers need not remain at the bottom of a hierarchy, but can find a career ladder from which to climb out of the ghetto or, more important, help transform the ghetto. Second, a key function of the indigenous worker is that of expediter. The expediter can facilitate interprofessional as well as interagency coordination, and thus affect the evolution of the professions in potentially positive ways. When consultation and supervision are added to the roles of mental health professionals, these duties can enhance the maturity of the persons occupying these positions.

In concluding, I return briefly to the crisis of mass violence, and the problems of the ghetto. How mental health professionals define their responsibilities in this area will greatly affect their future evolution. I believe that a balanced approach is possible, in the longrun through research, and in the shorter run through location of well defined mental health service programs in ghettos, without losing identity in the total social system, or becoming implicated in all aspects of social reform.

NOTES

1. Hearings before the Subcommittee on Departments of Labor and Health, Education and Welfare and Related Agencies of the Ninetieth Congress, *The Congressional Record*, First Session, Part 5, pp. 862-65.
2. *The Absurd Healer: Perspectives of a Community Psychiatrist* (New York: Science House, 1968).
3. *Community Mental Health—An International Perspective*, ed. Richard H. Williams and Lucy D. Ozarin (San Francisco: Jossey-Bass, 1968).
4. Philippe Paumelle and Richard H. Williams, "Issues in a Pilot Program," in *Community Mental Health—An International Perspective*, pp. 157-66.
5. Hearings before the Subcommittee on Departments of Labor and Health, Education and Welfare and Related Agencies of the Ninetieth Congress, *The Congressional Record*, First Session, Part 5, p. 863.
6. "An Emerging Scientist-Professional Role in Psychology," *American Psychologist, 22*:839-47 (1967).
7. Hearings before the Subcommittee on Departments of Labor and Health, Education and Welfare and Related Agencies of the Ninetieth Congress, *The Congressional Record*, First Session, Part 5, p. 863.
8. "Mental Health Manpower and Current Statistical and Activities Report No. 6," *Selected Characteristics of Social Workers* (Washington: National Institute of Mental Health, 1966).
9. *Employment Outlook for Social Workers*, Bulletin No. 1375-43 (Washington: U.S. Department of Labor, 1966).
10. "A Role Model for Social Workers in Community Mental Health Practice," *Social Work, 12*:21-26 (1967).
11. *Trends in Social Work Practice and Knowledge*, (New York: National Association of Social Workers, 1965), p. 142.
12. C. K. Aldrich, "The New Approach: Intervention and Prevention—The Clinical Psychiatry Model," *Social Science Review, 12*:268 (Sept. 1966).
13. "Changing Dimensions of Practices in the Mental Health Field," in *Trends in Social Work Practice and Knowledge*, pp. 111-12.
14. "Role of Social Work in Comprehensive Mental Health Centers," in *Trends in Social Work Practice and Knowledge*, p. 196.
15. "Training for New Mental Health Roles," *Mental Hygiene, 52*:85.

16. *Psychiatric Nursing in a Therapeutic Community* (New York: Macmillan, 1966), pp. *iii-iv*.

17. "Defining the Role of the Psychiatric Nurse," *Journal of Psychiatric Nursing*, 2:608 (1964).

18. Myriam David, "The Training of Nurses in Psychiatry in Paris," *JPN* 4:589-98 (Nov.-Dec. 1966).

19. Robert Reiff and Frank Riessman, *The Indigenous Nonprofessional: A Strategy of Change in Community Action and Community Mental Health Programs* Report No. 3 (Washington: National Institute of Labor Education Mental Health Program, 1964).

Current Status and New Directions in Mental Health Research

ROBERT J. KLEINER
SEYMOUR PARKER

In the last two decades an increasing sophistication in two basic areas in the social sciences has been evident. The first concerns the development of research methods, particularly survey techniques. Improved methods have enabled investigators to tap samples for information that yields statistically reliable conclusions. These samples reflect the heterogeneous characteristics of very large populations, in terms of ethnicity, race, urbanism, social class, history of migration, and other characteristics. The volume of data gathered in such large-scale studies has necessitated the concomitant use of computers and more powerful statistical tools. Thus, the lack of consistent results in many substantive areas can no longer be attributed simply to inadequate research methods.

A second basic area of development involves the role of theoretical models or explanations for social and psychological phenomena. More specifically, social scientists have become increasingly concerned with operationalizing concepts so that hypotheses derived from particular theoretical models can be validated or revised as the empirical findings demand.

_204_

Although some social scientists have taken very inclusive theoretical models as their point of departure, and others have utilized more limited approaches and attempted to explain behavior in terms of discrete social variables (for instance, explaining different behaviors in terms of social class) their ultimate objectives are the same.

These two areas of developing sophistication have important implications for evaluating long-standing theoretical models which have dominated psychiatric and social science approaches to functional psychiatric disorders, specifically, and to social deviance in general. Our aims in this paper are twofold: first, to discuss a few prevailing theoretical models and more limited explanatory points of view, and to illustrate the implications of recent social science research for them; second, to discuss several new research directions suggested by these same findings.

One widespread approach to the explanation of psychiatric disorders, often referred to as the medical model, views mental illness as some form of organic disease or defect in the brain or mind. Consequently, medically trained personnel usually head psychiatric facilities and determine the psychiatric diagnostic nomenclature. Not too long ago prevailing treatment methods were somatic in nature and included such procedures as shock therapies and to some extent neurosurgery. Even today treatment methods make extensive use of drugs. Surveys designed to determine the prevalence of illness depend on checklists of symptoms, largely of an organic nature.

This widespread acceptance of the medical model requires some evaluation and reconsideration. For example, there is relatively little empirical evidence to support it in terms of direct measurement or therapeutic success. The organic symptoms manifested by a given individual may reflect a definite organic disorder and have little relevance to a psychiatric disorder. On the other hand, the fact that an organic symptom may be related to a psychiatric problem does not validate the medical model.

This lack of direct organic measures of psychiatric disorders creates problems for the scientist in using the medical model. For example, in incidence or prevalence studies, when is a "case" to be counted as a "case"? This type of problem is a central one in epidemiological studies of psychiatric disorders in a community population. Such findings are always suspect because of the possible effects of the patient's sociological and psychological characteristics on the symptoms he manifests, which, in turn, influence the diagnostic label he is given, if he is even diagnosed as being ill at all. In addition social characteristics of the clinician may influence his diagnoses. The number and kind of clients brought to the attention of professional personnel may also be influenced by the social characteristics of those who interact with potential clients, and their definitions of illness. Unraveling the effects of these factors and identifying a case is further complicated by the unreliability of diagnostic classifications beyond the level of crude categories.

Finally dependence on the invalidated medical model involves considerable risk. The professional's theoretical approach determines by what means he will treat a patient. Thus, the medical model approach may lead to dependence on inappropriate treatment methods. We do not mean by this that the use of drugs is unnecessary, nor that psychiatric problems may not be associated with organic manifestations.

A second widely held but relatively untested view about the nature of psychiatric disorders may be called the anomie-alienation model. The ambiguity with which these two terms are used, as well as the unnecessary assumptions about what their use involves, hinders a definitive evaluation of this model. The concept of anomie was introduced by Emile Durkheim, in a sociological framework, to describe a state of normlessness in a social system.[1] Robert Merton has used the same term to refer to a disjunction between means and ends in society.[2] However, social scientists are not always clear about the particular usage to which they subscribe.[3] Sometimes the same investigator will utilize the concept in both ways, as if the two definitions were synonymous. Others view anomie as a social psychological phenomenon—that is, as describing a characteristic of the actor, rather than delineating the situation in which the actor behaves. Still others use the concept both in a sociological and a social psychological sense. Similar problems arise with the concept of alienation, and anomie and alienation are frequently discussed as if they were interchangeable.[4] These inconsistencies can only confound a clear understanding of this model.

Many of the approaches that treat anomie and alienation as distinct concepts also generally assume that the two are interdependent (for example, as anomie increases, alienation also increases; or knowing the degree of one implies that we also know the degree of the other).[5] For example, the ethos of success is assumed; therefore, the lower one's actual social status, the higher the degree of anomie and the higher one's concomitant alienation. In this context anomie describes the nature of the individual's social situation, and alienation refers to his social psychological characteristics. It is also implicitly assumed that individuals accurately perceive the nature of the social situation. This implied high degree of congruence between the two concepts is then used to explain psychiatric disorders and other forms of deviance.[6] However, a review of the meager literature does not provide strong support for the congruence notion. This model has another important limitation: since different forms of deviance are seen as manifestations of the same antecedent conditions (high anomie and high alienation), the model cannot predict the particular deviant behavior that will occur.[7] The assumption of a high congruence between anomie and alienation is tenuous, and, in fact, prevents realization of the potential value of this theoretical model.

The more limited theoretical frames of reference, alluded to earlier, relate such specific social structural variables as social class or social status, migration, and social mobility to rates of psychiatric illness. The social class view is probably the most widely used, and numerous studies underlie the assumption of an invariant inverse relationship between social class and rates of mental illness.[8] These findings have understandably given the model some explanatory value. However, its adherents also attempt to explain all differences among groups in terms of social class differences.[9] For example, if Episcopalians and Baptists show different rates of mental illness, the first step would be to demonstrate that the two religious groups differed in social class and then use class characteristics to account for the variations. Or, if groups varying in migratory status are found to differ in rates of illness, then efforts would be directed toward showing that the high-rate group was really lower in social class standing.[10] Thus, the social class model begins to take on magical explanatory power beyond that allowed by the evidence.

The social class approach also makes assumptions about the sociological and social psychological ramifications of social class differences.[11] As mentioned, anomie and alienation are assumed to increase as one descends the social class scale. Decreasing social class position is also taken to be associated with increasing frustration, and decreasing self-esteem. All these relationships supposedly have a cumulative effect which precipitates mental disorder. The appeal of the social class explanation derives from results of various correlational studies and from the compelling character of a commonsense explanation. However, reviews of the literature show the relationship between social class and rates of mental illness is not as definitive as is commonly believed.[12] Illness rate patterns vary according to the particular measures of status or class position used, and whether the generalization refers to a black or a white population. Findings that do not confirm the inverse relationship between status position and illness rates also raise questions about the validity of the assumed sociological and psychological ramifications of social status or social class.

A review of the research on social class reveals a number of methodological issues. Most measures of social class position, for instance, are multidimensional so that a given individual may simultaneously occupy quite different positions on several status continua.[13] An arbitrary social class level is derived by weighting these different positions and combining them into a single composite index. This procedure has questionable value, since the various status continua may differ widely, and each one may correlate differently with rates of psychiatric disorder; there is, in fact, evidence of this possibility. Thus, the meaning of what is being combined is not clear in such a multidimensional index. This issue becomes even more relevant when we realize that various social class indices are frequently computed on the bases of different components and weighting systems that may not be comparable.

A final objection to the social class explanatory view may be mentioned. Individuals arbitrarily assigned to particular status or class positions may differ in ways that are more significantly related to mental illness than is social class itself. The same class group, for example, may include individuals who are upwardly mobile, downwardly mobile, and nonmobile. Each of these mobility groups may manifest very different illness rates, which may be obscured when individuals are combined by class.[14] The status position of an individual varies from one measure to another. His many status positions may be referred to as his status profile. The same class group may include individuals with very different status profiles, and it has been shown that these profiles correlate differentially with various types of behavior. Clearly, any meaningful evaluation of the social class approach becomes a highly complex matter.

Another type of limited explanatory approach utilizes the migration factor. This approach assumes that migration correlates with high rates of mental disorder, from which culture shock is inferred as a causal factor.[15] Individuals who enter a new environment presumably face unfamiliar situations and confront conflicting role demands and role strain. These conditions create psychic stress and result in psychiatric disorder. The relevant literature raises several questions about this view.[16] The problem of defining migration seems to be a central one. The term may refer to movement from one country to another, movement within the same country, or movement from one part of a small area to another. Migration has at times been defined in terms of place of birth and at other times the locus of socialization.[17] Studies based on these different definitions reach conclusions that are dissimilar. Even studies that define migration in the same manner do not provide conclusive verification of a positive correlation between migration and rates of mental disorder. Finally, some studies demonstrate strong negative relationships between migration and illness rates. In the face of the conflicting evidence the utility of the culture shock explanation of mental illness is questionable.

A third limited approach attempts to explain psychiatric disorders in terms of social mobility and the stresses assumed to be inherent in this type of movement. The relationships between social mobility and mental illness have not been accepted with the unanimity that characterizes studies of social class and migration.[18] However, certain questions can be raised about the explanations offered in mobility studies. Some investigators treat upward mobility and downward mobility as two different types of psychological phenomena, or else attempt to explain the stressful effects of downward mobility and completely ignore upwardly mobile individuals. Downward mobility in this instance is considered a manifestation of failure, resulting in lowered self-esteem and the development of psychiatric disorder (or the social causation hypothesis). Upward mobility is viewed as a manifestation of success striving resulting in elevated self-esteem and positive mental health.[19]

Some explanations of downward mobility rely heavily on the social selection hypothesis.[20] According to this hypothesis, individuals move downward because they cannot function at their parental class level because of limiting constitutional or personality characteristics predisposing them to mental disorder. Thus, although explanations about mobility and mental disorder differ, findings agree that downwardly mobile individuals will manifest high rates of illness. Although this finding is reliable, no clearcut support exists for either the social causation or social selection hypothesis.

The findings for upward mobility present a confusing picture. The recent resurgence of interest in Durkheim and his concept of anomic suicide has led some to predict the same effects for upwardly as for downwardly mobile individuals. If we do not control status position in evaluating mobility status, we do not always find the highest rates of mental illness among the downwardly mobile, nor consistently low rates among the upwardly mobile. Recent findings show, however, that when status position is held constant, illness rates are higher for the downwardly mobile than for the nonmobile at the low end of the status scale, and higher for the upwardly mobile than for the nonmobile at the high end of the scale. Interestingly, it has also been shown that the two mobility groups have similar social psychological characteristics and differ in the same way from their nonmobile peers; the evaluation becomes more complex if one controls for direction of mobility and compares illness rates by status levels.[21] As we ascend the status hierarchy, illness rates for the downwardly mobile group decrease, and rates for the upwardly mobile increase. It becomes apparent, therefore, that rates of mental illness are a function both of direction and locus of mobility in the status hierarchy.

The brief evaluations of the medical and anomie-alienation models make it increasingly clear that these models, as currently defined and used, are of limited value. In addition, efforts to explain mental illness in terms of such gross social structural variables as social class and migration are not particularly helpful in light of all the problems attendant upon their definition and the limited consistency of findings with respect to rate variability.

Recognition of the problems inherent in current explanatory models provides a point of departure for more fruitful research directions. At the level of broad, far-reaching explanatory models, we propose the consideration of more systematic statements of social interaction or role theories of human behavior deriving from earlier role theorists which are beginning to emerge from social scientists' efforts to develop testable theories.[22] These theories are also different from earlier applications of role theories to mental illness because they do not require superimposition of social interaction theories on the medical model.[23] We should also emphasize that such models must encompass or consider the interaction of social structural and social psychological variables within the same frame of reference. The necessity for including social psychological variables leads us to propose the inclusion of cognitive consistency theories,[24] in this proposed point of departure. The proposal of these models derives not only from the social science disciplines, but also from numerous clinical precedents. The following clinical developments seem to reflect this thinking most clearly:

1) In recent years there has been a strong movement away from using the physical therapies (i.e., shock and operative procedures).[25]

2) Similarly there has been a decreasing dependence on intrapsychic manipulation in the treatment of psychiatric patients.[26]

3) Diagnostic evaluations are utilizing to a greater degree information about the social efficiency of the patient.[27]

4) Contemporary therapeutic approaches have been strongly influenced by the social psychiatric approaches of Sullivan, Fromm, and Horney.

5) Behavior therapy approaches have become increasingly popular with many clinicians who at one time stressed personality restructuring.[28]

6) There has been a widespread concern that psychiatric hospitals maintain social systems that promulgate patients' dependency and leave them devoid of social identity or identity as an effective individual.[29] This view has influenced the Joint Commission Report, which in turn has acted as a catalyst for the thinking of the clinical field as a whole.

7) Milieu or environmental therapy programs within the hospital setting or in the receiving community have concentrated on developing patients' feelings of identity and necessary skills for interacting successfully with community members.[30]

8) Family therapy focuses on the problems that may be involved in the patient's interaction with members of his family.[31]

9) The rapidly developing community mental health center movement emphasizes the need to maintain patients in active functioning social networks of which they are a part.[32]

10) Government agencies have been granting large sums of money for evaluating the various programs enumerated above.

The crystallization of social interaction and cognitive consistency theories draws specific attention to the social structural and cultural characteristics of a given situation (for example, norms and role expectations associated with status hierarchies and patterns of social mobility), as well as to the social psychological characteristics of the individual in that situation (for instance, perception of the social system, goal-striving orientation, self-esteem, and salient reference groups.) These theories also provide the means for defining mental illness in different operational terms, for example by contrasting an individual's perceptions and evaluations of a situation with the evaluations made of him and of his situation by significant others (his reference groups). Finally, this group of theories attempts to develop models that can be evaluated empirically or that allow for the derivation of testable hypotheses.

It is almost a truism that low self-esteem accompanies mental illness. However, self-esteem is measured in terms of traits that are often not tied to situational contexts. Social interaction theories focus on the many types of interpersonal relationships maintained by an individual. These theories lead easily to conceiving of self-esteem in terms of one's evaluations of his many important social relationships and roles. For instance, an individual evaluates his occupational, ethnic, and parental roles. Each of these evaluations may be called sub-identities of the self. Data relevant to such a profile of one's evaluations or sub-identities would include his role ideals, his role perceptions, his feelings about any discrepancies between them, and his view of how others evaluate him. Some investigators are currently working with this definition of self-esteem in their research on mental illness.[33]

We have discussed several problems with the anomie-alienation model. We feel that if these concepts were clarified, and a number of elaborations were made on the use of alienation, a more meaningful and testable theoretical model for understanding mental illness would emerge. Such a model would be compatible with some of the social interaction theories. We believe that anomie should refer only to the status of the many means-ends relationships prevailing in the social system—that is, the actual characteristics of the opportunity and prevailing modalities about achievement and success. Alienation, on the other hand, should refer to the ways in which an individual perceives his relations with his society—that is, his evaluations of his power to make his own decisions, his influence on the decision-making of others, how much he likes and is liked by others, and the degree to which his actions bring him desired rewards. Thus, alienation shall be used strictly as a social psychological concept. Only after specifying the empirical referents of each concept can we consider establishing a meaningful relationship between anomie and alienation.[34] The nature of this relationship will provide us with an operational measure of reality orientation, an important element in the definition of mental illness.

A specific illustration of this approach will be helpful. Parker and Kleiner have shown that in the context of a relatively closed opportunity structure a mentally ill Negro sample was more likely to view the opportunity structure as being open than a comparable sample of individuals in the general community.[35] In another study on a Negro population, juvenile deliquents and their significant adults are more prone to see a closed opportunity structure.[36] Thus, it is the lack of congruence and the type of incongruence between means-ends relations, and the perception of such relations, that provides insight into both the mentally ill and the delinquent populations. Further analyses reveal that the mentally ill, who assume a relatively open opportunity structure, also set high goals and maintain high expectations which are not realized. This psychological state correlates with low self-esteem. The delinquents, who assume the existence of a closed system, set low or different goals and have low or different expectations which may be realized, are in a psychological state which correlates with relatively high self-esteem. Clearly the opposite assumptions about the opportunity structure elicit different sets of logically interrelated attitudes. Both deviant populations come to the attention of different institutions and are labeled according to these differences.

A number of problems seem to pervade the treatment of alienation in the literature. Melvin Seeman initially subsumed under this term feelings of powerlessness, self-estrangement, normlessness, and hopelessness.[37] Subsequent investigators seem to assume that these feelings underlie most forms of problematic or deviant behavior.[38] On the other hand, individuals who do not display these feelings are frequently considered "healthy." Yet findings reported for a mentally ill population do not support these assumption. We feel that this alienation model is too limiting and does not fit the available data. We propose that the alienation concept be restated as an alienation-integration continuum. We have tended to concern ourselves with a limited segment of the total relevant behavioral continuum (i.e., with the part that deals with feelings of lacking something). We must also consider the part of the continuum that deals with feelings of having something. An individual may feel either powerless or all-powerful, each of which has very different consequences for mental health, when evaluated in terms of the social reality in which he functions. Mentally ill individuals, for example, seem to show strong feelings of hope on some measures, whereas delinquent youths apparently feel little or no hope, at least with respect to goals considered important by society.

An individual is frequently described as being alienated along one dimension or another, in effect being attributed with situation-free traits.[39] Statistical studies which have intercorrelated the scores on different dimensions of alienation to determine whether a general factor of alienation exists are inconclusive.[40] We prefer to view an individual as having feelings that approximate a point on the alienation-integration continuum with respect to a given social situation or role demand. This point of view derives from the necessity of considering the interaction between the situation and the individual. From this position we can derive the added idea of a profile of alienation-integration scores that correspond to the range of situations and roles in which the individual finds himself. It should also be clear that each score in the profile will vary in its salience or importance to the individual: the more salient the score, the greater its impact on his behavior. More specifically, given the profile of scores and the salience of each score, we should be able to relate these data predictably to the social structural and sociocultural context, self-esteem, psychiatric status, and other forms of behavior. These elaborations on the anomie-alienation model lead to innumerable hypotheses and research possibilites.

In a research endeavor that utilizes a social interaction and/ or an anomie-alienation model the investigator must consider the characteristics of the immediate social networks in which the individual's behavior occurs. Although survey and sampling techniques have become increasingly sophisticated, they have not been oriented toward obtaining information of this kind. This limitation has been dealt with by the concomitant assumption that individuals matched on such characteristics as occupation, education, age, or sex are also similar with respect to role ideas, norms, and other relevant social psychological characteristics. If this assumption is correct, large representative samples are appropriate. However, relatively little data from studies conducted in recent years support this working assumption. In a recent study by Parker and Kleiner, for example, heterogeneity in goal-striving stress, self-esteem, and orientation toward informal reference groups is found to be as marked *within* as *between* various status groups.[41] The trend appears for three different measures of socioeconomic status (education, occupation, and income). Such results indicate pointedly that the predictive value of these measures has been overstated. Even if the basic assumption is valid, surveys give us no information on the reference groups with which an individual interacts, other than the individual's own perception of them. They tell us nothing about how these reference groups perceive the individual and behave toward him—necessary information for evaluating his social psychological characteristics and role performances.

One's social reality is determined by the formal and informal reference groups constituting the social systems in which he moves. This social network may or may not coincide with the social structure as traditionally defined (in terms of occupation and education). These networks have their own stratification systems, meaningful roles, mobility channels, system of rewards and punishment, and means-ends relations.[42] Consequently, it becomes clear that we must concentrate on studying individuals in their social networks, an approach requiring us to use social interaction and role theories. This method also guarantees that we are working with meaningful social systems and not merely statistical constructs.

Kleiner and Lovald recently defined the urban environment in terms of the overlay of numerous social networks, each with its own dynamic system.[43] The interaction of these networks implies additional dynamics. Individuals participate in many different networks at the same time, as well as at different points in time. Anthropologists are beginning to formulate this type of strategy for studying the urbanization process in Africa.[44] Some of the literature on juvenile delinquency conceives of delinquent "subcultures" which retain certain characteristics of the larger society in addition to characteristics peculiar to their specific group or class.[45] There are scattered references to this approach in dealing with many problems, but such references do not show a well formulated methodology. Except on a very limited basis, we do not have the methods necessary to approach a meaningful evaluation of these networks. Adaptation of some anthropological field methods is required, not an easy task when one realizes that these methods will have to be applied to large urban environments.

Regardless of the type of study conducted, whether surveys or the kind of study we propose, two analytic procedures must be emphasized. The first refers to the types of sociostructural concepts that are used, and the second to the possibilities of taking the individual as the unit of analysis. A central question with standard measures of socioeconomic status is whether the position to which a person is arbitrarily assigned by the investigator has any meaningful social psychological ramifications for that individual. Concepts must be defined in terms that are most likely to have dynamic properties and social psychological implications. Social mobility status, for example, does fulfill these criteria. Social mobility status is usually defined by an individual's status in a current social context that makes different demands on him than those contexts in which he was socialized or in which he functioned at some time in the past. Changing social contexts require the individual to make numerous adjustments and adaptations.

Migratory status, which fails to satisfy these criteria, is usually defined in terms of birthplace. This definition has no dynamic implications unless certain assumptions are imposed on the concept, and such assumptions are not always sound. The idea of culture shock—rapid change in role requirements and demands—has been used to explain the higher rates of mental illness among migrants than among natives in a given area, when migrant is defined in terms of birthplace. However, this concept should be defined either in terms of an individual's locus of socialization or the pattern of environments through which he moved before arriving at his present residence. When migrant status is defined in terms of socialization, the social psychological differences between migrants and natives do not support the assumptions implied in the culture shock notion.[46]

Blalock has attempted to minimize the differences in definition between the status inconsistency and status mobility concepts.[47] He assumes that being at two different status positions at the same point in time (e.g., low occupation and high education) has the same implications for the individual as occupying two status positions at different points in time (e.g., moving from a low to high occupational position). However, it seems necessary to retain the distinction between the two concepts. We have shown that mental illness does not relate to status inconsistency but does relate to social mobility status.[48] An alternative and potentially fruitful concept is mobility consistency. There is considerable evidence to show that the several different types of social mobility have social and psychological implications; however, little has been done to evaluate how the interaction of different types of mobility affects the individual.[49] A person who is upwardly mobile in education and downwardly mobile in occupation, for example, should have different psychological problems and adjustments than one who is downwardly mobile in education but upwardly mobile in occupation. Thus, our proposed approach emphasizes the need for the development of concepts with dynamic properties.

Many large-scale surveys compare groups on one variable at a time. When two groups are found to differ significantly on several variables, it is assumed that individuals within one group differ in all these respects from individuals in the other group. The assumption, of course, is not warranted. In addition, all variables on which the groups do not differ significantly are omitted from further analysis, also a questionable procedure. Many analytical techniques now available allow us to compare individuals rather than groups in terms of several variables taken simultaneously. The underlying rationale is that although a variable may not differentiate between groups, it may gain discriminatory power when the individual is taken as the unit of analysis.

We have found this to be a fruitful approach.[50] Analyses considering each variable separately show significant differences between a community sample and a psychiatric sample on measures of goal-striving stress, self-esteem, and evaluation of one's achievements relative to his reference group. The responses that characterize the psychiatric population are called pathology-linked responses. Comparisons can then be made to see whether each of these pathology-linked responses characterizes particular subgroups in the community sample. However, only goal-striving stress differentiates significantly between such subgroups (for instance, downwardly mobile versus nonmobile individuals at a given status level). Ordinarily, one would conclude that the other variables have no fine discriminatory ability and should be discarded from further analysis. When community sample subgroups are compared in terms of the number of individuals in each group with multiple pathology-linked characteristics, however, reference group discrepancy and self-esteem scores are found to contribute significantly to our differentiating power. This procedure has been used to explain illness rate differences between groups differing in mobility status, migratory status, urbanism, and community of socialization.[51] This is not a new procedure, and although investigators will agree that the approach is more sensitive than doing group analyses on one variable at a time, few researchers have used it extensively.

In summary:

1. We have maintained that it is time to question the widespread dependence on the "medical" model to explain mental disorder. There are both clinical and social science precedents for this proposal.

2. We are taking issue with past efforts to explain mental disorder in terms of anomie and alienation. This position is based on the lack of conceptual clarity and inconsistency in usage associated with these concepts.

3. We have proposed that a different and potentially more fruitful point of departure would be to utilize the more systematic contemporary social-interaction and cognitive consistency theories developed in the social sciences. These theories lend themselves to prediction and empirical evaluation.

4. We have offered very specific definitions of anomie and alienation, and have also suggested a number of elaborations

on the use of alienation. We feel that these definitions and elaborations could provide still another fruitful theoretical model.

5. These alternative points of departure indicate the need for studying the nature of the social networks in which a given individual participates, as well as the individual himself.

6. Finally, we have suggested that many people in the mental health field tend both to utilize selected concepts beyond the point justified by the evidence, and also to overstate the predictive value of such concepts.

NOTES

1. *Suicide*, trans. J. A. Spaulding and G. Simpson (Glencoe, Ill.: Free Press, 1951).
2. *Social Theory and Social Structure* (Glencoe, Ill.: Free Press, 1957).
3. D. L. Meier and W. Bell, "Anomie and Differential Access to the Achievement of Life Goals," *American Sociological Review*, 24:189-202 (1959); R. Middletone, "Alienation, Race, and Education," *ASR*, 28:973-77 (1963); E. H. Mizruchi, "Social Structure and Anomia in a Small City," *ASR*, 25:645-55 (1960); J. P. Clark, "Measuring Alienation within a Social System," *ASR*, 24:849-52 (1959); Leo Srole, "A Comment on 'Anomy,'" *ASR*, 30:757-62 (1965).
4. D. G. Dean, "Alienation: Its Meaning and Measurement," *ASR*, 26:753-58 (1961).
5. Meier and Bell, pp. 189-202; Mizruchi, pp. 645-55; Srole, "Social Integration and Certain Corollaries: An Exploratory Study," *ASR*, 21:709-16 (1956).
6. R. S. Cloward and L. E. Ohlin, *Illegitimate Means and Delinquent Subcultures* (New York: The Free Press, 1960); Merton; Srole, "Social Integration and Corollaries."
7. A. K. Cohen, *Deviance and Control* (Englewood Cliffs: Prentice-Hall, 1966); Merton.
8. Joseph Cassel, "Social Class and Mental Disorders: An Analysis of the Limitations and Potentialities of Current Epidemiological Approaches," in *Mental Health and the Lower Class*, ed. K. S. Miller and C. M. Grigg (Tallahassee: Florida State University Press, 1966); R. E. Clark, "Psychosis, Income, and Occupational Prestige," *American Journal of Sociology*, 54:433-40 (1949); R. E. Faris and W. H. Dunham, *Mental Disorders in Urban Areas* (Chicago: University of Chicago Press, 1939); A. B. Hollingshead and F. C. Redlich, *Social Class and Mental Illness* (New

222   *The Mental Health Field*

York: John Wiley, 1958); T. S. Langner and S. T. Michael, *Life Stress and Mental Health: The Midtown Manhattan Study* (New York: The Free Press, 1963), II; Leo Srole *et al.*, *Mental Health in the Metropolis: The Midtown Manhattan Study* (New York, McGraw-Hill, 1962); P. M. Roman and H. M. Trice, *Schizophrenia and the Poor* (Ithaca: Cornell University School of Industrial and Labor Relations, 1967); Srole and Langner, "Socio-economic Status Groups: Their Mental Health Composition," in *The Sociology of Mental Disorders*, ed. S. K. Weinberg (Chicago: Aldine, 1967); Weinberg, "The Sociology of Mental Disorders: Analyses and Readings in Psychiatric Sociology," in *Sociology of Mental Disorders*.

9. H. W. Dunham, "Social Class and Schizophrenia," in *Sociology of Mental Disorders;* E. M. Gruenberg and A. H. Leighton, "Epidemiology and Psychiatric Training," in *Concepts of Community Psychiatry*, ed. S. E. Goldstein, U. S. Public Health Service Publications #1319 (Washington: 1965); S. K. Weinberg, "Psychiatric Sociology: The Sociology of Mental Disorder," in *Sociology of Mental Disorders*.

10. Gruenberg and Leighton; Weinberg, "Psychiatric Sociology," pp. 3-7.

11. Cassel; Hollingshead and Redlich; R. J. Kleiner and S. Parker, "Goal-Striving, Social Status, and Mental Disorder: A Research Review," in *Sociology of Mental Disorders;* Langner and Michael; Roman and Trice.

12. Kleiner and Parker, "Goal Striving, Social Status, and Mental Disorder"; and "Social Status and Mental Disorder," in *Mental Illness in the Urban Negro Community*, ed. Parker and Kleiner (New York: Free Press, 1966); Roman and Trice.

13. Hollingshead and Redlich; Langner and Michaels; Parker and Kleiner, "Social Status and Mental Disorder"; Srole *et al.*

14. R. J. Kleiner and S. Parker, "Social Mobility, Anomie, and Mental Disorder," in *Determinants of Mental Illness*, ed. S. C. Plog *et al.* (in press); "Social Mobility and Mental Disorder."

15. B. J. Malzberg and Everett Lee, *Migration and Mental Disease: A Study of First Admissions to Hospitals for Mental Disease, New York, 1939-1941* (New York: Social Science Research Council, 1956); H. B. M. Murphy, "Migration and the Major Mental Disorders: A Reappraisal," in *Mobility and Mental Health*, ed. M. B. Kantor (Springfield, Ill.: Charles Thomas, 1965).

16. R. J. Kleiner and S. Parker, "Migration and Mental Illness: A New Look," *ASR*, 24:697-90 (1959); "Migratory Status and Mental Disorder," in *Mental Illness in the Urban Negro Community;* and "Migration and Mental Illness: Some Reconsiderations and Suggestions for Further Analysis," paper presented at the Sixth World Congress of Sociology, Evian, France, Sept. 1966.

17. Malsberg and Lee; Murphy; Parker and Kleiner, "Migratory Status and Mental Disorder."

18. A. B. Hollingshead *et al.*, "Social Mobility and Mental Illness," in *Sociology of Mental Disorders*, pp. 48-54; Kleiner and Parker, "Migration and Mental Illness"; and "Social Mobility and Mental Disorders.

19. R. J. Kleiner and S. Parker, "Social-Structural and Psychological Factors in Mental Disorders: A Research Review," in *Social-Psychological Approaches to Mental Illness and Health*, ed. H. Wechsler *et al.* (New York: John Wiley, in press); and "Social Mobility and Mental Disorder."

20. Kleiner and Parker, *Ibid.*

21. Kleiner and Parker, "Social Mobility, Anomie, and Mental Disorder"; and "Social Mobility and Mental Disorder."

22. Gerald Gordon, *Role Theory and Illness: A Sociological Perspective* (New Haven: College and University Press, 1966); T. J. Scheff, *Being Mentally Ill: A Sociological Theory* (Chicago: Aldine, 1966); T. S. Szasz, *The Myth of Mental Illness* (New York: Harper and Row, 1961); A. R. Lindesmith and A. L. Strauss, *Social Psychology* (New York: Dryden Press, 1945); G. H. Mead, *Mind, Self, and Society* (Chicago: University of Chicago Press, 1934).

23. Faris and Dunham; Hollingshead and Redlich; Langner and Michael.

24. Leon Festinger, "A Theory of Social Comparison Process," in *Readings in Reference Group Therapy and Research*, ed. H. H. Hyman and E. Singer (New York: Free Press, 1968); E. E. Jones and K. E. Davis, "From Acts to Dispositions: The Attribution Process in Person Perception, in *Advances in Experimental Social Psychology*, ed. L. Berkowitz (New York: Academic Press, 1966), II; Albert Pepitone, *Attraction and Hostility* (New York: Atherton, 1964); J. W. Thibaut and H. H. Kelley, *The Social Psychology of Groups* (New York: John Wiley, 1959).

25. Joint Commission on Mental Illness and Health, *Action for Mental Health* (New York: John Wiley, 1959).

26. *Ibid.*

27. M. B. Sussman, ed., *Sociology and Rehabilitation* (Washington: U.S. Department of Health, Education, and Welfare, 1965); Weinberg, "Psychiatric Sociology"; and "Social Interaction as an Orientation to Mental Disorders among the Behavioral Sciences Prior to 1950," in *Sociology of Mental Disorders*.

28. Leonard Krasner and L. P. Ullmann, eds., *Research in Behavior Modifications: New Developments and Implications* (New York: Holt, Rinehart, and Winston, 1965); and *Case Studies in Behavior Modification* (New York: Holt, Rinehart, and Winston, 1965).

29. R. Sanders *et al.*, *Chronic Psychoses and Recovery* (San Francisco: Jossey-Bass, 1967).

30. G. W. Fairweather, *Social Psychology in Treating Mental Illness: An Experimental Approach* (New York: John Wiley, 1964); Fairweather et al., *Relative Effectiveness of Psychotherapeutic Programs: A Multicriteria Comparison of Four Programs for Three Different Patient Groups,* Psychological Monographs, General and Applied, 74:482 (Washington: American Psychological Association, 1960); Sanders *et al.;* R. M. Glasscote *et al., The Community Mental Health Center: An Analysis of Existing Models* (Washington: Joint Information Service, 1964); Weinberg, "Psychiatric Sociology."

31. Boszormenyi-Nagy and J. L. Framo, *Intensive Family Therapy* (New York: Harper and Row, 1965).

32. *Action for Mental Health.*

33. J. R. P. French, Jr., and R. L. Kahn, "A Programmatic Approach to Studying the Industrial Environment and Mental Health," *Journal of Social Issues,* 18:1-47 (1962); D. Miller, "The Study of Social Relationships: Situation, Identity, and Social Interaction," in *Psychology: A Study of Science,* ed. S. Koch (New York: McGraw-Hill, 1963), V; Parker and Kleiner, "Self-Esteem and Mental Disorder," in *Mental Illness in the Urban Negro Community;* L. I. Pearlin, "Alienation from Work: A Study of Nursing Personnel," *ASR,* 27:314-26 (1962).

34. Gordon Nettler, "A Further Comment on 'Anomy,'" *ASR,* 30:762-63 (1965).

35. S. Parker and R. J. Kleiner, "Perception of the Nature of the Opportunity Structure," in *Mental Illness in the Urban Negro Community.* Anomy," *ASR,* 30:14-39 (1965).

36. R. J. Kleiner and J. V. Buerkle, "Toward a Sociological and Social-Psychological Theory of Deviant Behavior," paper presented at the Society for Sociological Study of Social Problems meetings, Montreal, Aug. 1964.; and "The North Philadelphia Community: Aspirations and Values," (Philadelphia: Commission on Human Relations, 1966).

37. "On the Meaning of Alienation," *ASR,* 24:783-91 (1959).

38. Herbert McClosky and J. H. Schaar, "Psychological Dimensions of Anomy," *ASR,* 30:14-39 (1965).

39. R. Blauner, *Alienation and Freedom* (Chicago: University of Chicago Press, 1964); Clark; D. Gold, "Independent Causation in Multivariate Analysis: A Case of Political Alienation and Attitude Toward a School Bond Issue," *ASR,* 27:85-87 (1962); J. Hajda, "Alienation and Integration of Student Intellectuals, *ASR,* 26:758-77 (1961); Herbert McClosky and J. H. Schaar, "Reply to Srole and Nettler," *ASR,* 30:763-67 (1965); A. M. Rose, "Alienation and Participation: A Comparison of Group Leaders and the 'Mass,'" *ASR,* 27:834-38 (1962); Seeman, "On the Meaning of Alienation"; Melvin Seeman and J. W. Evans, "Alienation and Learning in a Hospital Setting," *ASR,* 27:772-81 (1962); L. A. Zurcher *et al.,* "Value Orientations, Role Conflict, and Alienation from Work," *ASR,* 30:539-48 (1965).

40. D. S. Cartwright, "Misapplication of Factor Analysis," *ASR*, *30*:249-51 (1965); Dean; C. R. Miller and E. W. Butler, "Anomia and Eunomia: A Methodological Evaluation of Srole's Anomia Scale," *ASR*, *31*:400-406 (1966); A. G. Neal and S. Rettig, "Dimensions of Alienation among Manual and Non-Manual Workers," *ASR*, *28*:599-608 (1963); and "On Multidimensionality of Alienation," *ASR*, *32*:54-65 (1965); A. G. Neal and Melvin Seeman, "Organizations and Powerlessness: A Test of the Mediation Hypothesis," *ASR*, *29*:216-26 (1964); G. Nettler, "A Measure of Alienation," *ASR*, *22*:670-77 (1957); Seeman, "On the Personal Consequences of Alienation in Work," *ASR*, *32*:273-85 (1967); E. L. Struening and A. H. Richardson, "A Factor Analytic Exploration of the Alienation, Anomia, and Authoritarian Domain," *ASR*, *30*:768-76 (1965).

41. Parker and Kleiner, "Social Status and Mental Disorder."

42. L. Coch and J. R. P. French, Jr., "Overcoming Resistance to Change," in *Basic Studies in Social Psychology*, ed. H. Proshansky and B. Seidenberg (New York: Holt, Rinehart, and Winston, 1965).

43. R. J. Kleiner and K. Lovald, "An Overview of Research on the Inner City," in *Ethnic Groups and Social Change*, ed. J. Jackson (in press).

44. A. L. Epstein, "The Network and Urban Social Organization," *Rhodes-Livingstone Journal*, *29*:29-63 (1961); "Urbanization and Social Change in Africa," *Current Anthropology*, *8*:275-84 (1967); "Comments and Reply to Comments," *CA*, *8*:284-94 (1967).

45. A. K. Cohen, *Delinquent Boys: The Culture of the Gang* (Glencoe, Ill.: The Free Press, 1955); W. B. Miller, "Lower Class Culture as a Generating Milieu of Gang Delinquency, *JSI*, *14*:5-19 (1958).

46. Parker and Kleiner, "Migratory Status and Mental Disorder"; "Migration and Mental Illness: Some Reconsiderations."

47. H. M. Blalock, Jr., "Status Inconsistency, Social Mobility, Status Integration, and Structural Effects," *ASR*, *32*:790-801 (1967).

48. Parker and Kleiner, "Social Mobility and Mental Disorder."

49. Kleiner and Parker, "Social-Structural and Psychological Factors in Mental Disorders."

50. Parker and Kleiner, "Interrelationship of Study Variables," in *Mental Illness in the Urban Negro Community*.

51. Kleiner and Parker, "Integration of Social-Psychological and Sociological Levels of Analyses," paper presented at the American Psychological Association Meetings, Washington, Sept. 1967.; and "Migration and Mental Illness: Some Reconsiderations."

The Role of Genetics in the Etiology of the Schizophrenias*

PAUL H. WENDER

In the past few years impressive data have emerged demonstrating the role of genetics in the etiology of the schizophrenic syndromes. I shall summarize these findings and discuss the relevance of these as yet not widely known studies. The schizophrenias are not uncommon disorders. The usual figure given for lifetime incidence is about one percent. This figure is based on hospitalized cases;[1] if the number of people hospitalized is only one-half to one-third of those who have the disorder,[2] the prevalent figure must be doubled or even tripled. But the problem may be even more extensive, since the boundaries of the syndrome are so unclear. It is possible that conditions which bear a phenomenological resemblance to schizophrenia, such as schizoid disorders and borderline states, may share etiological factors as well. These latter disorders are extremely common; some clinics report that as many as one-half of their applicants have been so diagnosed.[3] Clearly then what might be in question is the etiology of the

---

*This paper appeared in slightly revised form in the *American Journal of Orthopsychiatry*, 39:447-58 (1969).

disorder of a substantial proportion of the psychiatrically disturbed population.

The theories concerning the genesis of the schizophrenias primarily are explications of an observation of considerable antiquity: that there is a familial clustering of psychiatric disease. A suitably early reference may be found in Thomas Willis, who wrote in 1685 that: "It is a common observation, that men born of parents that are sometimes wont to be mad, will be obnoxious to the same disease." In the intervening 280 years studies exploring the etiology of the schizophrenias have implicated both genetic and environmental factors but have not yet been able to assess the relative roles of each factor in the development of the syndrome. These studies have employed two major lines of investigation.

First there are consanguinity studies—assessments of the prevalence of mental disease in the relatives of schizophrenic patients.[4] Such studies have demonstrated that there is a significantly higher prevalence of psychopathology among the relatives of schizophrenics as compared to the general population and that the closer the biological relationship, the greater the prevalence of psychopathology in relatives, culminating in the high concordance rate of schizophrenia in monozygotic twins. Results of such studies have been traditionally explained as results of the operation of genetic factors.

Second there are psychodynamic and family studies— studies of the psychological environment to which schizophrenic patients have been exposed.[5] These studies have revealed that schizophrenics have been reared in and exposed to a disturbed psychological environment. They have been interpreted to show that the disease is a learned reaction to, modeling after or identification with such familial pathology.

What makes interpretation of both types of studies difficult is the confounding of biological and psychological relatedness: the deviant psychological experiences have usually been received at the hands of the patient's biological relatives. One cannot decide to what extent the disturbance of the schizophrenic offspring has been genetically or psychologically transmitted, because the cognitive, affective, and childrearing abnormalities of the parents might be a manifestation of a genetic disorder in the parents rather than a cause of the illness in the child. The data accumulated are compatible with both the biological and the social transmission of schizophrenia and do not permit the evaluation of the relative contributions of either.[6]

In the past few years a method of resolving this dilemma occurred independently to several people: Leonard Heston, Jon Karlsson, and each of our collaborative team at the National Institutes of Health—Seymour Kety, David Rosenthal, and me.[7] This method involves the study of individuals adopted in infancy. Since in such circumstances the biological parents are not the parents who rear the children, the transmitters of biological heredity and social experience are separated and their relative roles may be evaluated. Why this method had not been previously applied to the problem of the psychoses and why it suddenly occurred to several people at once is an interesting question; the technique had been used to evaluate the contributions of nature and nurture in intelligence thirty years ago and to the problem of alcoholism twenty years ago.[8]

Studies utilizing adoption have employed three approaches attempting to answer three questions. The first question is: Does heredity play any role in the etiology of the schizophrenia and, if so, what is the manifestation of the genetic diathesis? Two relevant studies are those of Leonard Heston and Rosenthal *et al.*[9] Both have evaluated the personalities of adults born to schizophrenic parents but reared from infancy in foster homes (Heston) or adoptive homes (Rosenthal *et al.*). Both studies have employed the obvious control group of children born to normal biological parents and reared in foster or adoptive homes. Heston's evaluations of subjects were made primarily on the basis of clinical interviews, while the Rosenthal study employed psychological tests as well. At this time results of the Heston study have been fully analyzed, those of the Rosenthal study have not. In these studies the phrase "index group" refers to the offspring of schizophrenic parents reared in foster or adoptive homes, while the phrase "control group" refers to the offspring of nonschizophrenic parents reared in foster or adoptive homes. Table 1 presents the findings of each study and summarizes the results of both studies taken together. About 9 percent of the offspring of schizophrenic parents be-

Table 1
DISTRIBUTION OF SCHIZOPHRENIC DIAGNOSES
AMONG OFFSPRING OF SCHIZOPHRENIC PARENTS
(INDEX CASES) AND NONSCHIZOPHRENIC PARENTS
(CONTROL CASES)

	Schizophrenic	Borderline or Schizoid Schizophrenic States	Other	Total
HESTON (1966)				
Index Cases	5	8	34	47
Control Class	0	0	50	50

Schizophrenic + borderline schizophrenics + schizoid vs. "others," $p <$ .001 (exact probability test).

ROSENTHAL et al. (1967)				
Index Cases	3	6	4	26	39
Control Cases	0	1	5	41	47

Schizophrenic + Borderline schizophrenics + Schizoid vs. "Others," $p <$ .02 (exact probability test).

COMBINED DATA				
Index Cases	8 (9%)[a]	18 (21%)[b]	60 (70%)[c]	86
Control Cases	0	6	91	97

The probability that the excess of:
[a]Schizophrenics in the index group is chance, $p < .003$ (exact probability test).
[b]Borderline schizophrenics + schizoids in the index group is chance, $p < .001$ (exact probability test).
[c]Schizophrenics + borderline schizophrenics + schizoids in the index group is chance, $p < .001$ (exact probability test).

come schizophrenic when reared in adoptive or foster homes
as opposed to none of the offspring of nonschizophrenic
mothers reared in adoptive or foster homes. The rate of 9 percent is well within the range of offspring of schizophrenics
who become schizophrenic when reared by their own parents.
Likewise, about 30 percent of the index group manifested
psychiatric pathology in the schizophrenic or borderline spectrum as opposed to 6 percent in the control group. (These
differences are highly significant statistically, $p = .001$, exact
probability test.) About one-third of the offspring of one schizophrenic parent develop psychiatric disorders of a schizophrenic character when they are reared away from their
schizophrenic parents.[10] The studies show a markedly increased
prevalence of schizophrenic psychopathology among the biological offspring of schizophrenic parents, a finding strongly
implicating genetic factors in the development of some forms
of schizophrenia. The "some forms" is important, for logically
such a research design can (and has) shown only that some
schizophrenic parents genetically transmit the disorder to their
offspring. The design cannot demonstrate the converse—that
all schizophrenics have schizophrenic parents or that all schizophrenics have a genetic component to their illness.

Two additional results not cited in the tables are of considerable interest. Both relate to what seem to be other manifestations of the genetic tendency. Heston's study revealed that in
addition to the five schizophrenic subjects in the index group,
twenty-one index subjects manifested appreciable psychopathology, including nine sociopaths (Eight were noted as "schizoid psychopath" and have been included in the category of
"borderline schizophrenic" or "schizoid" states in Table 1.)
and thirteen other personality disorders (emotionally unstable
personalities and mixed psychoneurotic reactions). Among the
control group there were two sociopaths and seven personality
disorders. The difference in frequency between the two groups
is again significant ($p = .02$ for sociopathy, $p = .05$ for the personality disorders, exact probability test). The second unexpected result was that among the index subjects who demon-

strated no psychiatric pathology Heston felt that there were a large number of talented, creative, and colorful people—a provocative suggestion of the often mentioned relationship between madness and genius. Although there is a preponderance of psychopathology among the offspring of psychotic parents, there is some psychopathology among the offspring of the control parents. This fact does not necessarily demonstrate that such psychopathology can originate without a genetic basis. Neither study asserted that the parents of the control subjects were psychologically healthy but only that they had never received psychiatric attention. What fraction of persons with the schizophrenic syndrome do receive psychiatric attention at some time during their lives? Rosenthal found that of twenty persons who were schizoid, borderline, or schizophrenic only one had ever received psychiatric care. Judging from the Rosenthal data—as well as population surveys, such as *Mental Health in the Metropolis*[11]—only a small fraction of seriously disturbed persons do receive psychiatric attention. Accordingly, there is a fair probability that the control population's parents contained ill but undiagnosed persons. (It would seem that women giving up their children for adoption are more apt to be disturbed than those who do not). Preliminary analyses of the Rosenthal data suggests that severity of psychopathology in the parent is not closely correlated with the severity of pathology in the offspring; that is, borderline schizophrenic patients are as apt to have children in the schizophrenic spectrum as are chronically schizophrenic parents. If this is so, the psychiatric disturbance in the offspring of the control group may be due to genetic transmission, from mildly disturbed and undiagnosed parents within this group. A method which might permit clarification of the above problem would be to interview and screen the parents of the control group, including only the offspring of those parents who manifested no psychiatric disturbance. Hence, there is no reason for necessarily attributing disturbance of the offspring of the control group to psychological environmental factors. It is possible that the disturbances in both the experimental and control groups are entirely genetic. It is also logically possible that psychological factors do play a role in the development of psychiatric illness within both groups. One cannot make a decision between these two possibilities on the bases of these data. An obvious question is whether the experiences associated with adoption are psychologically noxious. One might then argue that some psychological experiences related to adoption interact with a biological predisposition to produce psychopathology in the index group. An admission that this is so is—because the control group did not in general become ill—tantamount to stating that the biological predisposition is so great that factors that do not make a genetically normal child ill will make a predisposed child severely disturbed; that is, genetically transmitted characteristics are at least necessary, if not sufficient. Virtually no disease is entirely genetic. Even phenylketonuria, which is generally considered to be a genetic disorder, has an environmental component. The child who has the disease will become ill only if he eats substances containing the amino acid, phenylalanine. If most edible substances did not contain phenylalanine, a child with phenylketonuria would become ill only if he ate special foods, those containing phenylalanine. Since most proteins do contain phenylalanine, an afflicted child becomes ill under any natural environmental circumstances. (When such a child is fed a diet deficient in phenylalanine the manifestation of the disease can perhaps be avoided). Similarly, the genetically predisposed child might not become schizophrenic if reared in an unusual way. These data show only that given an apparently adequate psychological environment, such a child does become ill.

The first experimental design answers one question: Can schizophrenia be genetically transmitted? The answer is affirmative. This design cannot answer the question: What fraction of schizophrenics are genetically produced? To answer this question another design must be employed. In this second design one starts with adult schizophrenics, adopted in infancy, and determines which of them have psychiatric illness in their biological relatives. If schizophrenia is a genetically transmitted disorder, one should find an increased prevalence of schizophrenia among the biological relatives of the schizophrenics as compared to the biological relatives of normal adopted adults. Likewise, if schizophrenia is a psychologically transmitted disorder, one should expect to find an increased prevalence of psychopathology among the adopting relatives of the schizophrenic subjects.

Such a study has been conducted and is reported by Kety, et al.[12] These authors report the prevalence of psychopathology among the biological and adoptive relatives of thirty-three adopted schizophrenics (the index cases) and thirty-three matched adopted nonhospitalized subjects (the control cases). The prevalence of schizophrenia and other psychiatric disorders among these relatives was determined by finding the number of such relatives who had received such psychiatric diagnoses from hospitals and clinics. The results are presented in Table 2.

The data reveal a significantly increased prevalence of schizophrenia among the biological relatives of the adoptive schizophrenics but not among the adoptive parents of these

Table 2
DISTRIBUTION IN THE RELATIVES OF
SCHIZOPHRENIC CASES AND THEIR CONTROLS

	Relatives with Schizophrenia or Probable Schizophrenia	
	Biological Relatives	Adoptive Relatives
Index Cases ($N = 33$)	11 (150)a	1 (74)
Control Cases ($N = 33$)	3 (156)	3 (83)

$p < .05$ (exact probability test, one-tailed).
Figures in brackets indicate the total number of relatives at risk. For example, for the upper lefthand cell, there were 150 biological relatives of adopted schizophrenics (index cases) and of these relatives eleven were schizophrenics or probable schizophrenics.

subjects. This result is highly significant statistically ($p = .05$, exact probability test). The finding is compatible with the genetic but not the psychological transmission hypothesis. Since Heston's study had shown that schizophrenic parents produced offspring with a variety of psychopathology, it was logical to reverse the process and to ask how many of the biological relatives of schizophrenic subjects have received comparable diagnosis. Accordingly, the following diagnoses were grouped together under the neologism, "schizophrenic spectrum disorder": schizophrenia; probable schizophrenia; psychopathy; neurotic character disorder; inadequate personality. The results are presented in Table 3.

The prevalence of all these illnesses is significantly greater among the biological relatives of the schizophrenics ($p = .01$, exact probability test), a result again compatible with Heston's finding of a general increase of psychopathology among the offspring of schizophrenic parents.

This study has one methodological and one logical weakness. The methodological weakness is that the diagnoses were made on the basis of formally recognized mental illness, and consequently, the rates of illness among the relatives are too low. Likewise the control group may have been far from psychologically healthy because a nondistinct criterion of health

Table 3

DISTRIBUTION IN THE RELATIVES OF
SCHIZOPHRENIC INDEX CASES AND THEIR CONTROLS

	Relatives with Schizophrenia, Probable Schizophrenia, Psychopathy, Character Disorder, Inadequate Personality	
	Biological Relatives	Adoptive Relatives
Index Cases ($N = 33$)	20 (150)	4 (74)
Control Cases ($N = 33$)	7 (156)	3 (83)

$p < .01$ (exact probability test, one-tailed).

was used: never receiving psychiatric therapy for mental illness. A logical weakness is that such a method could only set a lower limit on the fraction of schizophrenics who have a genetic predisposition. The reason is that any genetic trait which is not transmitted by a simple dominant gene will not be demonstrated by every child in the family with that trait. For example, if both parents are carrying a heterozygous recessive trait, neither will show the trait but perhaps one or more of the children will show it. This is common among the parents of children with phenylketonuria. In this study at least one child, an adopted schizophrenic, showed the trait in question. If the trait were a simple recessive one, one would expect that about 40 percent of the siblings would not manifest that trait.[13] That is, even if the disease were entirely genetic, 40 percent of the cases would have a negative family history.

In neither of the groups of studies discussed was the psychological environment of the adopted schizophrenic evaluated. Proponents of the psychological mode of transmission have clearly described the aberrant interpersonal and cognitive environment to which the future schizophrenic is exposed during his formative years.[14] Although such work is important, one cannot determine whether such an environment is a manifestation of illness in the parents rather than the cause of the illness in the child.

In an attempt to unravel this problem a third type of study has been conducted. In this study reported by Wender, Rosenthal, and Kety the adoptive parents of schizophrenics were compared with a group of parents who reared their own schizophrenic children.[15] The parents of these two groups and of a third comparison group, the adoptive parents of normal adults, were evaluated with psychiatric interviews and psychological tests. At present only the psychiatric interviews have been evaluated. On the basis of these interviews each parent was assigned a score on a global psychopathology scale, which is shown in Table 4. The average severity of psychopathology among the three groups was calculated, and the results are presented on Table 4.

Table 4

GLOBAL SEVERITY OF PSYCHOPATHOLOGY
RATING SCALE

1. Normal—without any disorder traits.
2. Normal—with minor psychoneurotic traits.
3. Psychoneurosis or mild character neuroses.
4. Moderate to marked character neuroses.
5. Severe character, schizoid character, paranoid character.
6. Borderline schizophrenia, acute psychoses.
7. Schizophrenic psychosis.

The biological parents were considerably more disturbed than the adoptive parents of schizophrenic patients. The difference is highly significant ($p < .005$, t-test). Likewise the adoptive parents of the schizophrenic adults were somewhat more

Table 5
FREQUENCY AND SEVERITY OF PSYCHOPATHOLOGY
IN THE THREE GROUPS OF PARENTS

GROUP		1-2	2.5-3	3.5-4	4.5-5	5.5-6	6.5-7	Mean
Biological Schizophrenic	Fathers	1	1	1	6	1	0	4.2
	Mothers	0	0	4	3	1	2	4.9
Adopted Schizophrenic	Fathers	1	4	3	2	0	0	3.3
	Mothers	1	3	4	1	1	0	3.5
Adopted Normals	Fathers	2	6	2	0	0	0	2.6
	Mothers	2	4	4	0	0	0	3.0

Significances, one-tailed t-test:
Adoptive Schizophrenic Parents vs. Biological Schizophrenic Parents, $p < .005$.
Adoptive Schizophrenic Parents vs. Adoptive Normal Parents, $p < .05$.
Adoptive Schizophrenic Mothers vs. Biological Schizophrenic Mothers, $p < .05$.
Adoptive Schizophrenic Mothers vs. Adopted Normal Mothers, NS.
Adoptive Schizophrenic Fathers vs. Biological Schizophrenic Fathers, $p < .05$.
Adoptive Schizophrenic Fathers vs. Adoptive Normal Fathers, NS.

disturbed than the adoptive parents of the normal subjects—this difference is significant but less so ($p < .05$, t-test). Some sampling problems and a methodological problem (the interviewers knew into which group the parents fell) dictate less than unqualified acceptance of these data, and a replication is planned. Nonetheless, the experiment again suggests that the psychopathology in the parents of schizophrenic individuals is a manifestation of genetically transmitted disturbance in the parents rather than the cause of illness in the patient. This last assertion contravenes the mandate of one's psychological intuition. It is virtually impossible to see how the aberrant psychological environments that have been described can fail to leave their pathological toll. Perhaps the psychopathology among the offspring of schizophrenic parents reared in adoptive homes would be still greater if these homes provided the type of environments which have been deemed schizophrenigenic. Nonetheless, if these data are correct, one cannot but conclude that the role of deviant psychological experiences in the etiology of schizophrenia has been overestimated.

Several questions have been raised but not answered by these studies. The first relates to schizophrenia spectrum disorders. One of the most surprising findings of the Heston and Kety studies was the increased amount of nonschizophrenic pathology (psychopathy, character disorders) among the relatives of schizophrenic patients. Because of the designs of these studies such pathology could not have been the effect of psychological causes but rather must have resulted from genetic inheritance. Not only do some schizophrenias have a genetic basis but apparently so do some phenomenologically nonschizophrenic psychiatric syndromes as well.

If a graduated continuum of psychiatric pathology—a spectrum—does exist, the nineteenth-century concept of a neuropathological trait with varying manifestations may have to be exhumed and resuscitated.[16] The efforts of nosologists to break the continuum of psychological malfunction into discrete psychiatric diagnostic categories may be impossible. Because of the difficulty nosologists have had in describing discrete non-overlapping psychiatric diagnostic categories, some psychiatrists (for example, Menninger) have argued that the reason for this continuum is that there really are no psychiatric diseases and that all apparently qualitatively different forms of mental illness differ only quantitatively; different forms of malfunction are the result of the degree of regression along a continuous path of psychological development common to all people.[17]

The demonstration of a continuum often leads to an incorrect conclusion: because a continuum exists, no diseases exist. Without quibbling about the meaning of the word "disease," we obviously know although intelligence is distributed along a continuum, certain biological pathological states (diseases) exist which produce low intelligence. Likewise, height is distributed along a continuum, but one would not argue that achondroplastic dwarfs or persons with pituitary giantism did not have diseases. In summary, the existence of a phenomenological continuum of psychopathology in no way excludes the view that biological diseases exist in the continuum. The data suggest that there may be an underlying continuum of biological disposition which is manifested in the observed symptomatic continuum.

Another question, related to the one already discussed, is what is transmitted. What are the primary psychological traits that are inherited? Are they any or all of the "fundamental" psychological characteristics posited by several authors to form the psychological anlage of schizophrenia? A partial list of such traits would include: dissociation;[18] introversion;[19] weakness of repression; overreaction to anxiety-producing stimuli;[20] and anhedonia.[21]

A second question is simply the mechanism of genetic transmission. What gene or genes are involved? What are the effects of their interaction? What is their degree of penetrance?

A third related question regards what is biologically transmitted. Using the computer as an analogy to the brain, we can consider at least three possible mechanisms. First, some of the components (neurons) may be aberrant. In this model some groups of cells have a metabolic abnormality which might be manifested in a variety of ways, including a raised or lowered threshold of excitability or lack of modification through use ("effective learning"). Such aberrant functioning might be detectible with present biochemical techniques. Second, the wiring may be aberrant. In this model the individual elements (neurons, vacuum tubes, transistors) function adequately but are interconnected incorrectly. Such an abnormality would probably be difficult if not impossible to ascertain with current biological techniques. Third, the inbuilt "programs" may be aberrant. In this instance both the elements and their interconnections are adequate but the instinctive programs are aberrant. In a normal child certain complex patterns of behavior emerge on a fairly predictable timetable: stranger anxiety during the second half of the first year; separation anxiety during the second year; oppositional behavior during the second and third years. Such preprogrammed behavior seems to fulfill an important role in normal development. As Levy suggests, without the period of preprogrammed rebellion a two-year-old might not begin to develop independence; one might easily see a child lacking this program as becoming an excessively dependent and "good" child closely bound to his mother—in fact, a child with some characteristics often described in preschizophrenics.[22] An aberration in which the mechanisms were intact but the neural instructions which govern were somehow malfunctioning would be an abnormality with a biological basis probably impossible to detect with current techniques.

The role of experiential factors is a final consideration. What have these experiments demonstrated with regard to the etiology of schizophrenia? They demonstrate that biological factors, almost certainly genetic, play a predominant role in the etiology of some fraction of the schizophrenic syndromes. The followup studies—studies of the offspring of schizophrenics reared in adoptive homes—can logically demonstrate only that schizophrenia can be genetic. Such studies cannot determine in what fraction of schizophrenias genetic factors are predominant. Studies of the relatives of adopted schizo-phrenics—the second type of study discussed—should provide some answers. Even if the syndrome were entirely genetic, un-less it were transmitted as a simple dominant trait (and it appears not to be), one would not expect to find a family history in all instances. (Certainly one would not expect all schizophrenics to be genetically produced. If some schizo-phrenic adults are, so to speak, "ex-schizophrenic children," then since a large fraction of schizophrenic children suffer from organic brain damage,[23] one would expect that the pre-dominant etiology of some adult schizophrenic syndromes would also be organic brain damage).

A most important question not answered by these studies is how and to what extent experiental factors influence the gen-esis of the schizophrenias. The adoptive parents study could only show that some schizophrenics have fairly normal par-ents. But what are the effects of disturbed parents? Can ex-periential factors alone produce schizophrenia? Some light may be shed on this question by a study now in progress of the psychological fate of the offspring of normal biological parents reared by schizophrenic, and presumably schizophrenogenic, adoptive parents. Finally, how and to what extent do experien-tal factors interact with the documented biological factors? Neither the Heston nor the Rosenthal study employ a compari-son group of adults reared by their own schizophrenic parents. Such a comparison group is necessary to determine whether or not deviant environmental factors contribute to the im-paired psychological and social functioning seen in schizo-phrenic individuals. It is possible that although schizophrenics' offspring reared in adoptive homes are as apt to develop schiz-ophrenic symptoms as when reared by their own parents (which the data seem to indicate), the severity and type of these symptoms may be affected by the circumstances of rearing.

Theories regarding the genesis of psychopathology are nu-merous, but facts are less abundant. Most theorists acknowl-edge the importance of both constitutional and experiental factors. Such assertions are not very useful, and what is essential is the specification of which kinds of experience, interacting with which kinds of biological background at various points, result in which kinds of personality development. The strategy of adoption studies may permit the construction of specific and useful theories, both for deviant and normal human psychological development.

NOTES

1. J. Book, "Genetical Aspects of Schizophrenic Psychoses," *The Etiology of Schizophrenia*, ed. D. Jackson (New York: Basic Books, 1960).

2. D. Engelhardt, "Drug Treatment of Chronic Ambulatory Patients," *American Journal of Psychiatry, 123*:1329-37 (1967).

3. E. Gaw, et al., "How Common is Schizophrenia?" *Bulletin of Menninger Clinic, 17*:20-28 (1953).

4. F. Kallman, *The Genetics of Schizophrenia* (New York: J. J. Augustin, 1938); E. Slater, and J. Shields, "Psychotic and Neurotic Illness in Twins", *Medical Research Council Special Report*, Series No. 278 (London: Her Majesty's Stationery Office, 1953).

5. Y. Alanen, "The Mothers of Schizophrenic Patients", *Acta Psychiatica et Neurolica Scandinavica Supplementum, 124* (1958); Y. Alanen, "The Family in the Pathogenesis of Schizophrenic and Neurotic Disorders", *Acta Psychiatica, 189* (1966); T. Litz, et al., "The Intrafamilial Environment of the Schizophrenic Patient: IV Parental Personalities and Family Inter-action," *American Journal of Orthopsychiatry, 28*:764-76 (1958); T. Lidz, et al., "The Intrafamilial Environment of the Schizophrenic Patient: VI Transmission of Irrationality," *Archives of Neurology and Psychiatry, 79*:305-16 (1958).

6. The studies of monozygotic (identical) twins do provide some definitive information regarding the role of genetics in the etiology of schizophrenia. This information is usually incorrectly interpreted. Since in no study conducted today has it been found that 100 percent of identical twin pairs are concordant with regard to schizophrenia, one can only conclude that the etiology of the disease cannot be 100 percent genetic. However, this does not document—as some people would seem to believe—that psychological factors necessarily play an etiological role in the development of the disorder. All that is nongenetic is not necessarily psychological; biological but nongenetic factors have been implicated in several such studies. (See J. Stabenau and W. Pollin, "Early Characteristics of Monozygotic Twins Discordant for Schizophrenia,"

Archives of General Psychiatry, 17:723-34 [1967].) The concordance rate of schizophrenia in monozygotic twins is approximately that of diabetes, a disease not generally regarded as primarily psychological in origin. (See B. Harvald and M. Hauge, "Heredity Factors Elucidated by Twin Studies," *Genetics and the Epidemiology of Chronic Diseases,* ed. J. Neel *et al.* No. 1163 (Washington: U.S. Government Printing Office, 1965).

7. L. Heston, "Psychiatric Disorders in Foster Home Reared Children of Schizophrenic Mothers", *British Journal of Psychiatry, 112*:819-25 (1966); J. Karlson, *The Biological Basis of Schizophrenia,* (Springfield, Ill.: Charles Thomas, 1966).

8. S. Kety, *et al., The Types and Frequencies of Mental Illness in the Biological and Adopted Families of Adopted Schizophrenics: A Preliminary Report* (in press); Rosenthal, D., *et al., Schizophrenics' Offspring Reared in Adoptive Homes* (in press); P. Wender, *et al., A Psychiatric Evaluation of the Adoptive Parents of Schizophrenics* (in press); M. Skodak and H. Skeels, "A Final Follow-up Study of One Hundred Adopted Children," *Journal of Genetic Psychology, 75*:85-125 (1949); A. Roe, and B. Mittleman. "Adult Adjustment of Foster Children of Alcoholic and Psychotic Parentage and the Influence of the Foster Home," *Memoirs, Quarterly Journal of Study of Alcohol,* No. 3 (1945).

9. Heston, pp. 819-25; Rosenthal *et al.*

10. Y. Alanen, *et al.* "Mental Disorders in the Siblings of Schizophrenic Patients," *Acta Psychiatica, 169* (1963).

11. L. Srole, *et al., Mental Health in the Metropolis* (New York: McGraw-Hill, 1962).

12. Kety.

13. In the Kety *et al.* study the average number of sibs per patient was three, or average number of offspring per biological parent four. The proportion of siblings who did not manifest a psychiatric illness was about 65 percent. For further reference, see any textbook on human genetics, for example Curtis Stern, *Principles of Human Genetics* (San Francisco: W. H. Freeman, 1956); Alanen, *Acta Psychiatica,* 124, and *Acta Psychiatica,* 189; Litz.

14. L. Wynne, and M. Singer, "Thought Disorder and Family Relations of Schizophrenics: I—A Research Strategy," *AGP, 9*:191 (1963); and "Thought Disorder and Family Relations of Schizophrenics: II—A Classification of Forms of Thinking," *AGP, 9*:199 (1963).

15. Wender *et al.*

16. The observation that mental disease, not particular forms of mental illness, cluster in families had been made considerably earlier. In his *Anatomy of Melancholy* published in 1651 Burton observed: "and that which is to be more wondered at, it [melancholy] skips in some families and goes to the son, or takes every other, and sometimes every third in a

lineal descent, and does not always produce the same, but some like, and some symbolizing disease." (Edition 185, ed. F. Dell and P. Jordan-Smith [New York: Farrar and Rinehart, 1927]).

17. K. Menninger, *The Vital Balance* (New York: The Viking Press, 1963).

18. E. Bleuler, *Dementia Praecox or the Group of Schizophrenias* (New York: International Universities Press, 1950).

19. C. Jung, *The Psychology of Dementia Praecox* (New York: Nervous and Mental Disease Publishing Company, 1909).

20. S. Mednick, "A Learning Theory Approach to Research in Schizophrenia," *Psychiatric Bulletin*, 55:316-27 (1958).

21. S. Rado, *Psychoanalysis of Behavior* (New York: Grune and Stratton, 1956).

22. D. Levy, "Oppositional Syndromes and Oppositional Behavior," *Psychopathology of Childhood*, ed. P. Hoch and J. Zubin (New York: Grune and Stratton, 1955).

23. M. Gittleman, and H. Birch, "Childhood Schizophrenia," *AGP*, *17*: 16-26 (1967).

Families and Schizophrenia: alternatives to longitudinal studies*

NANCY E. WAXLER

We now have abundant empirical evidence that families who have schizophrenic children are different in modes of interaction and styles of communication from normal families.[1] There is a general tendency to treat such findings as if they indicated that certain family processes are pathogenic. However, since most data are derived from families observed after the schizophrenia has occurred, the findings give no real assurance that the family has been an etiological factor in the illness. It is just as likely that the family processes labeled by clinicians as pathogenic are responses to the schizophrenic child rather than causes of or precursors to the schizophrenia.

There are at least four equally reasonable explanations of these empirical relationships, each supported by theorists or

---

*This work was partially supported by grants from the National Institute of Mental Health (MH 06276), National Science Foundation (GS 1225), and a National Institute of Mental Health Research Scientist Award (MH 38842).

I am grateful to Elliot G. Mishler for his useful suggestions and comments on earlier drafts of this paper.

clinicians familiar with schizophrenic patients and their families. The first explanation, the etiological one, states that predisposition to illness was present in the family structure as we see it and before the child's illness and, furthermore, had a part in the development of schizophrenia in the child. The theory developed by Theodore Lidz and his coworkers exemplifies this point of view.[2] The second explanation, which we have labeled "responsive," states that the family has developed new structures and processes in response to the illness, or deviance, of the schizophrenic child. In this instance the family process is the effect rather than the cause. Scott's description of the "closure" that occurs in the family at the time the schizophrenic child is defined as ill exemplifies a responsive theory.[3] The third explanation suggests that the modes of interaction in the schizophrenic family, and perhaps the schizophrenia itself, have developed as a response to a third variable. Here the cause may be one that is outside our theoretical concern with social variables; for example, genetic factors may explain both parental behavior and schizophrenia in the child. There are, however, other social variables not specific to schizophrenia that may affect both parental and child interaction. Hospitalization and consequent removal of the patient from the family is one of these. Finally, the fourth explanation of the relationship between family processes and the child's schizophrenia assumes that all of the above effects have occurred. Thus, the family processes that we observe after the fact of the illness may have been present along some dimensions before the child's illness; the family may have changed to some extent as a result of the child's illness; and it may have altered in response to other family experiences unrelated in any direct way to the schizophrenia. This last explanation, sometimes called a transactional or interactional theory, is represented by Wynne and is also discussed in relation to autistic children and their families by Bruno Bettleheim.[4]

The problem we confront in attempting to sort out which of these explanations is most reasonable is the time order in which the variables have their effect (as well as the extent of their relationship). Did the family process occur prior to the schizophrenia; did the schizophrenia occur prior to the family process, or, is there a complex interrelationship between these two? Lee N. Robins's discussion of the time-order problem in epidemiological research is related to our concerns; her proposals focus on nonexperimental methods.[5] The longitudinal study comes immediately to mind as the solution to this problem. A sample of families may be followed through a child's infancy to young adulthood to determine whether family process is abnormal prior to the development of schizophrenia or whether this abnormality is seen only after the illness has occurred. But longitudinal studies raise many methodological problems, which have been discussed in detail by Richard Bell.[6] The time required is prohibitive. Constant remeasurement of the same families may affect the dependent variables. Sampling may either be random, resulting in a small proportion of families that actually produce a schizophrenic child, or within a high risk group, thus omitting families within the low risk group that do produce schizophrenia. An explicit theory must guide the selection of variables. A special methodological problem inherent in the study of a relatively poorly-defined entity such as schizophrenia is the definition of the point in time at which the schizophrenia begins, since it is necessary to compare a family before the illness with the same family after the illness.

There are a number of solutions to these problems. Sarnoff Mednick has sampled from a high risk group that may produce a higher than expected number of schizophrenic children.[7] Control groups may be used at each point in time that a family is investigated to measure the effect of the measurement itself, or samples of families whose children are known later to have become schizophrenic may be obtained by examining early clinic records.[8] This latter method leaves the researcher with little control over data collection or sampling techniques. Each of these solutions will help provide answers to the original question and, as Bell has shown by creating hypothetical examples, findings generated by the longitudinal method, perhaps in modified form, may be crucial in some cases. However, we should give serious attention to alternative approaches that shed light on the time order in which the variables have their effect without having to confront the methodological problems and inflexibility of the longitudinal approach.

An alternative approach is the experimental method, in which the supposed causal variables are experimentally controlled, all other aspects of the subjects and situation are held constant, and a direct test of the effect of the controlled variables is made. This experimental paradigm allows investigation of many family interaction patterns (double-binds, reversed parental roles, and mystifications, for example) singly and in combination to test their effect on the child in the family. Such tests would provide interesting evidence for, or counter to, the etiological argument. However, the experimental technique rests on the assumption that there are theories about schizophrenic families which provide clear definitions of probable causal variables, the variables that must be manipulated. It requires that we know the causal variable and then operationalize and replicate it experimentally to measure its effect. Unfortunately, there are no such concretely specified theories. One example is Anthony Schuham's review of the definition of double bind communications.[9]

However, it is possible to use the logical principles of experimental design, to control or manipulate variables, and to do this within the context of a standardized experimental situation even though the supposed causal variables themselves (the family interaction or the child's behavior, for example) are not directly manipulated nor the time order of their occurrence controlled. The experimental technique we suggest consists of a multi-experimental group research design. Two experimental group types are selected, one the family of the schizophrenic child about which we have questions of time order and causality and the second a family type having a known time and causal relationship between the variables of family interactions and the occurrence of the child's illness. We also include one control group, a family in which there has been no illness. We observe each of these groups in a carefully standardized experimental situation; we assume all other variables to be randomly distributed. A comparison of the interaction in the three types of families will allow us to infer the probable time order of the events in the schizophrenic family, i.e., the modes of family interaction and the occurrence of the child's illness. More accurately, this experimental design aids in ruling out the least likely explanations of the relationship. Over a period of time, using a number of such studies, we should be able to arrive at one most probable causal explanation out of the four outlined.

How might one attempt to rule out the etiological explanation, the one that assumes the family processes were present before the schizophrenia and may have had a part in the development of the illness? Here we may select as one experimental group a family with a child who has an illness manifesting itself in deviant behavior, just as does schizophrenia, yet whose illness clearly is not caused by the interaction of parents with the child. In other words, we must find a family in which the time order of the variables is known; the illness must have occurred before the altered or abnormal family process. We know of a number of such childhood illnesses that clinicians and researchers have noted very often call forth changes in a family structure after they occur, yet have genetic or other nonfamilial causes. For example, Alfred Wood and associates describe interaction processes of parents of children with phenylketonouria (which has a known genetic cause) elicited by the requirement of controlling the child's eating habits.[10] H. B. Schaffer describes changes in family roles in response to a child with cerebral palsy.[11]

In this multi-experimental group design we compare the interaction patterns in families with schizophrenic children with those in families with children who have phenylketonouria or cerebral palsy, and with those in families with no sick or deviant children. If we find the styles of interaction in the schizophrenic and cerebral palsy families are similar and each is different from the normal family, then we could conclude that the responsive interpretation has gained support and the etiological interpretation is less valid. The schizophrenic family is similar to a family *known* to have responded abnormally to a deviant child, and this is evidence favoring the responsive interpretation. Here we do not argue that the child with cerebral palsy is the same as the child with schizophrenia, or that the illnesses manifest themselves in the same way, but that each illness has required the family to respond to the child as a deviant role player. There are, naturally, other possible findings than the one described. If the families of schizophrenic children differ from those with the genetically caused illness and these families differ from the normal families, then we may assume that the family etiology theory of schizophrenia remains logically possible.

A second explanation of the relationship between family processes and schizophrenia states that family interaction relates to a family experience such as hospitalization that is not specific to schizophrenia. A number of variables have been mentioned as possible explanations of the pathological family processes observed by clinicians who, by virtue of their work, see only a highly select sample of families, those having children defined by someone as sick. Pathological family processes may just as likely be a result of hospitalization, removal of the child from the family, definition of the child as deviant, or other variables. How might we rule out this explanation, using a multi-experimental group design? If hospitalization is assumed to be the most significant family experience affecting the family structure, then we need to keep all other variables constant except hospitalization; a control group of families having schizophrenic children who have never been hospitalized (or never treated) may be compared with another group of families having schizophrenic children who have been treated, and these may be further compared with a set of normal families. If both types of schizophrenic families are similar, and each is different from normal families, then we could assume that the third variable, hospitalization, has been ruled out. While methodological problems exist—particularly finding the nontreated schizophrenic children in the community and arriving at a reliable diagnosis, they are soluble.[12] Several studies of schizophrenic families have included control groups of hospitalized, nonpsychiatrically ill patients. For example, Amerigo Farina used parents having sons hospitalized for tuberculosis.[13] These studies have provided extremely interesting and useful findings, although from the point of view of our concern with control groups they mix the hospitalization variable with the medical illness variable and thus make interpretation of the source of family differences difficult.

How might we attempt to rule out experimentally the responsive explanation? Here the assumption is that the pathological family processes have been elicited by the deviant behavior of the schizophrenic child. Families have been forced to alter their structures and processes in response to a child who is different. Richard Bell calls this the "child effect," and discusses techniques for measuring this effect independent of the "parent effect."[14] Using the same procedure of the previous solutions described here, we should select a control group of families with children with a type of illness known to have been caused by pathological family interaction. We should then compare the interaction of this family type with the schizophrenic families. If we found that schizophrenic families are similar to this control group and both are different from normal families, then we could logically rule out the responsive interpretation and assume that the etiological explanation has more support. However, there are no diseases that clearly fit this type. An assumption that such illnesses as duodenal ulcers, or asthma, or that diagnostic category called character disorder, have a familial cause would certainly be controversial. For this reason we suggest a second experimental research strategy in which control groups and experimental groups of families are artificially constructed. Instead of asking whether it is likely that the family has responded to a schizophrenic child, and thereby altered family functioning, we will turn the question around and ask whether it is possible for a schizophrenic child to elicit abnormal responses from normal family members.

This experimental method consists of constructing families by placing a schizophrenic child with parents of a normal child, and by placing parents of a schizophrenic child with a normal child.* (This technique is similar to one suggested by Richard Bell, 1959-60). If we find that the schizophrenic child evokes abnormal behavior from the normal parents, and this behavior is similar to that of the parents of the schizophrenic, and if the schizophrenic parents appear to behave normally when with a normal child, then we could assume that it is possible for the patient child to have elicited a response from his family. Thus, the responsive interpretation is logically possible. On the other hand, if the parental behavior remains stable despite children, and the children's behavior changes despite parents, we would assume that the responsive interpretation can be ruled out and the etiological interpretation can be supported.

As in previous experimental designs there are methodological problems. To avoid the effect on interaction of previous acquaintance, all families, including the control groups of normal parents with normal children and schizophrenic parents with schizophrenic children should have the same degree of acquaintance. We must pay attention to the peculiarity of the experimental situation, especially to the family members' responses to being asked to interact with strangers. This technique—construction of artificial families—is not a new one, however, and work by Leik, who rotated normal family members across three groups, and by Siegel, who used adults paired with mentally retarded children unrelated to them, provides evidence that the method can be used to generate meaningful data.[15]

Each of the proposed experimental designs described here aids in ruling out one of three possible explanations of the relationship between family process and schizophrenia. In each a multi-experimental group design and a carefully standardized experimental situation provide a logical substitution for a longitudinal study. No single experiment provides satisfactory ev-

---

*An experiment similar to the one suggested here is currently being carried out by the author.

idence that one explanation may be finally ruled out. However, a combination of cross-sectional experiments, such as the three described here, in which measurement, sampling, and analytic techniques are identical, should result in data that will allow the researcher to reach the most probable explanation of the relationship between family process and schizophrenia.

A theory of family interaction and schizophrenia developed from the findings from this earlier series of experiments will in all probability have to consider all three interpretations. For example, the affective quality of interaction in the schizophrenic family—the relative coldness, the avoidance of interpersonal hostility—may have been present prior to the occurrence of the illness and thus may be treated as an etiological factor, while the style of communication—the controlled, rigid patterns of speech—may be a strategy developed by the family in response to the deviant child, and the high power position of the schizophrenic child may be a result of his having been defined as a deviant family member. Thus the experiments may lead naturally to the fourth explanation of family process and schizophrenia, the transactional one. However, at that point the transactional model will no longer be an assumption; it will have become a set of concretely stated relationships between variables, open to further test and refinement.

NOTES

1. *Family Processes and Schizophrenia: Theory and Selected Experimental Studies* ed. Elliot G. Mishler and Nancy E. Waxler (New York: International Science Press, 1968); Elliot G. Mishler and Nancy E. Waxler, *Interaction in Families: An Experimental Study of Family Processes and Schizophrenia* (New York: John Wiley, 1968).
2. *Schizophrenia and the Family* (New York: International Universities Press, 1965).
3. R. D. Scott and P. L. Ashworth, "Closure at the First Schizophrenic Breakdown: a Family Study," *British Journal of Medical Psychology, 40*: 109-45 (1967).

4. Lyman Wynne and Margaret T. Singer, "Thought Disorder and Family Relations of Schizophrenics. I. A. Research Strategy," *Archives of General Psychiatry,* 9:191-98 (1963); *The Empty Fortress* (New York: Basic Books, 1967).

5. Lee N. Robins, "Social Correlates of Psychiatric Illness: Can We Tell Causes from Consequences?" *Journal of Health and Social Behavior, 10:* 95-104 (June 1969).

6. "Retrospective and Prospective Views of Early Personality Development," *Merrill-Palmer Quarterly,* 6:131-44 (1959-60).

7. "A Longitudinal Study of Children With a High Risk for Schizophrenia: First Three-year Follow-up," *The Origins of Schizophrenia,* ed. John Romano, proceedings of the First Rochester International Conference on Schizophrenia, Excerpta Medica Foundation, Amsterdam, 1967.

8. Mary Waring and David Ricks, "Family Patterns of Children Who Become Adult Schizophrenics," *Journal of Nervous and Mental Disease, 140:*351-64 (1965).

9. "The Double-bind Hypothesis a Decade Later," *Psychological Bulletin,* 68:409-16 (1967).

10. "Psychosocial Factors in Phenylketonuria," *American Journal of Orthopsychiatry,* 37:671-79 (1967).

11. "The Too-cohesive Family: A Form of Group Pathology," *International Journal of Social Psychiatry,* 10:266-75 (1964).

12. Dorothea Leighton, *et al., The Character of Danger* (New York: Basic Books, 1963).

13. "Patterns of Role Dominance and Conflict in Parents of Schizophrenic Patients," *Journal of Abnormal and Social Psychology,* 61:31-38 (1960).

14. pp. 131-44.

15. Robert K. Leik, "Instrumentality and Emotionality in Family Interaction," *Sociometry,* 26:131-45 (June 1963); Gerald Siegel, "Adult Verbal Behavior with Retarded Children Labeled as 'High' or 'Low' in Verbal Ability," *American Journal of Mental Deficiency,* 68:417-24 (1963).

The Acquisition of Learning Readiness: task or conflict?

RUDOLF EKSTEIN

The child's mental health is defined as his capacity to love and to learn.

The pressures of our modern society, exerted on the learning child, his family, and the school system during a time experienced as crisis, produce reverberations in professional and scientific groups of clinicians and educators as well, and give rise to questions on every level of inquiry. In recent years we have been concerned with the Sputnik complex: the demand that we push serious study of scientific subjects into the earlier grades to compete in an international world full of danger for our civilization. We are concerned with the dropout child, the rebelling adolescent, segregation problems, the disadvantaged child, the Head Start program for bringing the deprived child up to a standard which will give him a fair chance when formal education begins. We face immense problems with rebelling adolescents, their often aimless search for purpose and identity, and their peculiar communities which express in bizarre forms their alienation from adult society. And frequently we have thought that we are powerless to bring them back into the educational process, regardless of whether we think in clinical, educational, or social terms. So great are the numbers of those afflicted that we have developed in our own ranks a new interest in mass problems which has even given rise to new clinical movements such as social psychiatry. It is against and in spite of this background that I contend that the development of the learning capacity of the child, in connection with the educational and clinical help which must be offered which in many ways will seem to be fruitless if considered against that vast social emergency to which I referred. Nevertheless, I still believe this the most vital opportunity to make a worthwhile contribution.

I will consider learning problems in terms of the individual, an outlook which has given psychoanalysis its vital strength and has led to the development of techniques, the development of educational and therapeutic resources, which then in turn have given impetus to the solution of these other much broader questions. The German philosopher Schopenhauer once suggested: "where counting starts, understanding stops." He was very pessimistic as to whether the kind of mass answers that are possible in other areas of science are truly applicable in the social field. While I would not agree any longer that the qualitative methods of psychoanalytic research cannot or should not be supplemented by quantitative notions, I do believe that we should turn matters around and start to understand before we start to count. If we are to understand the enormous problems of modern education, we may well start with an individual situation and see whether understanding cannot best be reached by examining once more the single case to learn something about the difficulties which children encounter in school today.

A boy, almost ten years old, came to our attention when he had completely failed in school and the public school system did not want to promote him from the fourth to the fifth grade. In this illustration I hope to separate the learning difficulties which are normal growth processes and which can be considered as the average task every child experiences in developing his capacities for learning and bringing about learning readiness from another set of difficulties considered to be truly pathological. The pathologic difficulties are regressions or fixations to a level where there is not as yet learning readiness, and where the solution of a task is impossible because of a lack of capacity for resolution of conflict. I have suggested elsewhere that the solution of learning tasks is mainly the domain of the teacher, the educator, who must match the child's learning readiness with his own teaching readiness, while the resolution of inner conflict is the domain of the child's therapist who deals with the restoration of those capacities defined as learning readiness, as learning capacity.[1]

Ricky's parents were advised by the school counselor to ask for psychiatric help. He is the oldest of four youngsters and has been described by the parents as very antagonistic toward his teachers, even in kindergarten. He has refused to do his work. Reports describe him as having a superior intellectual potential, but state that his performance is erratic and that he gives the impression of dealing with his own hostility in a passive-aggressive way. He struggles against parents and teachers, while at the same time using that struggle to reach them. He came to the current therapist at a point of total impasse.

Actually he had been seen by a psychiatrist who had responded instantly to this charming boy, who had a way of easily winning one over. The psychiatrist felt that he would be most useful to the child if he were to accept Ricky fully in the treatment situation, and he decided that the basic therapeutic intervention should consist of giving advice to the parents as well as to the teachers to bring about an entirely different social situation which would then permit this child to function. He seemingly made the decision to use the therapeutic material of the consulting room to get cues on how to change the environment of the child. Many of his therapeutic activities then consisted of replacing the child's passive aggression, his unwillingness to function, his not listening, not hearing, and not performing, through the active intervention of the adult, who thus becomes a kind of auxiliary professional ego for the child. Regardless of how much tact might be used, the outcome of that kind of battle is clear. I am reminded of one of the early books of a pioneer psychoanalytic educator, Oskar Pfister (1929) who wrote some four decades ago about the *Faults of Parents*.[2] He saw children's difficulties in terms of mistakes that parents and educators make, and his attempt, of course, consisted of influencing them and thus treating the problem as an external rather than an internal one.

This attitude which sees the technical problem in terms of a need to influence parents or teachers is still prevalent, and I leave as an open question whether it sometimes stems from a countertransference towards the child, an overidentification with his plight, an unconscious need to identify with him and then to fight against parents and teachers, or whether it is professionally mature insight into some of the external difficulties which may have to be changed. There is, of course, an external side to any kind of learning difficulty, and I am not suggesting that the psychotherapist who perceives in that way is necessarily wrong. The child will see such a therapist as a kind of magic helper who is stronger than the school and the parents and who will help the child to get over the isolation, to feel that he has someone on his side, but obviously this is not enough. External manipulation is hardly ever enough.

In this particular case we dealt with a father who had high ambitions for himself and for the child. The father believed in excellence and was very demanding but at the same time was aloof, except for the times when he would be experienced by the child as angry and threatening. The mother needed to be protected by the father, looked up to him like a child, and could not free herself to develop some sort of maternal autonomy. She literally had to be given permission to allow herself to be spontaneous and tender toward the boy. She had dealt with him in the past in such a fashion that the emotional climate between them had to be constantly protected by procedures of emotional antisepsis. Every word of love, every touch, every spontaneous act or expression of tenderness was filtered through objectivity, through diffuse anxiety, in search of permission or prohibition from professionals. She seemed to want to be guided in every step, but at the same time she reacted to their guidance, just as the boy did, with passive aggression and an inability to use such advice. The first psychotherapist experienced these parents as constantly opposing him, and after a while an atmosphere developed in which the situation between the therapist, on the one hand, and the teachers of the public school and the parents, on the other, was a replica in reverse of the basic relationship between child and adult. They had arrived at a dead end.

This impasse led to a reassessment and a new effort by the present therapist. The impasse described raises many questions concerning the kind of collaboration indicated between therapist and school. Some of these have been touched upon in *Professional School Psychology*.[3]

Ricky's first session did little except to allow for a sort of tentative identification with the helplessness of the parents and the teachers. What the therapist had found in the different reports seemed to be confirmed. The child was charming, aloof, jocular, pleasant, without any particular insight about why he had come or what he was supposed to want from the therapist. He maintained a level of humor, of little tricks here and there, with an air of being completely unconcerned. While one could not help but take to him, there seemed to be no way to focus on anything. He showed no overt anxiety and had a pleasant, manipulative air about him. He meant to convey that he had the therapist wrapped around his finger. As Ricky explored the room and the toys, he tried about everything and nothing. He touched the things, inquired about them, but like a butterfly that romps from flower to flower, he went from toy to toy and from question to question, barely touching something before leaving it again. He interrupted and disrupted the play or game before it even started. His attention span seemed to be very short, and he almost made the therapist feel that the impression of the parents and the teachers was absolutely correct. The professional helplessness that such patients arouse expresses itself frequently in beginning the treatment or referring him elsewhere, since a feeling of being shut out results from surface impressions. But the child also gave an eager indication that he wanted to explore some more and find out about all the other things that he had not yet seen. The therapist was able to use this quality easily as a bridge, which permitted the therapist to indicate that he too wanted to explore some more and to find out about all the other things that he had not yet seen, and to indicate some concern about how little fun Ricky could have when he started so many things but could not enjoy the outcome.

While the first session made one temporarily identify with the "diagnosis" of the demanding environment, namely that Ricky did not want to solve a task, there were indications that the truer problem was one of understanding this behavior as symptomatic of inner conflict. The sudden, and actually unexpected turn of events, that took place as soon as the second hour started surprised even the therapist.

Apparently the therapist's influence on the child was underestimated, as was his not imposing a task upon the child but giving him permission to say whatever he wished to, such as expressing through this erratic beginning what the problem really was. Ricky was really given permission to say what he wanted, and he first tried out the therapist by talking in sentences that began but did not end. I am, of course, not referring to the spoken word but to the language of his play. The therapist thus had established the basic rule of the session, rather than identifying himself with the parents, who wanted to establish the basic rule of the learning situation in which a task is completed. While in therapeutic action he identified with the therapeutic situation, in assessing the child's behavior the therapist had a kind of temporary and fleeting identification with the helplessness of the parent. If that identification with the helplessness of the parent had been the dominant and overwhelming one, he might have done exactly what the first therapist did; that is, become active, if not in regard to the child, who would have given him a feeling of helplessness, then in regard to the parents and the school whom he might have thought he should dominate and manipulate because of his professional authority.

During the second session, the boy inquired about a basket filled with crayons, and when given all the crayons and paper, he wanted to develop a cartoon story and tell the therapist something funny. The therapist thought that this attempt to draw a story would end up exactly the way all other attempts had ended and was prepared for a beginning without any ending. The therapist thought that anxiety would prevent Ricky from completing the task that he had set himself.

But from then on Ricky was a changed child. Actually the beginning of the session had given the therapist a cue. The therapist had opened the door to the waiting room when he had seen the red light indicating that someone had walked in. As he opened the door, he saw no one; but Ricky, who had been hiding at one side, quickly sneaked into the room and rushed to the button which controlled the red light and turned it off. The therapist found the boy under the desk and shared with him the pleasure of having tricked the therapist.

As the boy decided that he wanted to develop a story about a young boy and wondered about a name for the hero, the therapist suggested "Tricky the Trickster." Ricky was delighted with the name, and for a number of weeks he developed his little book of many pages, sometimes compulsively redrawing and reworking it to come out with his idea of perfection, but never letting up, and frequently through a slip of the tongue indicating that the story of Tricky the Trickster was an autobiographical account of Ricky the boy with a severe learning difficulty. What follows covers the work of a number of weeks, still during a period which had not yet led to a full commitment toward a treatment program. This is important, because the material that follows must be understood as the child's insight into his difficulty, his acceptance and understanding of the therapeutic situation, and his way of committing himself to treatment, his way of promising to make use of the treatment situation.

Ricky starts to draw a classroom scene. A little boy sits at his desk, head in his hands, and faces a tall teacher, more than twice his size, in front of a huge blackboard, with a long pointed stick in her hands. Between them is a small window through which the sun is shining. The boy does not work, the teacher gets excited and yells. The drawing of the child on the second picture gives the impression that he is falling apart, exploding. He wants to play a trick on the teacher. Ricky accompanies the different drawings with comments, and sometimes writes comments into his drawings. His hero, Tricky the Trickster, thinks of the wonderful sun outside. He knows magic tricks and decides that he will trick the teacher by disappearing so that he can be with the sun.

He flies right toward the sun, and the sun is smiling. But just at this moment, when he seems to have achieved his end of being away from the demanding teacher and having fulfilled his longing for the smiling sun, he discovers concern on the face of the sun because a terrible thunderstorm is starting. It rains and there is lightning, he has to escape from the thunder, and black clouds cover the sun. He is back in the dreary classroom facing the teacher again, who does not know what is happening and who seems to be helpless toward the magic of Tricky the Trickster and at the same time angry that he is not paying attention to her. While the helpless teacher wonders what to do with Tricky, the boy sits at his bench and has a fantasy. In this fantasy he considers how to get around the terrible thunder and rain between him and the shining sun. Tricky is a clever boy and knows about science. He thinks that if he could rise above the clouds, if he could stand on top of the clouds, the sun would not be covered, and the rain would not drive him back into the classroom. He could be reunited with that shiny sun. He again uses all his intelligence to outwit the teacher and uses his magic to escape once more from the dreary school situation and sees himself again on top of the clouds with the shiny, smiling sun. But as he starts to enjoy his triumph, he again sees distress on the face of the sun. The smile turns to worry and anxiety, since the sun has discovered that the cloud is starting to rain and is thus melting away. The boy has nothing to stand on and cannot remain united with the sun. As the rain cloud melts away, he starts to fall down through the sky. But Tricky, even in terrible moments of distress, is not without resources. A parachute opens and saves his life. He slowly comes down to earth, and although he gets stuck in a tree and has lost the sun, he finally saves himself. But there he is, back in the classroom, and again he faces the dreary teacher. What a beautiful illustration of phobic and counterphobic mechanisms.

Frequently when Ricky could not cope with the learning situation and did not obey orders, the teachers had sent him to the principal, and he was often sent home, only to face at home the anger of the parents when he wanted to be reunited with a loving mother. We see this child gravitating back and forth between the demanding image of the teacher—demands he cannot meet—and the longing for the smiling image of the mother, whom he sees primarily in oral terms, without demands, without rules that guide the life of the school child. His need for love does not include the need for the child's work, the development of learning capacity, his performance. His conditions for love are to receive it unconditionally, and he is constantly driven back into a situation where he faces conditions which he cannot meet, or does not want to meet. It depends, of course, entirely on the diagnostic estimate as to whether one assumes he actually cannot meet these new conditions for approval, or whether he has an option and stubbornly chooses to refuse to meet them. The educators and the parents experience his refusal and his escape into the fantasy world as stubbornness, while he tries to convey to us the lack of satisfaction, which causes him to feel alienated from parents and teachers. But we are dealing here with a situation that had existed as early as kindergarten and was most likely true even in earlier years.

Tricky the Trickster then faces the teacher again. The teacher tries once more to force him to do his work. The next picture reveals a change. The window and the sun are gone, and instead of the cloud that keeps him from the sun, there is now a similar huge area drawn in red, and on it one can read the words "do your work." Tricky is described now as needing to look for a new way out. He does not try to escape again to be united with the sun. He decides to do magic work. As he submits this magic work to the teacher, she looks at it and becomes very angry. Ricky writes on the next page, "magic work fails," and draws a dejected little boy who has received a failing notice. He must leave the school and take the marks home. As he comes home to show the report card to his parents, he crosses his fingers for magic protection, full of anxiety as to what they will do with him. Ricky describes Tricky the Trickster as a boy who has his own fantasies as to what would happen to him. Ricky stresses that this is not what really will happen, but that these fantasies are just on his hero's mind.

We notice here a subtle reference to the boy's capacity to differentiate between fantasy and reality, but the fantasy is so strong that it is almost like reality. As he discusses his pictures and the story and his creation of the thoughts of Tricky the Trickster, he makes sure that the therapist realizes that Tricky does not always know where the fantasy begins and where reality begins. It would be too far-reaching to discuss in detail certain of the finer points of psychic organization which are described through the accounts that Ricky gives of his hero. Suffice it to say that Tricky expects that his father may hang him, may shoot him, and worst of all may kill him by a guillotine or by chopping off his head with an ax.

I believe that the development of the story shows clearly how insight grows. It becomes clearer that the material principle, reflected in his conception of the demanding teacher opposed to the smiling sun, is understood in terms of helplessness. The teacher cannot get him to do the work, and the smiling sun cannot stop the rains and the thunder and cannot convince him that he is loved and that he can do the work, and thus magic must fail. The paternal principle, described at first through the thunder and the clouds, and the threat of falling, becomes humanized toward the end of that part of the story when he cannot escape any more to cloud nine or above cloud nine, but sees himself facing angry parents for having failed the work. He sees himself as being threatened with annihilation and castration and finds it impossible to cope with his anxieties, except that he finds hope to make him believe that all the threats he faces will not really come true and are only in his mind. They also mean, perhaps, that the parents never quite mean it and are, therefore, in many ways as helpless as parents as the teachers are as teachers, and also as he is as the learning child.

In one of the scenes he describes what really happens to Tricky the Trickster. The mother looks critically at the report card, and the boy is being "mildly spanked" by the father. Tricky now goes back to school, and he hands in to the teacher the report card, which was signed by mother.

During all of this time the therapist had done no more than admire the many wonderful tricks that Tricky had devised, but at the same time he had voiced sympathy that the tricks did not work and that Tricky did not get what he wanted. He had not moralized but had identified with the position of the hero and always wondered what Tricky really could do to be a happy child, to feel that he is accepted by teachers and parents, and to really enjoy the smiling sun. The therapist and the child sometimes had enjoyed together vicariously the wonderful tricks of the hero. They had responded to the thrills, the dangers, the adventures as if they were a fairy tale, while the therapist had left it entirely up to the child to develop that part of the story which would be considered in a fairy tale as its cautionary aspect. The child showed the hero being punished, showed him being tamed, showed him finally accepting reality, and showed, when he was given the initiative, that he has actually identified with the demands of reality, as he wishes to please the therapist and thus to indicate what the purpose of the therapeutic work should be.

As Tricky was made to come back to the teacher, a discussion ensued between Ricky and the therapist about the words the teacher may use to help the child. It was only at this point, after a number of weeks of developing the story theme, that the therapist helped Ricky in developing the teacher's part of the story. Their little book contained the words: "Teacher says: You have trouble with your work because you are afraid of your father. You think he will hurt you or kill you if you get bad marks. Are you angry at him?"

On a later page the red area which offers space for the teacher's words now carries her new message to Tricky: "Tricky is the best worker in the class."

One year later—an interesting prediction on the part of Ricky concerning the effectiveness of therapy for him—Tricky has a test and the teacher tells him that the work is good and she gives him an "A." The child runs home with his report card while the beautiful sun shines and smiles at him. His mother, who has on a yellow dress like the sun, says: "Oh, darling!" and his father gives him rewards, green dollar bills, while Tricky, seeing all that money, says with delight: "Oh, boy!" There is another page indicating that this is the end of the story, except that Ricky writes a postscript on a final page. This picture shows Tricky taking all the money to the store to buy candy.

This story sounds almost too contrived to be true, too much like a textbook story, a cautionary tale with moralizing built into it, but nevertheless it is the free invention of this child. The new division of labor is one in which the therapist turns into the one who admires Tricky the Trickster, while Ricky turns into the person who creates in his fantasy figure, joining the adult world, a new conscience, a vital superego, and an effective capacity to work.

It was much easier now to ask Ricky to what degree he was really functioning like Tricky, and to what degree he also worried as desperately as Tricky did about terrible punishments. In addition, if he thought that his wishes to be close to the sun had much to do with the hope that mothers should never demand and should only feed and satisfy, and how that will be interfered with by the stern anger of all those who expect something of him. We started to work slowly on all the issues that prevented Tricky, that is, Ricky, from doing his work and forced him to believe in magic and flying to cloud nine. Can he really keep that promise, or was that promise just a way to restore love,[4] to make the world, the sun, and mother shine on him again? But there was also some reality in that promise, inasmuch as the work itself that he accomplished during these next few weeks showed that there could be concentrated effort and uninterrupted work and that at least in psychotherapy this capacity for prolonged attention was undermined only rarely.

At one point the father brought the child to the waiting room, and as the therapist opened the door, the father stopped him in front of the child and said that he wanted him to see a note he had received. He handed the therapist a failure notice from school. The therapist tried not to pay too much attention to it, beyond acknowledging it, but during that therapy hour the boy was diffuse. He was full of anxiety again, and interpreting did not help. The hour was under the sway of the disruption that had occurred when the father tried to make the therapist into his own extension and to expose the child's weakness. This time there was no story about Tricky, but only aimless attempts at random activities.

This case provides rich materials for conjectures and inferences concerning the contributing factors in this example of a learning problem. The demanding teacher and the smiling sun are but different aspects of the mother figure. The smiling sun could never be reached, and the demanding teacher could never succeed in establishing inner discipline. One may well wonder why he must maintain this split for such a long time in his looking at the maternal figure. One might also wonder what is revealed about his relationship to the father, and what is revealed about the paternal object representation, if we see the father in the story of Tricky the Trickster not as a person at first, but as an impersonal threat: thunder, lightning, rain and clouds, and dangerous parachute jumps and how the father appears only much later, as does the mother, as a real person.

While the triangular situation is obvious, and while much of the material has the coloring of the oedipal situation—the longing for the possession of the mother, and the castration threat—we see that many of these elements are really of a non-phallic nature and have to do with much earlier problems in the development of the ego organization. Some of the problems perhaps go back to a time where there were only unsteady object representations and when there was at times a kind of autistic isolation from the parental figure.

A few additional illustrations from the therapeutic material will illustrate these points. At the point when Ricky got Tricky the Trickster off the hook and had the parents reward him, we learned that the reward was expected in tangible services. He got money, a kind of impersonal expression of the father's esteem, and he went to buy himself some candy. At that moment Ricky discovered a play candy machine among the many toys and got the therapist to stock the machine with candy. He developed a candy store. During the next few weeks he dealt with the candy store as he had dealt with the story at first. He worked painstakingly, using whatever doll furniture and boxes he could use to build the store. Some of the things to be sold were actually candy, while others were make-believe candy. Ricky and the therapist stocked the store, and he now had a subtle way of getting the parents to join the play. He would sell them some candy for a penny, or would buy himself some candy, or the therapist would buy candy, and the next few weeks were a kind of stagnant situation, looking like a playing out of a kind of feast. He suddenly and spontaneously would want to feed the therapist candy and take some candy for himself. There was harmony and happiness, but there was for a while no movement in the story. It seemed that he had regained attachment to the food, and occasionally, when opening the door to the waiting room, the therapist saw the child now sitting very close to the parents. They were telling each other stories, and the mother had found a newly gained spontaneous capacity to react to the child with tenderness and acceptance, and the same was true for the father.

At some given moment Ricky added to the candy store the doll house and the doll furniture and brought in a disturbing element. A certain period of establishment of a new basis seemed to have ended, and he seemed now ready to face new material. In the doll house were all kinds of family dolls, among them doll babies. He took the doll babies and had them go into the candy store during the night. They were supposed to sleep in the candy, without parental supervision. Tricky the Trickster, or should we now say Ricky the Trickster, now introduced new humor, which was anal humor. The babies would do all kinds of "doo-doo" in the candy store, and Ricky would sell the therapist or his parents candy which actually was left there, he suggested, by the babies, mixed perhaps with the "dirty things" that babies do at night. Hilarious laughter characterized the giving of these new gifts, at his having tricked everybody in play into accepting as candy what was really fecal matter from the babies. These were the tricks of babies, of phantom twins. Then he began to build the doll house. At first he worked on the babies' room. These babies, a strange dual expression of himself, took furniture from every other room. Their room contained a little bit of living room furniture, bedroom furniture, and kitchen furniture. They had a refrigerator and all kinds of foods, liquids, and solids. They decided to barricade the room. The babies were isolated and fenced in, and the parents and other children were not allowed in. Whenever the therapist made some comment about the isolation of the babies, and how they might be longing for the parents, Ricky insisted that they did not care for the parents and did not need them. The babies had everything there. Theirs was an autistic paradise; they were completely independent, and the parents would never be allowed to go in there. Paul Bunyan never had it so good in his quest for omnipotence.

The therapist commented that these courageous and independent babies, rebelling successfully against any outside force that might take away their freedom, must be lonesome and helpless sometimes. Would they not want their parents at night, to reassure them, to tell them fairy tales, talk to them, and the like? Ricky countered with certainty that they did not need the parents, denying any dependency need on their part. As a matter of fact, he described the rest of the home as chaotic. He simply turned all the other rooms of the house into chaotic storage rooms. When the therapist wondered what had happened to the rest of the family, and whether the babies had really destroyed them and had made themselves completely independent, Ricky developed another theme. The house and the other rooms slowly emerged. There were all the siblings, and there was a dining room where the family gathered together happily to have a beautiful meal, except that the babies maintained their vigilance and barricaded themselves against the other members of the household. Their isolation was described as one caused not by the parents, or other children, or the outside world, but arranged by them and wanted by them. The therapist's interest in the babies and their potential loneliness led in future sessions to Ricky's comment that someday they might give up the barricade.

A situation developed, according to Ricky, which indicated that the babies were sick. Finally, something had to be done for them. The rest of the family was not allowed to enter, but the babies or somebody had called a doctor. The doctor was described as a friendly doctor, but he had to work his way into that multiple purpose room of the babies. He could not come in through the door nor through the ordinary windows. He somehow got to the babies only after quite a struggle and a guarantee that nobody else could enter the room. He was a friendly doctor, and he wanted to help the babies with drugs and with foods. All his help was oral in nature. The time had now come for Ricky's therapist to introduce the doctor as somebody who was not just interested in drugs and food. He wanted to understand the babies and see what really was on their minds. Slowly, he was allowed to be more than a friendly doctor. The babies and he talked together. By the time this happened, Ricky himself seemed to have more access to the parents, the rest of the family, to other children, and seemed to have made a better beginning in the new school year. The friendly doctor was on his side, on their side, and more frequently it was possible to tie up the story with Ricky himself. The barricades were not down yet, but there was a bridge between that autistic world described and the parents outside. The friendly doctor was that bridge.

I am not able presently to carry the case further, but there seems to be a trend, a promise toward higher integration. No single case illustration can encompass all the questions concerning learning problems, but I believe this illustration can lead toward a more systematic way of studying pathological learning problems—the treatment issues, as well as the educational issues. Learning problems are indeed the most frequent complaint brought to the attention of clinicians. There are so many different types of learning disturbances that as soon as the psychoanalyst goes beyond the symptom, beyond the presenting facade, he does not find too much use in that type of diffuse classification. Learning difficulty can be compared to work difficulty in the adult personality, simply an external sign of an emotional or mental disorder which has to be understood in dynamic, economic, and structural terms—in terms of object relationship difficulties, ego disturbances, etc. Ricky's case is no exception. I could well see that one could discuss this case as a mere clinical entity.

Freud's definition of mental health in terms of the capacity for *lieben und arbeiten* (love and work) can also be paraphrased in the case of the child. The child's mental health can be defined in terms of his capacity to love and to learn. Learning is his way of working. The notions of love and learning have to be examined in process terms. These notions are not static, absolute concepts but change as the child's mind develops.

I have elsewhere referred to the Freudian and Eriksonian concepts of emotional development to define the ingredients necessary to bring about learning readiness, another notion that I want to be understood in process terms. From every phase of the child's development emerges a new ingredient toward learning readiness, which the child will then bring into school in an integrated way. The first ingredients are very much tied up with his capacity for love. One might say that the small child who develops trust out of the separation and weaning conflict at that time lives through a phase in which learning and loving, love and work, are merely two sides of the same coin and are not as yet truly separated. This phase of orality—the loving of, the working on the breast, the separation from the breast, the search for it, the finding—somehow combines love and work; and he learns there for the first time loving and working, uniting and separating, and moves toward the capacity for basic trust in others and himself.

As we look at the clinical material concerning Ricky, we realize that this establishment of trust, this learning via trust and self-trust, is indeed on shaky grounds. The long story that he wrote during sessions—the vacillating between facing the strict taskmaster and escaping to the smiling sun, the vacillating between magic and true effort, between the hope for unconditional love and the fear of terrifying separation and sadistic punishment and the isolation of the barricaded babies, who mixed food with feces, who do not want parents and claim that they do not need them—gives us beautiful clinical illustrations which demonstrate that Ricky at that time had indeed not worked through the issue of trust, that important ingredient which the teacher needs to inherit from the parents when formal schooling starts. Ricky starts to live in an isolated world and prefers to live on cloud nine, in the hope of reaching the warm, smiling sun. The thunderstorm, the rain, the melting of the base, drive him back to the impossible task, a little version of Don Quixote between the windmills and Dulcinea.

I have not specifically discussed the fact that the issue of trust, its specific outcome in this case, can also be used as an indicator of the child's particular capacity for object relations. The fantasy material is full of examples in which the object is depersonalized, barricaded against, and seen as strict and sadistic, and whenever Ricky does reach the object in a positive way, he sees it primarily in oral terms. The rewards consist of money and candy, and the long phase of play activity around the candy store and the babies' use of food during the night refers to oral and anal need gratification, most of the time without objects. Only toward the end phase of that particular beginning do we see objects emerge which move from food to personal friendliness, from drugs to verbal interaction, and to some feeble attempts to reach out and to let the babies reach the external object world of parents and siblings.

If we examine the problems Ricky has with autonomy and control, we find that the trust deficit described earlier has created immense difficulties in facing that second phase of development. What he will bring to school then will be almost autistic autonomy. He will be free on cloud nine. He is free in his internal fantasy life, but he has no autonomy for learning, for the use of teachers, or for the use of the school. He sometimes makes sporadic attempts, and since he is a bright child, he occasionally makes rapid advances, but he cannot maintain them.

Just as he cannot maintain more than autistic autonomy, he cannot accept control. His inner control is poor, and his capacity to accept control from others always leads to a deadlocked struggle. He becomes inaccessible. No punishment helps, and he escapes over and over into fantasy life to that fantasied mother, the warm sun that smiles and feeds. Sometimes he tries to get himself to work by inventing powerful, sadistic controls on the part of the adult world. It is as if he wished to have castrating, punishing parents, as if the threat of being shot, of being hanged, or of being guillotined might get him to work. He almost prescribes control activities to the teachers and provokes sadistic, angry behavior on the part of the parents. This part of the fantasy is not only an attempt at reconstruction, but also describes his attempt at solution. But the solution of conflict fails; therefore, he cannot solve the learning task. He is still deeply engaged in the resolution of inner and external conflicts.

This conflict situation leads him toward an attempt to bring back the anaclitic object, to restore unconditional feeding love by means of promises which he cannot keep, the learning by magic, the work by magic, which is a promise made to restore love but cannot be kept. The struggle between autonomy and control finds him developing intensive stubbornness, and whatever capacity there is for relating to objects is involved in tricking the object, and then coping with the ensuing anxiety. All his learning initiative and his curiosity are in the service of tricks, of attempts to escape, of developing fantasy solutions; and whenever this initiative is turned into an attempt to cope with the real task, it breaks down and leads to a sense of inferiority or a feeling of incompetence. Any attempt to identify with the aloof but demanding father fails, and every attempt to regain mother's unconditional love fails as well. He becomes isolated like the phantom babies who live in the barricaded room.

Anna Freud and her coworkers have developed a psychoanalytic profile in which the development of the child is followed through these different phases in such a way that inferences can be made concerning the therapeutic task.[5] This profile goes beyond the ordinary psychiatric workup of a child. It is oriented around psychoanalytic thinking and tries to assess the child's strengths and weaknesses.

I suggest that a similar undertaking could be tried with regard to learning failure in a child. As we follow Ricky, we can develop a psychoanalytic profile around all the aspects of the living situation and can design it to serve the work of the therapist. But we may also write the profile primarily focusing on the learning difficulty itself to try to see how every deficit, as well as asset, contributes to the learning difficulty and contributes eventually to its solution. Such a profile could be developed not only for the therapist but also for the educators and teachers who work with children like Ricky.

As Ricky enters the school system, that phase of developing capacity for industry which, as Erikson suggests, turns into a feeling of inferiority if the establishment of that ego capacity fails, is one that Ricky indeed has not passed through with a sufficient degree of stabilization. From what we have learned from his early therapy we can see that he is not without capacity for industry, not without capacity for compulsive and orderly working, but that this capacity is severely impaired. The capacity is available to him only temporarily and in the service of resolution of conflict. If it is primarily to be in the service of the task imposed by the outside world, he must flee, search for the warm and smiling sun, and he becomes unavailable to the teachers and for the learning task. In turn, of course, he arouses in the teachers strong feelings of failure, of inferiority on their part, and of wishes to control him as if he were as yet capable of accepting and using their control.

Interestingly, the first therapist thought in terms of controlling the teachers. The second therapist did have some contact with the school system and used this to bring about mutuality of purpose without dictating or suggesting what the school should do. He made few comments about the child and encouraged the school staff to live with its own limits. The school staff instantly countered this with the suggestion that they recommend a social promotion, rather than set him back and that they wanted to give him a full year to see whether he could catch up. They said they would be very happy to meet with the therapist and exchange information. Interestingly, they then started to describe some of Ricky's assets, such as that frequently he really knows quite a bit about various subjects but cannot put it into work, cannot put it into the task, cannot deliver in terms of the demands of the adult world, but obviously does achieve quite a bit when he can be permitted to remain in his own world. That is, of course, exactly what happened in psychotherapy when the condition of producing something was in terms of his own needs, in terms of the equivalent in child analytical work for the basic rule in adult analysis. It would be interesting to discuss what teachers could do if they knew the learning profile of such a child, described and developed along analytic lines such as the one the therapist attempted to use in this instance.

I suggest, of course, that I wish to separate the functions of psychotherapy and of teaching; and I suggest that teaching techniques can be developed for such a child, side by side with the therapeutic process, complementing the psychotherapeutic process, deriving cues for teaching techniques from the learning profile of the disturbed youngster so that the teaching task would not have to be abandoned. In this particular case the mere indication on the part of the therapist that he did not wish to interfere with the autonomy of the school, that he wanted to give them an absolutely free hand as to whether they wanted to promote the child or hold him back, instantly brought about a change in attitude. Occasional case conferences in which no intimate material would be given away, and in which the psychotherapeutic secrecy would be maintained, but that nevertheless allow for sufficient contact, would help us develop a leaning profile which the teachers could use and apply to their own functions. The psychotherapist in turn might gain immensely from observations which would go beyond the usual factual reporting of success or failure.

I am referring to the host of problems that exist in this complex world where many professional people carry different functions, work in different places and agencies or in private practice, and cannot afford for practical or emotional reasons to maintain the kinds of cooperation that would be necessary to bring about an optimum program from such a child.

The work with this child suggests a model of professional cooperation, as well as cooperation to be worked out with the parents. What seems to be particularly important in the case of learning difficulties is the bringing about of a new kind of collaboration between the teaching and clinical professions. I envision activities which will bring teachers and clinicians together, in which learning difficulties will be discussed around the same profile of a child, the learning profile and in which his ways of learning and his way of resisting learning will be described in terms of the therapeutic problem, as well as in terms of the teaching problem. The knowledge that we have today about ego development, the growth of psychic structure, the development of object relationships, the development of capacity for imitation and identification, the development of learning readiness and the development of capacity to use teachers, should be utilized in such a cooperative process.

I suppose one could get to Ricky's problems in more than one way. The ordering of data relates always to the techniques available. Much that we can apply to the learning and teaching process, the developing capacity of the learner, stems not from our experiences with children but from our experience with adults. I refer to the training of professionals. Let me give as an illustration of certain concepts, some examples which I believe to be applicable to the problem of Ricky and children like him in the same phase of development or at a later phase, such as puberty or adolescence, and which stem from teaching devices that have been elaborated as supervision of professional skills, such as psychotherapy, psychoanalysis, and social casework.

Robert Wallerstein and I referred to certain typical aspects of supervision which exert regressive pull on the professional student as typical constellations repeating themselves over again, and we called them problems about learning and learning problems.[6] The former ones were described by Peyton-Jacobs as learning resistance, while the latter ones were described as the student's typical learning style which may be useful or may actually turn out to be an obstacle in case the specific learning style is not appropriate for the subject to be learned.[7] In some other context he has referred to these problems as "blind spots" and "dumb spots." Blind spots refer to inabilities in the development of a capacity to learn, having much to do, for example, with certain inhibitions, as if certain material were taboo and should not be known. There are, for example, children who have difficulty reading anything in order to avoid learning about things which would create anxiety in them. Some of Ricky's difficulties are of that nature. The dumb spots refer to lack of knowledge and lack of skill, and frequently also to learning styles developed which are not applicable to the subject matter. To these characterizations I can add a third one, which came to mind as I thought about the three monkeys who see no evil, speak no evil, and hear no evil. They are blind, dumb, and deaf. Their blind spots would refer to their incapacity to see or to understand certain things because of inhibitions and taboos. Their dumb spots would refer to lack of knowledge or lack of learning skills, and the deaf spots would refer to difficulties they have with authority—teachers and parents. These generic characterizations, somehow a part of every learner, can also be used to develop a learning and nonlearning profile of the child. Ricky, for example, could not allow himself to see certain things as long as he felt that the adult would oppose this knowledge and would be critical of him. We see, for example, that during treatment certain desires, such as the babies mixing feces with candy, could only be discussed later when he felt that he could trust the therapist, but at first they were taboo subjects, a difficulty that indeed would show up in his developing learning inhibition. His learning style was best characterized perhaps through the name that he and the therapist gave the hero of his fantasy life. Tricky the Trickster had a way of learning, of trying to achieve autonomy, knowledge, and skills, even though it got under the skin of adults. His learning style was in the service actually of learning resistance, was a means of opposing parents and teacher, and thus was a cramped learning style inasmuch as he could not really use the school and the teacher and thus developed deaf spots. Much of his learning style is typified through the picture he gave us of the autonomous babies who barricaded themselves against the adult world and tried to develop their own Paul Bunyan-like world of learning, where one does not need teachers or adults and is self-sufficient, but without outside contact and without outside initiative. Such babies have no one to identify with and no one to imitate and much of their learning remains hidden from the adult world.

Actually the teachers never saw these private learning worlds, could not give them sufficient credit, and could not exploit his learning style and match it with an appropriate teaching style. In developing a teaching style which takes into account whatever the child has available at that time to learn the teacher would also have to use the child's resistance to learning. It becomes clear that a learning profile for Ricky would have to be matched by a kind of teaching profile to fit him. Individualized teaching and learning would try to adapt the teaching style to the learning style of the child, rather than meet the child's difficulty with teaching resistance provoked by him.

Much of the learning style of any child has to be understood as an investigation of his capacity for insight, his ways of acquiring insight, his creative methods of problem solving, and his cognitive style. The functions, studied so well by Piaget and also important for psychotherapy based on insight, have not been given quite as much attention in our work as they deserve. We have to catch up with that part of psychology which has so far remained a stepchild in psychoanalytic work, in spite of our frequent reference to the work of Piaget. The usual tests of youngsters in the realm of intelligence, achievement, and cognitive functions unfortunately are deficit-oriented most of the time, rather than based on investigating the positive aspects as well.

It seems to me that a continued collaboration between teachers and clinicians around a case like Ricky's would not only benefit the child but would help us to create models of collaboration around the issue of learning. There is no doubt that many children can be helped without such cooperation, but I believe that the more serious disturbances certainly will need it.

I have selected a comparatively easy case, and I certainly have selected that part of the case material with an obvious meaning. But as soon as we get into more difficult situations, particularly where there are cognitive deficits, or cases of individuals in adolescence, we will get to issues which I believe cannot be solved well without collaboration.

We know, of course, that learning during puberty and adolescence contains a new ingredient which will decide the way of learning and the way of resisting learning. I suggest that the adolescent will be confronted more and more with purpose, with goals, with identity struggles, with conflicts over separation from the home, and that all these will either enhance or cramp his learning style by bringing a new variable into the total learning profile. These struggles are a part of learning rather than its obstacles.

Ricky's purpose in learning, beyond the joy that he experiences playing tricks, presently seems to be entirely one of trying to restore the shining sun, love, and the supply of candy, of oral gratification. There are not as yet dominant functions which indicate that his ego has turned passivity into mastery, imitation into identification, and that he has learned to develop the pleasure function of learning, the joy of discovery and of mastery. Much of his story indicates that he yearns for love and is far from having reached the stage of development where he also may love learning and may identify with the teacher's love of subject matter or love of skill, interest, and curiosity.

One of the great teachers of psychoanalysis who was deeply interested in children, adolescents, and the profession of the educator was the late Siegfried Bernfeld. He once described the teacher, and he may as well have included the psychotherapist, in terms of certain narcissistic preoccupations, of certain tendencies toward professional megalomania, that made him think about his task in overidealized rather than technical terms. Bernfeld suggested that the teacher could be compared to the gardener who thinks that he makes flowers grow, when all that he does is remove stones, fertilize the ground, provide water, and create conditions for growth. It is nature that causes the seed to develop into a certain flower, while the gardener can at best provide optimal conditions. I think it is useful to add to his simile that a gardener will do best if he knows a great deal about the seed and if he can develop a growth profile of the different plants he wishes to grow. If he had such a growth profile, he could then develop a profile to describe his own activities on behalf of the plant.

Our thinking suggests that learning disturbances, as well as normal learning conflicts, have to be understood along developmental lines, a concept Anna Freud and her coworkers have elaborated as they have developed psychoanalytic profiles of children.[8] We want to follow these developmental lines in relation to the learning task and the unresolved learning conflict. The case of Ricky gave us an opportunity to view such an outline and to look at the task from both sides—the side of reality, that is, the task of the teacher and the parents; and the side of the child's inner world, inner psychic development, referring to the task of clinical intervention. We do not want to fully separate these tasks, and neither do we want to merge them. We want to create a bridge between them without destroying their functional difference. This will require an intensive effort in collaboration, both in actual practice as well as in research. Like Ricky's fantasy about Tricky the Trickster, such a program is but a promise. May we have enough optimism and enthusiasm to see to it that such a promise will not merely serve to restore love among us or to avoid conflict, but rather will turn into a professional and scientific commitment, a way to solve a task.

NOTES

1. Rudolf Ekstein, "The Child, the Teacher and Learning," *Young Children* (New York: Basic Books, 1967), pp. 195-209.
2. Oskar Pfister, "The Faults of Parents," *Zeitschrift für Psychoanalytische Pädagogik,* 3:172-84; 205-11; 251-61 (1929).
3. Rudolf Ekstein and Rocco Motto, "The Borderline Child in the School Situation," *Professional School Psychology,* ed. M. G. and G. B. Gottsegan (New York: Grune and Stratton, 1960), pp. 249-62.
4. H. J. Schlesinger, "A Contribution to a Theory of Promising: I: Primary and Secondary Promising" (unpublished manuscript, 1964).
5. Anna Freud, *Normality and Pathology in Childhood; Assessments of Development* (New York: International Universities Press, 1965).
6. Rudolf Ekstein and Robert Wallerstein, *The Teaching and Learning of Psychotherapy* (New York: Basic Books, 1958).
7. Personal Communication, 1967.
8. Freud.

Social Class and Child Psychiatric Practice: the clinician's evaluation of the outcome of therapy*

JOHN F. McDERMOTT, JR., SAUL I. HARRISON,
JULES SCHRAGER, ELIZABETH W. KILLINS,
AND BARBARA L. DICKERSON

This report, one of a series emerging from a long-range investigation of social class factors and child psychiatric practice at Children's Psychiatric Hospital, attempts to determine ways in which the clinician's evaluation of children's improvement as a result of psychotherapy is associated with the children's social class. We wish to emphasize that it is the clinician's perception of improvement which is the focus of this study. We recognize that in psychiatric practice the therapist is his own therapeutic evaluation instrument, making particularly evident our responsibility for continual examination of our clinical practices.

Although many investigators have studied the various relationships between social class and therapeutic outcome in adult psychiatric patients, few studies have involved children. In one, Maas found no correlation between class and negative outcome of treatment.[1] He found, however, that the upper

---

*This paper appeared in slightly revised form in the *American Journal of Psychiatry*, 126: 951-56 (1970).

class children tended to have a higher incidence of positive outcome, with the children of families with lower occupational status more often being referred elsewhere on termination. Rosengren described class-related behavioral differences in response to treatment, as well as differences in the therapists' attitudes toward the patients, finding a greater tendency by therapists to view middle class boys objectively and to describe them in psychodynamic terms, whereas the view of lower class boys was often one of "blame" and control of behavior.[2] The problem of unconscious discrimination of therapists against lower class patients is discussed by Hunt, McDermott and coworkers and Harrison and coworkers.[3]

Malmquist noted that it is harder to get lower class families to participate in treatment as practiced in child psychiatric clinics.[4] He points out that the lower class family demands immediate symptomatic relief and lacks a long-range perspective and understanding of the basic problem, such as in the resolution of a school phobia. Crecraft found that children cannot benefit from treatment until "permitted" to do so by their parents.[5] Although we regard children as our primary patients, their response to therapy will in part be determined by the parents' attitude toward therapy and the parents' ability to relate to the child differently, whether on the basis of their own intrapsychic change or the development of new interactional modes.

Coded data from both the original psychiatric evaluation and treatment summaries of 364 children ages two through fourteen (264 boys, ninety-nine girls, and one unidentified case) treated in the outpatient service at the University of Michigan's Children's Psychiatric Hospital from 1961-1967 were examined and compared. All parents were seen in casework therapy as well, and data on them was included in the treatment summaries. The majority of cases were seen on a once-a-week basis.

Children were assigned to three broad socioeconomic groups based on their father's occupation. In other studies occupation has been found to correlate well with various other determinants of social class position.[6] The first group included ninety-seven professional-executive and upper white-collar workers which we designated as the upper middle class. The second group, 121 lower white-collar and skilled workers, were called the lower middle class; and the third group, 146 unskilled workers and unemployed, were called the lower class.[7] Summary code sheets, filled out by the therapist at termination of therapy, were examined for variables relating to the clinician's evaluation of therapeutic improvement. The chi-square test, with Yates' correction where necessary, was performed on the social class variable and those relating to therapeutic improvement. Goodman and Krushkal's gamma was also calculated with ordinal variables to investigate the direction of association of the chi-square.

The several major areas of association studied included: 1) social class and duration of treatment; 2) social class and child improvement (coded as improved or not improved) as assessed by the therapist. In one-fourth of the cases there was no improvement rating coded by the therapist. These cases were analyzed separately and are referred to as the "no report" sample. We also investigated 3) social class and severity of condition upon termination (coded as mild, moderate, or severe); 4) whether a child terminated against medical advice in relation to social class; 5) social class and parent improvement (coded as improved, slight change, or not improved); and 6) social class and the primary form of therapy employed (supportive or uncovering). For this last item there was a reduced sample of 268 children, other forms of treatment being disregarded.

The sample was found to be homogeneous across the three groups for age ($x^2=6.956$, df=10, N.S.), sex ($x^2=4.759$, df=5, N.S.) and major diagnostic categories ($x^2=7.899$, df=8, N.S.). The average duration of treatment for all children was 7.87 months. Durations were coded as less than six months, six to twelve months, and more than twelve months. Social class and length of treatment were significantly associated, the upper middle class continuing the longest and the lower middle class the shortest ($x^2=32.115$, df=4, $p<.001$).

There was no significant difference among the three social

class groups on coded improvement rates at termination. However, this finding is incomplete, since in one-fourth of all cases there was no report from the therapist regarding the degree of improvement perceived. The failure to evaluate improvement occurred significantly more frequently than statistically expected from the distribution of the rest of the sample in the lower and lower middle class groups and significantly less frequently than expected in the upper middle class group ($x^2=19.171$, df$=1$, $p<.01$). The distribution of ages and diagnoses for this "no report" sample did not differ significantly from the distributions of these variables for the rest of the sample, but the "no report" sample did differ significantly in regard to duration of treatment ($x^2=55.346$, df$=1$, $p<.001$), with a much higher than expected proportion of cases with duration of less than six months. Also, there was a significantly greater number of children in this sample than in the rest of the sample who terminated against medical advice ($x^2=22.405$, df$=1$, $p<.001$). Severity of clinical condition and parent improvement were almost never known for the "no report" children.

Investigating other variables associated with improvement, we found that in our upper middle class group increasing duration associated significantly with greater perceived improvement ($x^2=6.605$, df$=2$, $p<.05$). The same tendency exists in the other two groups, but neither reaches a significant level of association. Increased severity of illness in the upper middle class and lower middle class patients associated significantly with less improvement rated ($x^2=13.028$, df$=2$, $p<.05$) and ($x^2=8.441$, df$=2$, $p<.01$), but in the lower group we found no such relationship. There is also a significant association between social class and perceived parent improvement ($x^2=13.116$, df$=4$, $p<.02$), with a much higher than expected number of parents in the lower class coded as "slight improvement" and also a much higher than expected number of parents in the lower middle class who made "no improvement." The highest rate of improvement appeared for the upper middle class parents, the least in the lower middle class parents. One-eighth of the total sample terminated against advice, but this was not associated with social class.

There were no differences in the use of "uncovering" or "supportive" therapy as noted by the therapist by social class. However among those whose primary treatment mode was considered to be supportive, we found that with rising social class, duration of treatment increased (x^2=17.096, df=4, p<.01). In those cases treated with uncovering therapy there was also a significant relationship between social class and duration of treatment (x^2=14.642, df=4, p<.001). The significance arose largely from the greater than expected number of cases in the lower class patients with durations longer than twelve months and from the greater than expected number of cases in the lower middle class patients treated for less than six months.

As patients of a university hospital, our patient population was probably not typical of community-based, service-oriented clinics. The selection of cases for therapy was based largely on the training needs of the therapists rather than the ability to pay. Thus, presumably those children represented in all classes were considered the "best treatment candidates." This may account for the fact that there was no significant dropout rate by social class, which in other studies has been noted to be significantly greater in lower groups.[8]

Differences in duration of treatment have received special attention as an important variable relating to improvement. In our study longer duration of therapy seems to be directly related to perceived improvement in the upper middle class group but not significantly in the other two groups. While the coding does not reveal which of the patients in our sample were planned as short-term candidates, as opposed to those who became short-term, this finding would seem to support the current trend in some clinics of selecting lower class patients more frequently for short-term goal-oriented treatment. This tends to confirm studies which point out that the lower class family demands immediate symptomatic relief and tends to lack the long-range perspective and understanding of the basic goal as defined by the therapist, i.e., the development of insight.[9]

However, these findings are somewhat different from those of other institutions. Meyers and Auld noted that the length of therapy relates directly to the judgment of improvement.[10] While this tendency exists in our three social class groups, the only significant relationship found was for the upper middle class group. This raises questions about what is meant by improvement and whether this term can be used in the same sense from class to class. Kahn, Pink, and Siegel investigated treatment at three institutions which serve primarily lower, middle, and upper class patients, respectively.[11] The institution serving upper class patients had the highest proportion of patients treated in traditional psychotherapy, with lowest average of improvement, while the institution serving the lower class patients had a higher proportion of somatic therapy treatments and better rates of improvement. The authors suggested that varying discharge ratings reflect variations in criteria used for evaluation of improvement—the higher the person's social background, the more complex the criteria employed. They also suggested that differences in treatment are related more to staff attitudes and social class than to psychiatric differences in the populations.

The question of relating overall perceived improvement to social class differences is complicated by the fact that there were so many "no reports" in our lower middle and lower groups. For the reported cases no association exists between social class and perceived improvement, but since the "no report" cases were significantly associated with social class, we do not know how they would affect the distribution of improvement by social class had they been rated. It would appear that therapists at our clinic seem to demonstrate difficulty or reluctance in assessing change in both the lower middle and lower class children whom they treat in comparison to those of the upper middle class. This seems true even though the "best" treatment candidates from all classes were selected.

The therapists' greater difficulty in rating improvement in the lower middle than in the lower class patients is surprising and puzzling to us. It may be that recent emphasis on understanding lower class life styles has made us more able to empathize with their values and life stresses than with those of the lower middle class, a marginal group "floating" between classes. Rating the upper middle class may present less of a problem for the therapist, since these children are more like himself. A study currently in progress relating to the social class backgrounds of staff and trainees at Children's Psychiatric Hospital indicates that most of our therapists come from what we are designating here as the upper middle class.

The difficulty in assessing change in children of the lower middle and lower class groups may be a function of lack of clarity of the therapeutic goals with these families and/or a discrepancy of goals between the patient and the therapist. Heine and Trosman have speculated that patients and psychiatrists may entertain expectations in the treatment which are not complementary and hence are particularly disruptive in early stages of the therapeutic relationship.[12] It may well be that the short durations in many of the "no improvement report" cases resulted from a lack of engagement between therapist and family, leading to discouragement of both parties. Sociological data, deriving from an examination of social class and parental values in child rearing, shows that upper class parental values are developmental.[13] They want their children to be curious and eager to learn, to be healthy, happy, and well. Working class and lower middle class values, on the other hand, are considered traditional. They want their children to be neat and clean, to obey, and to respect adults. The therapist's own background and therapeutic frame of reference may be in sharp contrast to the values of this lower middle group. This group is also described by Kohn as more resistant to new childrearing methods than the upper middle class group.[14]

The therapist's uncertainty concerning patient improvement may also reflect the question of transferability of intrapsychic improvement into the life situation. The child's existing life circumstances may make it more difficult for a lower middle or lower class patient to translate effectively any internal change into behavior.

Therapists also seem to have difficulty rating improvement

in children from any social class who terminate against medical advice. This is not surprising, and we may assume a degree of disappointment, anger, or sense of inadequacy on the part of the therapist, as well as the actual absence of sufficient material on which to base his judgment. For the entire sample treatment was of shorter duration with the lower middle and lower class groups than with the upper middle class group. Frank observes that remaining in therapy seems to be a function of such factors as class, occupation, and social integrity, as well as the relation of the treatment situation itself to the patient's own life situation.[15] There were no higher rates of termination against medical advice in these two classes as often happens with adult patients of the lower class. However, other factors within the therapeutic relationship may have contributed to the shortness.

Perhaps therapists are unable to shift therapy techniques according to the patient's needs and intrapsychic orientation, attempting rather to employ a traditional psychodynamic approach in all cases. The therapist's interpretations of the patient's "distortions" may reflect the therapist's need to translate his own inadequate understanding of the patient's reality and frame of reference into psychopathologic terms. An example is the finding that in the upper two classes less improvement associated with a more severe rating on clinical condition, but that in the lower class the patient was rated as more severely disturbed regardless of his degree of improvement. The question must be asked: Are these lower class children really more severely disturbed, remembering that diagnosis was homogeneous across classes, or do we just see them that way in reference to our own world?

Because of the possible discouragement and emotional disengagement of the therapist, the process of "turning the patient off" may occur and termination eventually be made by mutual agreement, with no real psychological endpoint having been reached. This may be a new and more subtle way of rejecting the patient. This turning off may account for the therapist's inability to rate improvement when he looks back upon the treatment.

In regard to duration of therapy and improvement, our findings that upper middle class patients are both held in supportive therapy longer and are more often perceived as improved may in part be accounted for on the basis of greater gratification to the therapist. If this is true, however, and the therapist fails to receive comparable gratification from his lower class patient, how then might we account for his holding them longer in uncovering therapy? Possibly he holds to his hope that despite slow progress, he will ultimately see the patient achieve a degree of introspection and a translation of intrapsychic change into new, more adaptive patterns of behavior. It is also possible, however, that a lack of flexibility on the therapist's part prevents him from perceiving altered goals on the part of the patient, and that he simply persists in trying to fit the patient to his uncovering model.

Our society presently does not provide a broad, flexible continuum of services which can provide genuine help for the complex, interrelated social and emotional problems of our less privileged population. The therapist may have inadequate training to understand fully the synthesis of his lower class patients' social and emotional characteristics, only vague awareness of actual social resources which might aid his patients and a general sense of discomfort with the adequacy of available services.

While our findings do not indicate either a different basic approach or an overall discrepancy in effectiveness on a class-related basis, they point out subtle difficulties in the application of our traditional therapeutic modes to lower middle and lower class patients. The development of social and community psychiatry is based in part on this recognition. Until we can confidently realize that our patients will in fact receive adequate and appropriate services in our social system, we may cling to these patients out of a vague awareness that to refer them elsewhere would be a termination or abandonment.

NOTES

1. H. Maas, "Sociocultural Factors in Psychiatric Clinic Services for Children," *Smith College Studies of Social Work*, 25:1-90 (1955).
2. W. Rosengren, "Hospital Careers of Lower and Middle Class Child Psychiatry Patients," *Psychiatry*, 25:16-23 (1962).
3. R. Hunt, "Social Class and Mental Illness: Some Implications for Clinical Therapy Theory and Practice," *American Journal of Psychiatry*, 116:1065-69 (1960); J. F. McDermott, S. I. Harrison, J. Schrager, and P. Wilson, "Social Class and Mental Illness in Children: Observations of Blue Collar Families," *American Journal of Orthopsychiatry*, 35:500-508 (1965); S. I. Harrison, J. F. McDermott, J. Schrager, and P. Wilson, "Social Class and Mental Illness in Children: Choice of Treatment," *Archives of General Psychiatry*, 13:411-17 (1965).
4. C. Malmquist, "Psychiatric Perspectives of the Socially Disadvantaged Child," *Comprehensive Psychiatry*, 6:176-83 (1965).
5. H. Crecraft, "Treatment in a Child Guidance Clinic," *Journal of Diseases of Children*, 98:11-14 (1959).
6. A. Reiss, *Occupation and Social Status*, (New York: Free Press, 1962).
7. Father's occupation was originally coded on the basis of six occupational groups: a) no occupation or habitually unemployed ($N=5$); b) unskilled or semi-skilled laborer (employed for tasks involving either no training or a very small amount of training, e.g., assembly line worker ($N=92$); c) skilled laborer employed in manual activity which requires training and experience, e.g., machinist, self-employed small farmer ($N=67$); d) lower white-collar worker involved in small business or in clerical or similar work which is not primarily manual and which depends on some educational or special background, e.g., policeman, sales clerk, typist ($N=54$); e) upper white-collar worker employed in more responsible administration white-collar positions, e.g., supervisor, large scale farmer, school teacher ($N=76$); f) professional or executive employment depending upon professional training beyond the college level, or involving important executive responsibilities or high financial status, e.g., university teacher, attorney, engineer ($N=70$). The six occupational groups were then collapsed into three main categories for statistical purposes: lower (a and b), lower middle (c and d), and upper middle (e and f).
8. N. Cole, *et al.*, "Some Relationships Between Social Class and Practice of Dynamic Psychotherapy," *American Journal of Psychiatry*, 118:1004-12 (1962).
9. Malmquist, pp. 176-83.
10. Myers and R. Auld, "Some Variables Related to Outcome of Psychotherapy," *Journal of Clinical Psychology*, 11:51-54 (1956).

11. R. Kahn, M. Pink, and N. Siegel, "Sociopsychological Aspects of Treatment," *AGP*, *14*:20-25 (1966).
12. R. Heine and H. Trosman, "Initial Expectations of the Doctor-Patient Interaction as a Factor in Continuence in Psychotherapy," *Psychiatry*, *23*: 275-78 (1960).
13. E. Duvall, "Conceptions of Parenthood," *American Journal of Sociology*, *52*:193-203 (1946).
14. M. Kohn, "Class and Parent Child Relationships: An Interpretation, *AJS*, *68*:471-80 (1963).
15. J. Frank, *et al.*, "Why Patients Leave Psychotherapy," *Archives of Neurology and Psychiatry*, 77:283-99 (1957).

The Adolescents: on the care and cultivation of weeds

JOHN L. SCHIMEL

It is an old observation that what characterizes any particular age is not typical of it. It is rather the atypical that determines the character of a period, and this is certainly true today when the two most newsworthy groups of adolescents tend to characterize our life and times. The disenfranchised bitter black youths and the milder middle class hippies not only vie for housing in Haight-Asbury, but also, albeit innocently, for the role of determinant of the character of the 1970s. Neither group is typical of current American youth.

"Typical" is a word that has to do with numbers and statistics and refers to majorities. We tend to speak as though we were discussing the majority of the people when we speak of the Golden Age of Greece, the Renaissance, the Age of Enlightenment, or the Lost Generation. Such periods were actually characterized by the sports or atypical specimens that appeared within the population at the time. Certain conditions, the soil, must have made the mutations possible, and many studies have focused precisely on this question. In our time the majority of youth are middle class and my observations are derived from a small in-depth sample of middle class youth.

I refer mainly to those young people who have consulted me about problems in living to which they are heir. The observations I offer have come from intensive psychotherapy with adolescents and young adults in private practice. The intellectual context of my observations is that of a psychoanalyst who can be termed neo-Freudian or, perhaps more accurately, Sullivanian. An inclination toward catholic tastes has made me aware at least of some of the contributions of the other social sciences. This has been buttressed by an interested scanning of the reporting and essays that regularly appear in the mass media.

I reviewed the cases of twenty current and recent patients who were between the ages of fourteen and twenty when I first met them. They were all analyzed in some depth, but certainly do not constitute a random sampling of young America. Numerous channels or tracks are available to young Americans when they seek help. Those who reach me are preselected.

The group utilized was preselected by my referring sources, who tend to eliminate the seriously psychotic and the financially indigent who are shunted elsewhere, sometimes to the clinical services of the William Alanson White Institute of Psychiatry, Psychology and Psychoanalysis with which I am associated. The selection limits my private practice to the offspring of parents who are for the most part successful and well-to-do. Suffice it to say that the microcosm of my firsthand knowledge involves the children of the affluent or even the super affluent—the true inheritors of middle class America.

Almost without exception, the fathers are handsome, talented, hard-working and successful. Most are professionals or businessmen, men of power and authority, which does not, however, quite reach into the home. Although seven of the mothers are professionals, all showed a diligence in managing their homes and offspring that rivaled the father's diligence in the office.

I believe my sample, which includes only those who reached a psychoanalyst's office, resemble their middle class counterparts in several significant aspects. These youngsters are exactly like their fellows, only more so. They are for the most part basically lively and spirited, well-mannered and even charming, extremely verbal, even to the point of glibness, brash and self-indulgent, and also shy, but related. Practically all appeared at a period of crisis in their schooling, often interwoven with an episode of love. A few of the older ones came at a point of social or career failure. Of the thirteen who were actual school dropouts nine returned during the period of their therapy.

Psychotherapy was almost uniformly successful, if one applies the societal criteria of improved school and work performance and more harmonious personal relationships. It would seem clear that the private practice of psychoanalysis fits the Communist definition of it: a bourgeois invention to serve the interests of the bourgeoisie. What I have indicated thus far also fits Kingsley Davis' observation that the mental health professions necessarily serve the interests of society in which they are practiced. This same observation has not escaped the attention of Thomas Szasz who, although a psychoanalyst, argues that a process which results in the individual conforming more closely to the social norms is a violation of individual liberty. Szasz pursues this theme with a simpleminded logic to the point where any intervention in the career line of a psychotic or even a suicide is seen to be a violation of his civil rights. These matters plague youngster and therapist alike. Matters of freedom, conformity, choice, life style, and values are significant parameters for "The Inheritors" of the middle class way of life.

Young and old debate the role of values in life. Let me define the word "values" in terms of usage. In my experience the concept of values in interpersonal affairs emerges as a matter so vague and unformed, so variously pursued and interpreted, as to mean all things to all men, and hence is a word or concept virtually undefinable and unknowable. I can now perhaps be more coherent in suggesting that my young patients, their parents, their educators, and the philosophers of youth have a most pressing concern with words and concepts which are virtually undefinable and unknowable. The old values have been lost, we are told, and with them man has lost his sense of purpose. A new set of values is needed. Some admire the hippies because they have renounced our "materialistic" set of values and reverted to simpler ones, not unlike the early Christian values.

I am not speaking for or against values, since I have no position on the undefinable. I am pointing to the soil and climate in which our young weeds, the adolescents, grow in a semantic thicket. On close analysis a remarkable number of words reveal themselves to be undefinable in situations in which they are used. They include honesty, dedication, sincerity, loyalty, freedom, consideration, conformity, sharing, work, and love. So-called liberal parents and educators cause more confusion in their use of words involving values than do the authoritarians or even the authoritative. Believing in "freedom," they attempt to persuade and exhort, invoking ethical issues concerning matters of preference or custom. They are generally oblivious to the coercive use of invoking questions over values. Often they fail in the struggle to influence, because bright youngsters easily become adept in the manipulating of ethical concepts for the purpose of confounding their elders or their peers. They do succeed, however, with middle class youth in legitimizing dealing with self and others in ambiguous terms with ethical implications.

In this soil there are three chief kinds of sprouts that grow. There are the stunted and distorted plants, sometimes schizophrenic, for whom the soil and climate of words and attitudes proved drastically inhospitable. For these unfortunates the things of our culture, our words, ideas and ideals do not perform an orienting function. Words indeed, as in Lewis Carroll's writings, mean precisely what you say they mean, just that and nothing more, and they change when you decide they change. Concepts are simple, awesome, frightening, and evanescent. Their attachment to reality, i.e., words, concepts and their referents, is vague, transient, and replaceable. The vicissitudes of these young people, with particular emphasis on their family milieu, have been described by Lidz, Bateson, Weakland, and others. They are not related to the concerns of Puritanism or egalitarianism, and they float in isolation without the orienting notions which guide all. Some give up in despair and suicide.

A second group includes those who seek refuge in a simplistic view of self and others, a haven in a semantic storm. Some find simpler subcultures in which to live. These include some who become Timothy Leary's followers, the disciples of this or that guru, the members of right wing political groups, converts to fundamentalist religious groups, hippies, and some radical left wing activists. There is overlapping between the two groups. Many manage to stagger along on a more or less even keel, although buffeted by verbal storms.

My young patients fall into a third category. They are simple-minded Puritans. They tell me that values are the answer. They can believe in the undefinable or excoriate it. Some years ago, one student inveighed that we must rise up against conformity en masse. This is a sticking point with many young Americans and their elders. They are stuck at the intellectual level Piaget described as moral absolutism. They know there is a right way to think, feel, and behave. They actually believe that human relations are simple but that in some manner the simple solution has eluded them, or worse, that they have found it. In the child moral absolutism is an essential part of the developmental process. He must master the rules of marble playing as adhered to in his schoolyard. When he visits a friend in another neighborhood, he is convinced that since his friend plays by a different set of rules, his friend must be wrong. It is not only a developmental epoch but an emotional, intellectual, and ethical milestone to the realization that there can be two or an infinite number of sets of rules for playing the game of marbles, which Piaget termed moral relativism.

Harry Stack Sullivan suggested that neurosis is a disease of certainty. Although a patient may present himself with complaints of extreme indecisiveness and frequent vacillations, closer knowledge of the patient reveals rather astounding convictions concerning such unknowable matters as what (all) women are like. In all there is the certainty that somewhere certainty exists. I am naturally aware that in some circles such matters are considered primarily in terms of the wish to return to the womb or to the breast, and I have no particular quarrel with these fleshy metaphors. Of more particular concern, however, is the defective perceptive or problem-solving aspects of these matters as they appear in my young charges and their mentors.

I have referred to my patients as young Puritans. Their concerns in relating to themselves and others are experienced in the context of the Puritan ethic with its emphasis on hard work, thrift, diligence, and abstinence. The anguish of their parents in regard to them is similarly expressed in terms of failure to adhere to the terms of this ethic. There is room for confusion and controversy here. The diligence expressed in the pursuit of pleasure by some youngsters I believe to be the same driven diligence of their elders. The inner experiences of guilt and shame also run parallel. The notion of "fun morality" is an old one by now. It reflected studies which indicated that the shame which once attended all pleasurable activities still survives but is attached by many to those situations in which one "fails" to have fun.

The simplistic notion of being right permeates all concerns, a point of view which deplores confusion and uncertainty and is profoundly anti-intellectual in its outlook, although to be an "intellectual" is, by and large, a very conscious goal for most. This is reinforced by the condemnatory fulminations so dear to American journalism and publishing. Scarcely an aspect of American life has not been studied, documented, and soundly thrashed in some volume. Young people's inability to proceed in one direction or another is often a reflection of the interplay of the desperate and unrealistic notion that there must be a "right" direction and uneasy apprehensions about doing the wrong thing. The wish to rise "against conformity en masse" is a potent one, whether found in graduate school students or among dropouts. The pressure to be individualistic, inner-directed, and even unique interdigitates with the need to be conforming enough to fit in with some group of peers. I once had a two-year run of young patients who, to a man, confessed that the only "acceptable" course for them would be to write the great American novel. One presumes that this might require some degree of the alienation so deplored by some social scientists and psychiatrists. I suggested that some degree of alienation, of detachment, perhaps painful, is necessary for creative acts. But our youngsters are supposed to be engagé, and they are painfully aware of it. With a Puritan spirit and a condemnatory environment, a number become stymied for shorter or longer periods of time. For them even the most exalted callings are experienced as shoddy, contaminated by possibilities of self-aggrandizement on the one hand, and failure on the other. They seek the pure and unquestionable. Attempts to ameliorate such a situation by offering "proper" values or a sense of purpose add to the semantic jungle we and they inhabit. Therapy for them involves among other matters the explication of moral concepts, the recategorizing of interpersonal relations, the defusing of explosive words and ideas, and the decoding of the hortatory activities of their elders, who are then often seen as rather amusing after all, rather than awesome or evil.

These youngsters are a decent lot, if not particularly involved in the issues of the day. Of my twenty, seventeen were more or less opposed to the American position in Vietnam. Perhaps the other three were also opposed. If so, it never became a matter of analytic concern. All twenty struck me as apolitical, although their hearts were in the right place. (Seymour M. Lipset reported in the Winter 1968 issue of *Daedalus* that among college students the Young Democrats and Young Republicans have a total combined membership of only 250,000, while the Students for a Democratic Society has some 7,000 members.) Politics is an area in which their ever-ready dynamisms of shame, guilt, and conflict formation did not appear, except in those youngsters threatened by the draft. The latter tended to ruminate about the various postures possible in this situation. They considered activism, flight, conscientious objector status, and "bugging out" via psychiatry. None considered an heroic prowar or "patriotic" American stance, although this may have existed beneath or along with an apathetic, "I can't do anything about it" attitude. By and large, going off to war struck most as a frightening irrelevancy in their scheme of things. A considerable portion of their fears evolved around the prospect of conforming to a lockstep Army existence. Perhaps such notions as "individuality," "freedom of choice," and "nonconformity" are subtly constricting and only possible for a small elite after all, as it always has been. Army propagandists would be well advised to stress the amount of individuality possible in the services. A few of my returned youngsters felt less regimented in the Army than they had back home with liberal Mom and Dad or in their liberal or libertine college environment.

These youngsters were characterized by a desire to get along. They did not want to violate family and social expectations, and yet they were failing in school, uncomfortable with their peers, and not "making it" too well in heterosexual encounters. Only three had experienced any strong wish for self-improvement prior to therapy. This is not to say that all had not entertained wishes for success and happiness or Walter Mitty fantasies of conquest and glory. In psychodynamic terms the reasons for their difficulties were varied. In common, however, they did not burn with zeal for outer cause or inner self. Even after therapy only an additional three had acquired a zest for improving the inner self. Each of these had realized in treatment, with considerable shock, the extent of their prior dehumanization, and this presumably sparked a certain zeal for self-development.

During my review the lack of zeal for insight and understanding on the part of my sample was surprising. I assumed that as these young people came to know me and as we shared a lively and rewarding experience, they would share my lively interest in what makes people tick. I now realize that by and large they did not. I wonder why this facet only stood out for me as I reviewed these data. I surmise it is in part a patronizing or nonegalitarian attitude on my part. They learned to function, to "make it" in their terms, under my tutelage and departed better off and delighted, if not wiser. This satisfied me as well, and no doubt was a form of "making it" for me, although they had achieved less than an ideal result. I had always regarded psychoanalysis as a preparation for a lifetime of self-analysis.

Some youngsters, as has been noted by other authors, departed only to return when confronted by some other issue such as pregnancy, marriage, parenthood, or divorce, to plumb further the mysteries of the psyche. Some analysts believe an adolescent cannot be fully analyzed. Perhaps this is so. Perhaps it is sufficient to note that analyst and patient do not have to share what I consider to be a primary humanistic and therapeutic attitude for useful change to take place.

The wish to get along reflects the desire to perform adequately and nothing more. Failure to "make it" is painful and striving to "make it" may be energetic, even desperate at times. It is not, however, the expression of a wish to create or to transcend. This observation, if valid, raises several problems. It appears to contradict what I have described as an enduring adherence to the Puritan ethic. It might even suggest a deterioration of aspiration on the part of youth; or, to revert to an older vocabulary, it could indicate a prevalence of laziness, self-indulgence, and selfishness, as has been asserted by parents and public officials. I do not think so any more than I feel such qualities to be nonexistent.

I do not feel that the frequent observations about the competitiveness of getting into the right secondary school or Ivy League college constitutes a contradiction. "Getting along" or "making it" can involve among middle class youth a very high level of achievement without a particular concern for self development, excellence, or transcendence. "Getting along" at M.I.T. well enough to get a place and a scholarship in graduate school is not a mean performance. Psychologically, once a student is on such a track and relatively stable, he can often be seen to be living up to a particular standard, conforming to a set of expectations without going beyond them.

The wish to "make it" economically sums up, as in dream symbolism, a complex amalgam of forces. There is the wish to perform adequately, particularly to have one's adequacy acknowledged by contemporaries, to reap the resulting rewards, which are not only material but sexual and also spiritual in the form of feeling that one's activities are rewarding, fulfilling, gratifying, and worthwhile. A large order, it is true, and quite indigestible, I assure you, and yet it is a societal prescription. It includes the notion of rightness but not the notions of trial-and-error learning, failure as part of life, or anxiety as an acceptable aspect of human functioning.

It is a neat and unresolved, although crucial, problem to distinguish the factors which lead one anxiety-afflicted youngster to choose one solution or life style and another similar youngster to choose a quite disparate solution. It is also a neat problem for the therapist to temper an inclination to interpret social action as acting out, or conversely, to hail social action as being authentic, genuine, or mature. What the therapist does about his own accretions of anxiety in these matters is in itself worthy of serious study.

The youngsters noted have been strangely unfamiliar with the ubiquity of human apprehensions, loneliness, longings, and fears. Their idealized image, their model, seems to be one of a smooth operator or "cool cat" who achieves effortless successes while maintaining a serene interior. They respond to their own inner experiences with accretions of anxiety. They are intolerant of inner process, whether ferment, frustration, or fear, and they respond with self-disdain and diminished self-esteem. They are surprised and unbelieving when they hear that others suffer inner torments. They are unreconcilable. In my early days of practice a young schizophrenic explained to me that it was not anxiety that was the troublesome factor; it was anxiety about anxiety. This is their hangup.

I believe that these factors account at least in part for the popularity of the theater of the absurd, youth's poets and balladeers, Camus and other writers who appeal to these youngsters. These artists hold up to view unrelated, purposeless, and sometimes horrible happenings without connecting links. This must be the view of those without a view, or with a false view, of the nature of man. In such a context Arthur Miller even in his new works seems hopelessly dated as he portrays the perplexities of his protagonists as they wrestle with complex ethical issues. Moral absolutism seems to be the order of the day, at least for those in the public view, and ethics are represented to be as simple to comprehend as the plot of a cowboy movie, extended to include race relations, international affairs, and more closely (and absurdly) related to my own purview, interpersonal relations.

I should point out that I have seen no convincing data that the psychological events I am describing are anything new, although the number of middle class youths has risen sharply. I do not know societal remedies for this group or whether what I am describing can be properly labeled individual or group pathology, or pathology at all. There is, however, a sense of an evolution going on in the quality of personal relations in the middle class milieu. I do not believe in any Golden Age notion of a time when men were better than they are now. Nevertheless, I offer some predictions.

Although there is a strong ideological thrust in the direction of shunting the focus on the mental health professions from the middle class to the lower classes, the need for such services for the middle class will not abate but increase. A primary reason will be the perceptions and expectations the sexes have of each other. An egalitarian ideal subtends sex and family relations and is combined with a Puritan seriousness and sense of purpose. For them love is no laughing matter. It is shot through with egalitarian imperatives: to share, to be fair, to expect and demand an equal return for every caress and favor. Their marriages tend to be disasters. My young charges cannot tolerate the *angst* in themselves in heterosexual relations. They tend to immerse themselves in fits of love in which the object of that love is remarkably distorted and the disillusionment which can only be suffered by the illusioned is ever close at hand.

There is little authentic interest in sex but a great preoccupation with "making it" in the sexual area. The concept of courtship is prevalent as is the chemical theory of the divination of love with its palpitations and ecstasies. They are as preoccupied with orgasms and reciprocity in love making as are their elders. Again, there is an intolerance of any apprehensions. They have a remarkable certainty that there is a right way to make love. Mutual orgasm is not only idealized but required, and anything less is regarded as failure. This is a right for many rather than a preference, a privilege, or an accident. Anything else tends to be considered a perversion or a tragedy.

In his expectations, apprehensions, and behavior regarding sex, the middle class youth reflects more clearly than in any other area his misapprehensions, his disappointments, his failures, his catastrophes, his lack of knowledge of human possibilities, his intolerance of human frailties, his certainties of rightness, and his pigheaded and wrong-headed idealism, his human condition.

Withal there seems to be cause for optimism. The very concepts which are confounding in a state of moral absolutism hold much promise for those who break through to a position of moral relativism. The widespread notion of "making it" may have within it the seeds of a less competitive and more compassionate society. In the soil of the affluent society there may be sprouting a sufficient number in this generation who can be secure enough about "making it" to be comfortable enough with and detached enough from the inequities and problems of our age to do something constructive about them.

Infantile Autism and Childhood "Schizophrenias": a cybernetic approach to mental development

ROY M. KAHN AND MICHAEL A. ARBIB

By pointing up similarities and differences between brains and computers we discuss cybernetic concepts which may prove relevant to the mental health worker in his investigation of mental processes. We focus especially on the mental development of the child and use as tentative illustrations the problem and symptomatology of infantile autism and the so-called "childhood schizophrenias."

A brief introduction to possibly new vocabulary will be required to help in our discussion of ways in which cybernetics, computers, communications and systems theories *may* be of use to the mental health worker in the future, and to make the discussion of infantile autism which follows truly intelligible.

Sigmund Freud in his "Project for a Scientific Psychology" anticipated that neural substrates would be found to his theoretical formulations.[1] The error has been ours if we have assumed that these substrates would have to be tied to specific locations rather than involving the type of process formulations and systems analysis we are here seeking to describe, and which do involve neurochemical systems. When we think of ego psychology terminology and psychoanalytic formulations, we find that all too often the efforts to deal with process rather than labels, and end products have fallen short of the intent. Computers are eminently suited to such efforts.

The human being rarely functions with the logic of science, though science tries to understand him through its logic, leaving a conceptual gap too often filled by semantic refinements of theory. Essentially, the normal brain will learn almost anything you teach it, but the developing normal young child has tremendous difficulty in comprehending that he cannot be in two places at once (physically); cannot be both big and little at the same time; and cannot have and not have at the same moment. He gets unhappy, furious, tearful, and vacillating when confronted with this. We do not speak solely of frustrated wishes, but of a state of being as concerns brain function more implicative than has been recognized.

In Aristotelian models a thing or an experience cannot be and not-be at the same time. People, however, function this way all the time. They want and do not want at the same time. The fact that clinician speaks of mixed feelings or ambivalence does not mean that the feelings are, in fact, mixed (as salt and pepper), but may represent primarily the effort of the clinician to comprehend the actual state of affairs (being and not-being simultaneously) through imposing his familiar digital conceptions on the situation. To what extent has our learned approach for understanding and classifying mental and emotional functioning led us to confuse our systems of analysis with the actual basic functioning processes of the thing being dealt with?

Information theory, computer science, and cybernetics may help us evolve a more appropriate, objective frame of reference for our consideration of these matters. Our fundamental emphasis is on process, of which digital behavior is but a manifestation. From this perspective symptoms, such as disordered behavior, must be regarded as the outward signs of malprocess. It is the underlying processes which cybernetics must tap to be of use to the mental health worker. The analogy to finding and correcting the errors in computer programs is clear, though as yet the gap between the form of our computers and the understanding of our brains is too great to make it fruitful.

Computers and cybernetic theory may be useful in mental health efforts, as in this example focusing on the symptomatology and possible cybernetic formulations of the condition known as infantile autism, which we seek to separate from the so-called "childhood schizophrenias."

A Westerner might have difficulty in comprehending a Chinese series of symbols, but he would not feel it to be James's "buzzing, blooming confusion." "Confusion," cybernetically, occurs at points in development when information being received is on the verge of being encoded, but cannot quite be grasped. That causes confusion.[2]

Watzlawick, Beavin, and Jackson have distinguished between digital communication, which is based on an arbitrary system of symbols such as those of Western language conventions outside of which "there exists (almost) no other correlation between any word and the thing it stands for," and analogic communication in which there is something "thing-like" in what is used to express the thing.[3] They cite "posture, gesture, facial expression, voice inflection, the sequence, rhythm and cadence of the words themselves, and any other nonverbal manifestation of which the organism is capable, as well as the communicational clues unfailingly present in any context in which an interaction takes place."

A similar distinction will be used here in talking of information, digital information being that conveyed in the crisp this-or-that terms of a well defined symbol system, while analogic information may be somewhat inchoate, expressed by a continuum of interacting variables and of varying intensities. We mean to stress the distinction between the logical mode of expression society teaches a child and the emotional-neural-chemical substrate which is the child's initial endowment. Digital information eventually comes to claim more and more attention, but the analogic substrate is always there. Only by realizing this can we come to grips with the problem we have raised.

"Meta-information" refers to data which tells how other data are to be used, thus giving meaning to the data rather than just storing it as a string of symbols. The question of most interest and to which we shall sketch the beginnings of an answer, is: How does the analogic information possessed by the neonate come to provide the meta-information required to handle the digital information provided by the environment?[4] (This is not just a uniquely human problem as we sometimes think—the baby octopus must learn that the visual pattern of a crab shell is a symbol for a meal!)

Viewing the brain as an information processing device, and feelings as information, albeit of an analog type, we see that the human organism, like the computer, can misoperate on two major bases: 1) something may be wrong with the "hardware," such as the wiring, circuitry, dampers, or unmodifiable aspects of the overall program (say, genetically), or the internal environment (as in biochemical defect); or 2) something may be incorrect about the "software," or program, such as the information fed into the machine for processing, or the way or sequence in which it is fed, such as words, cues, or attitudes of mother or society.

With our emphasis on process we should like to take special pains to protect the reader from the error, all too common in psychological literature, which sees each mental process as requiring a separate region of the brain and vice versa. In systems theory we often analyze a system "S" and find it to be equivalent in behavior to an interconnection of systems "S_1" and "S_2," each with well defined functions—and feel that we have learned much about "S" from such a decomposition— even though there is no way of carving up "S" spatially in such a way to yield two systems equivalent to "S_1" and "S_2," respectively.[5] This implies that systems and processes need be examined rather than their end products, behavior, to comprehend the bases of mental health and illness.

FIGURE 1: A Simple Neuron Net

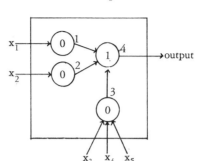

Consider the simple neural network of Figure 1 made up using the simplest of all neuron models—the McCulloch-Pitts neuron.[6] The network behavior is determined by which nerve fibers are firing at regular intervals, say a millisecond long, with specified thresholds which, when surpassed, cause the neuron to fire at the appropriate time.

Neuron 1, like 2, is just a delay element. Its output fires when triggered at adequate threshold levels by inputs X_1 or X_2. Neuron 3 detects whether any of its inputs are firing—by firing if and only if one of its inputs has fired. Neuron 4 is the most interesting. Its threshold requires two inputs for it to fire. If the input from neuron 3 is firing, only one more input is required to trigger it, and it will fire if neuron 1 or neuron 2 has fired (or both); however, if the input from neuron 3 is not firing, it needs two more active inputs and so it will only fire if both neuron 1 and neuron 2 fires. In the first case we say it acts as an "Or" gate, in the second case as an "And" gate.

In a sense then we may consider our four neuron "brain center" as having two "data" inputs, X_1 and X_2, and three "control" inputs, X_3, X_4, and X_5. The box will act as an "And" gate unless one of the control lines is activated, in which case it will act as an "Or" gate.

Functionally, then, we might represent the box as in Figure 2, but we know that in the actual structure of Figure 1 the "And" and "Or" circuits cannot be separated.

FIGURE 2: A Block Diagram for the Neutral Net of Fig. 1

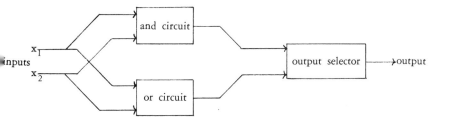

If one of the lines X_3, X_4, or X_5 were to be severed, then the box would exhibit an apparently erratic behavior, failing to act as an "Or" gate on many occasions when it should. Or suppose a "disease" were to cause X_3 to go into a mode of continual firing. Then neuron four would always function as an "Or" gate, and the function "And" would never be activated. (We may emphasize the problem the psychologist, as opposed to the neurologist, faces, or does not have to face, by noting that exactly the same malfunction would result from a "chemical change" which lowered the threshold of neuron 4 from two to zero.) This example emphasizes that we cannot deduce, just because a function is missing, that an actual brain locus is not activated. Failure to activate a function does not imply failure to activate a neuron net, only failure to activate the net in a certain way. Thus, we may have a brain in which all neurons are activated, all gross neural tracts are connected appropriately, but errors of detailed connections or thresholds may lead to malfunction. We can also describe neural networks wherein not only does each neuron take part in several functions, but also where functions are distributed over several anatomically distinct parts of the network.[7]

People and present-day machines are different in a variety of ways. Age factors are crucial in a child's developmental sequence. It is not true that unless you program a computer at a specific point in time, it may fail of development and never be programmable. The machine does not have an inherent developmental sequence of its own, which can develop well or poorly but will develop. Factors not found in machines do exist in people. However, computer programming is sufficiently flexible that we may simulate such developmental factors in the computer, albeit at the information processing level, not at the hardware level. Our human concern that computers could never be used to deal with such seemingly intangible and amorphous aspects of human functioning as feelings and nonverbal communication may not be as real as we believe, provided the psychologist can provide analogs and measures, or definitions and parameters, suitable for definition and redefinition in or by computer programs. We think that analogic information processing exists internally as well as interpersonally and is a normal mode of information processing in humans—one which may be amenable to computer analysis as process. Indeed, we consider analogic forms of information processing as necessary precursors in normal brain development which persist as forms of information processing throughout life and as potentially highly relevant to theories of affect.

What is needed is the development of more accurate and more subtle computational systems for integrating intersystems feedbacks to interplay digital and analog-simulation programs in order to cope with psychological concepts. With such development, processes occurring in interactions in the machine will actually define each term as a process, and not merely as a static verbal concept.

All this must not be taken to imply that at this moment computers exist which can perform all the operations we suggest in their full complexity. Nor should we rule out the possibility of biochemical factors affecting various systems under discussion, as indeed they do.[8] Rather, the appeal is for an openness of attitude to allow for modifications: 1) in leading to a re-examination of frames of reference for understanding mental processes; 2) in helping to avoid the pitfalls of theoretical language which tends to freeze process into labels, since it can neither make internal process visible nor describe variations in intensity from moment to moment adequately; 3) through making process observable, they may clarify our thinking about brain function as it actually operates (rather than through its end products like behavior), and may enable us to replicate certain hypothesized internal conditions and vary them at will to learn about the effects of such variations on end products and do this without injury to persons or feelings; 4) in providing leads and eliminating blind alleys in our efforts to comprehend theoretically or modify clinically certain internal processes. It may be possible to examine and test our own psychological theories and fantasies about how the brain works through using computers as an arena in which informational input can be selectively controlled, modified, and observed while it is in the process of being processed. This cannot be done normally in the human brain, yet would yield invaluable information about the process of processing itself, in brains; 5) in determining treatment approaches, regardless of whether the frameworks be psychoanalytic or operant conditioning, or anything in between, for the focus would be process. Additional aspects of the cybernetic view of normal development have been discussed by the authors elsewhere.[9]

The normal process of development in children moves from general to specific. This seems true in motor spheres and interpersonal relationships and also appears to be true in information processing. In cybernetic terms the brain function moves from reactivity on analogic bases (analogically processing as variations of intensity of the internal state or external inputs) to digital-with-analogic data (using cues blending intensity and, say, form or sound). In normal development the mother eventually comes to be recognized (digitally) as a precursor to tension relief. But tension in the infant is essentially an analog state—a matter of intensity rather than of specific locus. Tension relief is merely a variation in intensity, from the infant brain's point of view, a change in state which registers in an analog fashion. Eventually as memory develops and the self becomes separated from the mother and the world an internal model of the environment is created in the brain; and with learning, digitally based reactions become more and more predominant.[10] We shall view psychosis in children and infants as an arrest or failure in this progression to the normal processing of information.

The autistic child is like no other child, but the diagnosis remains extraordinarily difficult. This is partly because behavior, which is the end product of process, serves as the criterion for diagnosis, and true autistics show behavior similar to, and sometimes identical with, behaviors found in a large miscellany of other conditions. Yet they are different enough to constitute a separate classificatory group—infantile autism—and we shall discuss them to illustrate some of the possibilities existing in the cybernetic world for viewing mental process.[11] While we find some clues in these illustrations, we do not as yet feel we have proved a difference in process but only strongly inferred such a difference.

The classical descriptions of infantile autistics describe the child as "different from birth," or "like a sack of flour,"—assumedly unresponsive in infancy, and "undemanding."[12] The later behavior of the infantile autistic suggests that great inner tensions exist, but these remain focused on inner states and on maintaining a state of "sameness" in the environment, usually in some specific regard.[13] How does this come about, cybernetically speaking? We posit here that the processes which normally serve to build up the internal model of the world are subverted at, before, or very soon after birth. The child makes no systematic digital or analogic association between mother and tension relief. We further posit that, as a result, the operation of the brain's homeostatic mechanisms dealing with inputs or feedbacks tends to be highly restrictive. The introduction of new materials would undo a balance, and thus all input would tend to be shut out by the homeostatic mechanisms which would be incapable of modifying more than a small segment of the internal systems—and such modification itself would then throw the balance off without adjustments elsewhere. To maintain some semblance of process continuity new inputs would have to be "excluded" when the balance was threatened. Many inputs, perhaps including those from the child's own body, would not be subject to feedback modification. In a sense tension relief, which is a feedback process, would not be possible, or be only minimally possible in a restricted sphere, for tension relief is dependent on feedback processes and analogic variations in the brain which register as variation somewhere along the line.

As concerns affects: Affects are either nonexistent overtly (as in any demonstrations of pleasure, capacity for play, body relaxation, or joy) or they are wildly exaggerated as in violent rages which suddenly and inexplicably arise. Affects seem to be randomly expressed in motor activity against objects, people, or self, and laughter is a very rare and unclear in significance.

Since pleasure expressions imply a modification in internal state, usually associated with a lack of tension, or tension release, this inability to show pleasure—which is long standing—suggests that internal modifications of analog systems (or feeling systems) either does not occur or occurs via disruption of an established pattern or program. Initial infantile pleasure may be an analogic state of information processing based on variations occurring as the result of feedback from the infant's viscera. Without such information processing, what kind of program of tension relief is possible?

Pribram, in a neuropsychological theory, has viewed emotion as essentially a set of processes reflecting the state of relative organization or disorganization of an ordinarily stable configuration of neural systems, one which also reflects the mechanisms which operate to redress any imbalance—not through action but through the regulation of input. Pribram essentially suggests two types of feedback in the organization of emotion. One process entails the incorporation of input into existing neural systems through an alteration of neural mechanisms or models operating inside the person. This is called "participatory." The other alters input to make it congruent with the existing neural mechanisms (even if it excludes new inputs to effect this) and is called "preparatory." Pribram has stated:

> When preparations are directed to input processing channels (tending to shut them out), they have the disadvantage of not disposing of the source of the inputs responsible for the disequilibrium.[14]
> Under such circumstances preparations become chronic, repeated preparations progressively lead to hyperstability of complete internal controls, the organism becomes divorced from reality; the plans of action become inflexible. Thus more and more inputs become appraised as irrelevant. When this hyperstable inflexible state is finally disrupted by an input which cannot be eliminated, then the entire system become perturbed and, as the saying goes, "all hell breaks loose."[15]

The above description is relevant, as the reader can see, to the affectual functioning of infantile autistics, even in later years.

Withdrawal is a second hallmark of the autistic. Since much of the autistic's behavior involves a shutting out of as much input as possible, his behavior seems equivalent to saying "get out of my universe—you are messing it up." There is the implication here of a rigid, static internal universe, according well with our suggestion of the restrictive function of homeostatic brain mechanisms in the autistic. In an organism with ten billion brain cells, and with neural systems smeared over large geographic areas of the brain, withdrawal seems more related to systems functioning than to parts functioning. It also relates to the behavior one sees in the autistic called "a need for sameness" by ego psychologists and psychiatrists.

If there is any predictable reaction in the older autistic child, it is his rage when his internal universe is disturbed by an input somehow incompatible with what was there before. This need for sameness in the environment can be extensive and pertain to many objects or just a few, or even to a sequence of events—a schedule. This is a capricious bit of fuctioning, however, for the sameness makes no objective sense.

Why do the shoes have to be just there, and facing just in that direction, in the middle of the bathtub? We can eschew for the nonce esthetic reasons, and will bypass dynamic interpretations. Though the behavior ties in closely with rigidity, something cybernetically comprehensible may be adduced. Normal children learn to deal with the world by filtering incoming information and by using universals in their storage of data. Even with ten billion brain cells it is hardly a useful strategy for one to store everything as discrete pieces of information. The autistic, when he insists on sameness, may be indicating that material (or input) has streamed in, but that he cannot do anything with it. It remains digital—stored as datum without any instructions (meta-information), save perhaps in terms of matching up (super-imposing, as it were) the external input and the previous internal datum registration. The rage he demonstrates is inappropriate from the outsider's point of view, but it may reflect an upsetting of digitally-oriented homeostatic brain mechanisms (when change occurs) and not a real emotional connection between past experiences, nor an investment in the objects themselves. A program has been upset. Normals build, slowly, an internal model of the world about them—a cognitive map, as it were, which they cruise freely picking the best possible routes ("optimizing," cybernetically) or one that will do ("satisfying," cybernetically). This enables them to manage their trip through the world and include new territories. The autistic seems to have no internal use of such a map. He has only a template to match the world with, a template of bits of data. He has a still photo for a cognitive map rather than a motion picture. There is experimental evidence that monkeys and cats whose brains have been modified surgically can react to movement with recognition, although the same object at rest seems unperceived by them. Viewed thusly, the concepts of pleasure-displeasure may not be meaningful concepts for the understanding of the autistic. The process involved here is significant, however, for one implication is that the nature of memory in the autistic fits with the basic process of memory in nonautistics, but is different in terms of analogic connectivity. The autistics' reactions seem to operate like a fire alarm which switches on and off in response to a signal, without having an ego which is protesting the presence of fire. The need for sameness occurs in terms of location and in terms of daily routine at times.

Autistics react unfavorably to movement of the static object, but can and will manipulate simple moving machines endlessly (possibly because the unvarying nature of the machine's motion does not stir the homeostatic mechanisms into action). Novelty is an arouser of brain function. The autistic child in his repetitive movements may be demonstrating what have been called displacement activities,[16] which are characterized on a neurophysiological basis as reflections of a homeostatic process operating toward cancelling the arousal increment. Hutt and Hutt's electroencephalogram studies of autistic children give evidence for believing that the need for sameness relates neurophysiologically to maintaining a higher physiological level of arousal to shut out new inputs.[17] Interestingly enough, the autistic may not react overtly at all if something is removed from the field of vision—and frequently what he insists on is the presence of a thing, a human body perhaps, to fill a given space, rather than on the presence of a specific, real person. The outer world must match the spatial template or the alarm goes off.

One may speculate about a continued dominance of analogic communication and information processing as the basic mode of brain operation in autistics in a clinical setting. On one ward an autistic ten-year-old was particularly prone to sudden and unheralded violence. In this ward were only other autistics; yet the child must have given off some minute clue that no one was ever able to spot (perhaps an analogic variation in the intensity of his minimal activity), for the other children would retreat to safety just before he would rampage. Had this flight not been instantaneous, mutual, and simultaneous among the ten other patients, there might be a case for saying their flight provoked him. But clinically one would have to consider seriously the reverse: they fled as the result of an apparently nondigital clue he emitted.

The precocious talents and excellent motor coordination uniformly reported in autistics—taken together with digital storage—might make the autistic appear brilliant, and yet he would actually be functioning at a severely retarded level. It would appear that rather than brilliance the autistic has registrations without any meta-information. In trying to build an internal model of the world he simply has bits of data in his memory, rather than actual useful intelligence which would imply a different information processing system, one with meta-information feed-in and modification occurring through feedback. The possibly real talents of the autistic unfortunately do not seem aimed at any recognizable end and exist in isolation.

A peculiar variability in behavior towards physical inputs has been noted in infantile autistics, even when older, be these inputs in the form of sound, light or touch (pain).[18] The thresholds seem variable with regard to effectiveness of input registration.[19] Cybernetically we would view this more as a variability of output. An input of the same stimulus strength might well register every time, but, at one moment, yield no apparent output, and at another time produce a reaction all out of proportion to the input strength. Perhaps some of the sudden "inexplicable" rages are delayed from previous inputs—but this is unanswerable speculation right now.

Delayed responses and responses unconnected to immediate stimulus appear to be arbitrary, capricious, and inexplicable. Since inputs do not find immediate appropriate (or inappropriate) affectual or motor responses, the impression of variability of input threshold may reasonably be created. In programming for a computer the difference between variability of input and variability of output would be a major one—and we raise it now as the kind of question a cybernetic theorist would ask. With regard to the seeming lack of response to input it would appear that, in Pribram's terms, the inputs are being handled in a preparatory fashion by the autistic's trying to adjust the input registration rather than modifying the internal brain processes or neural system to make the inputs acceptable. (This again is reminiscent of the reactions of children and infants where the internal affective or physical state constitutes the entirety of the universe and where analog variations are the only measures and systems of internal functioning. The analytic concept of fixation seems relevant here.) The analogic functioning here seems dominant, but is divorced from the digital.

The sense of self is based essentially on internal modeling processes. Within the ego phychology framework much of the internal model is based on basic trust. Viewed cybernetically, these may be translated into problems of long-term memory and of time. In many ways the autistic appears to have no sense of self. Frequently he behaves as though his own body parts are not attached to any central self. There is, however, much controlled bizarre posturing, and strange repetitive motions are indulged in endlessly; facial grimacing and ritual-like touching abound.[20] But through all this the appendages appear to have a separate existence, just pieces of data. The apparent lack of self-image accords well with the lack of a central coordinating system for integrating proprioceptive experiences and feedbacks into an ongoing internal model in long-term memory. The feedbacks from proprioceptors do not get integrated into a single entity. The excellent motor coordination reported exists without unitary representation in the brain, as a series of automatic righting reflexes, visual-motor coordination units from short-term memory and feedbacks from balance centers. This does not vitiate the presence of both long and short-term memory functions in autistics (in the computer sense) but strongly suggests a communication problem or a difference in system functioning (a weakening, as it were) in the way they function in processing information.

In the development of the normal child, data fed into the system and stored as long-term memory is eventually integrated and comes to constitute an internal model of the self, the outside world, or anything else that is so treated. Such an internal model, with a clear distinction between self and external world, appears to be lacking or deficient in the autistic. Long-term memory in the autistic seems to comprise disjointed data, without correlation and without the making of adaptive generalizations. Basic trust theoretically comes into being via consistent tension relief. Eventually this tension relief—which is first analogic and internally based in terms of feedback from viscera—becomes connected and registered digitally to its source (usually the mother) along with the analog components of relief.[21] Then these cues (mother) come to have meaning, and serve as signals for impending tension relief for the child. Meta-information then comes to exist. We stress here the word impending, for it implies a sense of continuity in the child—an ongoing time sense with the previous and present somehow connected experientially. Basic trust (the confidence of tension relief) starts after what Anna Freud has described as the "need-object" phase—a phase the autistic does not seem to enter at all. The autistic's need for sameness implies a sense of environmental discontinuity based on template matching rather than any time sense of continuity. Any disruption of the template threatens or disrupts neural homeostasis, thus bringing homeostatic mechanism into play, and also producing rage reactions or a more massive denial of the external environment. Which of these occurs would depend on the momentary condition of the internal state. In either case neither basic trust nor its precursive need object phase can develop, and in the autistic neither does. Prerequisite to both is a sense of time continuity. In terms of mother-child interactions we also note that the lack of object relationship and of empathy in autistics are common observations,[22] and one wonders about their relationship to maternal feedback systems.[23]

The usual lack of speech in autistics may be one of the clues to the nature of defective systems in the brain. In the autistic speech is rare, and where it occurs it is usually either echolalic or just sound utterances. Some autistic children are said to have had speech and then (usually around age eighteen to twenty-four months) to have lost it. Speech is seldom attached to needs, wishes, or feelings and usually is limited to a specific object or phrases. Kanner and Eisenberg found that out of nineteen autistic children without speech by the age of five, only one seemed to improve enough to go to school, while out of twenty-three who were said to have shown some speech by the age of five (whether later lost or not), thirteen were capable of such improvement.[24] Is it possible that speech system (not area) activation, when it occurs, somehow impinges on, activates, or otherwise creates new available systems, areas, or processes in the brain for development? The use of speech, of course, also implies digital thinking, for labels are possible. The absence of speech to a great degree impedes this. Recent work hints that timing and sequence of systems activation may be crucial to normal information processing in the brain. Salk notes that babies in incubators for one to two months have less tactile stimulation than full-term babies, as well as maternal deprivation, and that these lacks can lead to irreversible structural changes.[25] In this regard he also explores imprinting processes. There is also evidence that no differences exist in intellectual functioning between a group of children who at six months of age had received visual input with only minimal social interaction and a comparable group of children who had received both.

One wonders why the age of five or five-and-one-half should loom so important, although it is clinically evident that it does. Rimland thinks that at five-and-one-half learning moves from conditioning paradigms to more cognitive understanding types of functions, and thinks that operant conditioning succeeds because conditionability is still intact from earlier phases of brain development.[26] Studies of reading readiness have found that a jump in the curve of *readiness* occurs at age five-and-one-half in normal children. Freud believed that the ages four to five-and-one-half were the oedipal period, culminating in a new system functioning for the superego. In certain EEG studies Gray Walter concluded that the changes at age six paralleled the acquisition of the concrete operations of Piaget's scheme.[27] In the cybernetic terms we are using here this would be a changeover from primarily analogic information processing techniques and relationships to a marked modification of process leading to a greater use of digital modification of inputs and meta-information, although the process of changeover may have been germinating for some time. It also appears that after the age of five-and-one-half the special diet for phenylketonuric children may not be as effective, or possibly not necessary, since changes in myelinization occur at five-and-one-half.[28] Seventy percent of the parents of autistic children surveyed by Rimland said their children had changed at age five-and-one-half, but they all remained autistic.[29] Kuttner theorizes that the CNS becomes less plastic as it matures and that language must activate before the CNS fully matures if the individual is to make full use of it.[30]

This age factor suggests that the concept of "crucial periods," as applied to child development, may be significant. These have been touched on by Weiland and Rudnik, Spitz, and Coblinger, and Bettleheim among others.[31] Scott has suggested three crucial periods.[32] We place any crucial failure at zero to three months in the autistic. In terms of the analogic functioning and digital functioning of the autistic this time estimate appears reasonable. Relating the crucial-period phenomenon and imprinting to the study of infantile autism raises many interesting questions. In animals the period for imprinting can be relatively short—a day, an hour, or a week or two.[33] Whatever evidence we have relating to imprinting phenomena in more complex animals suggests that any period for imprinting (or perhaps we should call it learning in humans) would probably extend over a longer period of time than in lower phylogeny. There may be an activation of neural systems by an imprint or a memory, or there may be a failure to activate neural systems, or at least a failure to activate them in a certain way. This leads us into the question of misprogramming, which we shall take up in the next section. Rather than consider infantile autism as a thirty or fifty-point on a continuum, we should recognize that the total failure of process-developmental sequences to occur is a form of process different from an abnormal unfolding of development, in which process still occurs, but along lines distorted more by software factors than by basic hardware injury. Basic hardware injury precludes maldevelopment of normal process by aborting the process itself, while software injury distorts or blocks process without totally aborting it and is also more specific about the processes involved than is the more generalized hardware defect in the autistic.

Are we merely translating one set of clinical ego psychological abstractions into another set of computer cybernetic abstractions—and perhaps injuring these complex abstractions in the process? Answers and techniques are being sought to investigate process as such. The aims here are to determine ways to begin setting up computer programs to replicate autism and to study its process functioning. Basically, in autism inputs and responses seem divorced or not connected through metainformational processes or fail because of lack of processes to integrate digital and analogic information. In the so-called childhood schizophrenias the inputs and the responses, however, do not seem to be divorced. The responses, though inappropriate, do occur. Cybernetically, so to speak, infantile autism appears to suggest at least as a meritorious hypothesis a basically different process from the so-called childhood schizophrenias and in this sense should not be considered an extreme example of the schizophrenic process at all. We do not consider this word play, for if cybernetics can demonstrate that the realities of brain functioning underlying the two systems are different in terms of processes and systems, we will know at least where to begin looking in each of these conditions.

Computer simulation aids the investigation of process (rather than behavior) by allowing internally observable programs, which are the determinants of process for the computer. Just as the behavior of a person constantly feeds back and modifies his next behavior, so the computer program may be modified by the execution of a routine or subroutine. In present-day computers hardware is not so modified, but it will help our model making if we think of all processes as involving both hardware and software. Viewing mental illness and health as processes, certain psychoses need not involve structural changes, while others may.[34] In normal functioning, brain systems actively seek information from the environment and are not merely ones of passive registration.

At this stage we shall find it useful to distinguish between incompatible and misprogrammed systems as follows:

A misprogrammed system may result when the external significant other or environment has consistently or inconsistently fed information into the brain which is either 1) not congruent with reality as perceived by other senses; 2) inconsistent with itself (e.g., the words and feelings do not go together and may be contradictory—yielding a new affect process not adequately described in digital terms); or 3) incongruent with the ongoing internal state of the child (e.g., mother fails to pick up or reflect accurately the needs and separateness of the child). The double bind is a form of misprogramming.[35]

An "incompatible" system is based on a hardware defect where internal states 1) are incompatible with each other (leading to mechanisms for reducing general input), such as underlies the "allergy" theory of infantile autism; 2) lead to failure to develop processes for refinement of analog information by digital information inputs; or 3) produce unacceptable internal feedbacks or feedbacks incompatible to ongoing internal brain systems (for example, tension relief fails to be processed, or internal input fails to activate or to dampen certain ongoing processes). Basic to incompatible systems is the concept of an inbuilt process (defective or not) or structure such that inputs produce a consistent pattern within an already damaged system, yielding consistently atypical behavior (which itself need not be consistent), or a rigidity of internal systems so great that it breaks down early and then fails to develop. The rigidity of the inbuilt system (hardware) may then cause a breakdown in developmental sequence so that the stored data and the meta-information fail to classify the input data, and the child stores data without any instructions about how to use them. At the same time that this is going on, both analogic (quantum or feeling relationship) information processing and digital information (content) fail to modify each other or to develop processes for such modification. The child fails to learn how to learn. Thus the end product behavior remains inappropriate or nonexistent with regard to a given input.

There are other forms of childhood psychoses, and these appear more related to misprogramming than to hardware defect: the brain has been taught to malfunction, or is misprogrammed. This can result from the acceptance into a normally functioning system of inappropriate inputs, which have modified an originally adaptive system so that it malfunctions. Since the normal brain can learn almost anything you teach it, the system can adopt (or create) programs of instructional data execution of which, if they consistently yield disasters, eventually are modified so that they do not yield the disaster. If the input is inappropriate, but countering the input yields, for example, rejection, the program will eventually come to accept the inappropriate input as though it were appropriate. One result can be that feedback modification begins to destroy the basic structure of the system itself. Lidz and associates and others have pointed to family interaction patterns which fit this paradigm at the interpersonal level—to the double bind situation[36] in which digital data and analog data (in the sense of nonverbal communications or instructions) are noncongruent, which results in an absence of appropriate meta-information. The adaptive system may maladapt to reality in the double bind situation to avoid the conflict between input and feedback. Computers may prove useful in varying programs to see whether this occurs and under what kind of reprogramming the adaptive aspects of the system which do remain may best be used for corrective purposes. At present in these cases psychotherapy or family therapy may be efficacious, and the concept of transference becomes a relevant one. However, in infantile autism many basic processes seem not to develop at all, and the child is often and classically seen as having been different from birth. It is not as though he has been taught not to learn, for example, but as though storage and memory systems and analog processes make only certain aspects of input recoverable and almost nonusable. This contrasts to other psychoses of childhood (and to normal functioning), where recovery of data modified by meta-informational processes produces partial reverberatory anxiety types of responses.

In the childhood schizophrenias—to use one term for a multitude of different disorders—a range of affects or analogs are invariably expressed, albeit inappropriately to the situation at times. Efforts seem to be made to modify internal neural processes to accommodate inputs, but unlike the normal these inputs are then processed inappropriately, and the resultant accommodations are maladaptive. Pribram calls this process "participatory." In contrast to the "preparatory" operations of the autistic, "participatory processes deal with incongruity (of input) by searching out and sampling the input and accommodating the internal system to it. . . . The experience becomes part of the organism, and the plans of action are appropriately modified."[37]

Where inputs are inappropriate the internal system of the childhood schizophrenic (which has already moved to the point of being competent to execute participatory processes, and is thus more than three months old developmentally) will also modify itself to accommodate or gain congruence with the inappropriate inputs, yielding mislearnings or childhood schizophrenia. The normal adult can tolerate a moderate amount of inconsistency in his internal model; mental disorder results when the inconsistencies yield gross instabilities. The younger the child the less developed is the model and the more disruptive the misprogramming.

The basic processes involved in infantile autism (as derived from the symptomatic behavior, and from theoretical considerations) and those of childhood schizophrenia thus appear cybernetically different. In this sense they may be thought of as not parts of the same continuum.

We have suggested that a separate clinical condition exists which may be labeled infantile autism, involving chronic malfunction within the brain system (as against a progressive disease or transitory disorder), in the analysis of which the study of neural malfunction (whether structural, functional, or the result of the disordered biochemical genetic environment) is relevant. An analysis of the so-called childhood schizophrenias, however, may well be done at the level of psychological interactions.

We have shown that these problems may be presented in terms of cybernetic concepts and language, and that such models cast light on underlying processes. We stress that this entails no assumption as to unicausality and no assumption about locus at the outset. There is an assumption that events external to the organism can modify internal functioning. Infantile autism may come to be shown to result from a biochemical error, as has been done for PKU, or DNA/RNA error, or other body deficit. Our present models neither imply nor deny such a causation, but rather seek to elucidate the information processing development of the child to analyze what deficits may yield results similar to infantile autism, irrespective of their cause. While we postulate that infantile autism is a condition in the neonate, the existence of this very internally generated condition may so disturb the mother (the primary source for external inputs) that it causes impaired mother-child interactions, thereby further aggravating the condition. Thus cybernetic analysis of mental health and disorder must take into account both internal malfunction and relational malfunction.

Cybernetics, computers, communication theory, and system analysis help to clarify the functional nature of differences between mental health and various disorders and aid in the elaboration of the neural mechanisms involved. In this fashion, we may provide new definitions for the theorist and process-management suggestions for the clinician, leading in the future to new concepts of the processes underlying mental and emotional functioning.

NOTES

1. New *Introductory Lectures in Psychoanalysis* (New York: Norton, 1933).

2. M. A. Arbib, "Cognition—A Cybernetic Approach" in *Cognition—A Multiple Approach*, ed. P. Garvin (in press).

3. Their distinction was based on the distinction between digital computers, which store numbers as strings of symbols (as binary or decimal notation), and analog computers which store numbers continuously (for example, by setting a voltage to a value proportional to the number to be stored). By programming the equations of an electrical circuit into a digital computer we can make that digital computer simulate an analog computer. Thus, when, in what follows, we talk of the utility of simulating a model on a computer we shall mean that the model is represented as a program for a digital computer even if the model involves what we define as analogic information. P. Watzlawick, J. H. Beaven, and D. D. Jackson, *Pragmatics of Human Communication* (New York: Norton, 1967).

4. M. A. Arbib and R. M. Kahn, "A Developmental Model of Information Processing in the Child," *Perspectives in Biology and Medicine, 12*: 397-416 (1969).

5. M. A. Arbib, *The Algebraic Theory of Machines, Languages and Semigroups* (New York: Academic Press, 1969).

6. W. McCulloch and W. Pitts, "A Logical Calculus of the Ideas Immanent in Nervous Activity," *Bulletin of Mathematical Biophysics, 5*: 115-33 (1943).

7. M. A. Arbib, *Brains, Machines and Mathematics* (New York: McGraw-Hill, 1964).

8. R. M. Kahn, "Childhood Schizophrenia: An Approach Based on DNA/RNA Functioning, Conditioning and Mis-Learning" paper presented at the annual convention, American Orthopsychiatric Association, San Francisco, 1966.

9. M. A. Arbib, "Cognition"; Arbib and Kahn.

10. Arbib and Kahn.

11. For detailed clinical and nosological descriptions of infantile autism, the reader is referred to these works: L. Kanner, "Early Infantile Autism," *Journal of Pediatrics 25*:211-17 (1944); L. Kanner and L. Eisenberg, "Notes on the Follow-up Studies of Autistic Children," *Psychopathology of Childhood*, ed. P. Hoch and J. Zubin (New York: Grunne and Stratton, 1955), pp. 227-39; L. Kanner and L. I. Lesser, "Early InfantileAutism," *Pediatrics Clinics of North America 5*:711-30 (1958); B. Rimland, *Infantile Autism* (New York: Appleton-Century-Crofts, 1964); D. E.

Reiser, "Psychosis in Infancy and Early Childhood as Manifested by Children with Atypical Development," *New England Journal of Medicine, 269*:844-50 (1963); Bruno Bettleheim, *The Empty Fortress* (New York: Free Press, 1967); M. S. Mahler, "On Child Psychosis and Schizophrenia: Autistic and Symbiotic Infantile Psychoses," *Psychoanalytic Study of the Child, 7*: 286-305 (1952); and "On Early Infantile Psychosis: The Symbiotic and Autistic Syndromes," *Journal of the American Academy of Psychiatry, 4*:554-68 (1965); and M. S. Mahler, M. Furer, and C. F. Sattlage, "Severe Emotional Disturbances in Childhood: Psychosis," *American Handbook of Psychiatry*, ed. S. Arieti, (New York: Basic Books, 1959), I, 816-39; *Early Infantile Autism*, ed. J. K. Wing, Pergamon Press, 1966.

12. Not all autistics are so described, and such clinical pictures have been presented in detail. However, it is also true that in recent work Rimland found a bimodal curve on a checklist of infantile autistics' behavior—as seen in later childhood—and if one restricts the term infantile autism to the lower hump of this curve, those definitely autistic, a correlation may be obtained with early nonresponsiveness. In this regard the autistics with speech by the age of five differed considerably from the never-speaking ones (personal communication, 1967).

13. L. Eisenberg, "The Autistic Child in Adolescence," *American Journal of Orthopsychiatry, 26*:607-12 (1956).

14. By disequilibrium here is apparently meant neuronal patterns or activity representing affectual states arising from noncongruence of input with some internal plan—or process—or model. The concept advanced by some that infantile autism represents a condition in which certain biochemical body products are noxious to other body chemicals or each other yielding bizarre behavior, the "allergy theory" of autism, may be better viewed in terms of two or more internally originating neural processes which are mutually antagonistic, precluding the reduction of internal equilibrium, or of tension relief.

15. K. H. Pribram, *Emotion: Steps Towards a Neuropsychological Theory* (Palo Alto: Stanford University School of Medicine, in press).

16. J. D. Delius, "Displacement Activities and Arousal," *Nature, 214*:1258-70 (1967).

17. J. S. Hutt and C. Hutt, "Stereotypy, Arousal and Autism," *Human Development, 11*:277-86 (1968).

18. Arbib and Kahn; W. Goldfarb and S. Gurevitz, "Pain Reaction in a Group of Institutionalized Schizophrenic Children," *AJO, 28*:777-85 (1958).

19. Another note of some interest is that while older (seven to twelve-year-old) autistics seem peculiarly impervious to the usual punishment inputs, such as spanking, Lovaas has found that, for as yet unknown reasons, the mild electrical shock of a standard conditioning goad or floor grill will get through and bring about immediate rage reactions. The

autistic will then modify behavior under a well planned and well executed conditioning program. Why electricity more than any other input carried neurally from the body periphery should work (where even toothaches will not) is an interesting problem. Similarly, why conditioning techniques should be efficacious in a system otherwise generally not self-modifying and nonresponsive to normal external stimuli is an open matter. The present paper does not account for this, and this suggests one direction in which it needs extension. Lovaas also found that once he had conditioned autistics to talk, they had nothing to say. They had data, but did not have anything to do with it. (I. Lovaas *et al.,* "Aquisition of Imitative Speech by Schizophrenic Children, *Science, 151*: 705-707 [1966].) It has been mentioned that modifications in the autistic's internal system would be isolated and not generalized, if they occurred, especially if no connection existed between analog and digital systems of functioning. Perhaps the conditioning modifies isolated segments in the brain system through the presence of "inescapable" (electrical) input initially, which forces the homeostatic mechanisms to modify in those areas or minor systems.

20. The reader may experience this for himself by holding his arms up at eye level out forwards and the elbows slightly bent so that the hands are now fifteen to twenty inches forward from the temples. Focusing eyes directly forward vaguely across the room, and moving the hands around, may produce the impression that hands may not be attached to the body, but are acting as independent agents.

Sometimes in the framework of ego psychology, the bizarre motions are referred to as magic rituals, and, indeed, at times they seem to serve some defensive role. However, if communications and cybernetic theories can reduce conceptions of magic to systems operations and neural functioning, a certain clarity will indeed have been introduced into our thinking about human behavior; although at the present the concept of magic is a useful and somehow very attractive one.

21. Arbib and Kahn.

22. L. Eisenberg and L. Kanner, "Early Infantile Autism, 1943-1955," *AJO*, 26:556-66 (1956); R. M. Kahn, S. Anenias and P. Peterson, "Psychotherapy of an Autistic Child," unpublished manuscript, Metropolitan State Hospital, Massachusetts, 1962; M. S. Mahler, "On Early Infantile Psychosis: The Symbiotic and Autistic Syndromes," *JAAP*, 4:554-68 (1965); R. Rabinovitz, panel presentation at annual convention, American Orthopsychiatric Association, 1965.

23. Kilmer and McCulloch have described computers and programs wherein two computers, each with only partial information, interact and modify to refine each other until final consensus as to behavior is reached. The analogy to mother-child interactions is evident, and mother-child programs may be able to be created or simulated in machines.

24. Pp. 227-39.

25. L. Salk, "On the Prevention of the Schizophrenic," *Diseases of the Nervous System, 29S*:11-15 (1968).

26. D. Rappaport, *Emotions and Memory* (New York: Science Editions, 1961).

27. *Psychobiological Development of the Child* (London: W. H. O. Publication, 1956).

28. While no one should attempt to diagnose infantile autism on the basis of the foregoing description of clinical highlights, the clinical picture also should not be confused with that of Phenylketonuria (PKU), which is similar in some respects. PKU is, of course, a biochemically-based disorder. Some differences clinically are: (1) the autistic *always* walks, while the PKU child often does not; (2) the autistic's motor coordination is excellent, that of the PKU is not; (3) 80% of high grade PKU show abnormal EEGs, the autistic usually does not; (4) 66% of the PKU children show hyperactive reflexes—not the case with autistics; (5) 68% of PKU children show microcephaly. There are no reports of this in autistics. The PKU child is described as "having a stiff gait, with short steps, a stooping walk" or "stumbling gait," not the case in autism. Some points they share in common are: a tendency towards incessant action, either with part or all of the body (hyperkinesis); restless hyperactivity (only at times in autistics), speech disturbances, and emotional outbursts. In both types "none could be described as friendly, placid or happy. They are restless." [20] But the PKU child is described as overly "fearful"— something which does not show in the autistic. In both, the mood, if any is ascertainable, is one of tension or withdrawal.

29. B. Rimland (personal commnication, 1967).

30. Kanner and Lesser.

31. H. I. Weiland and R. Rudnik, "Considerations of the Development and Treatment of Autistic Childhood Psychosis," *Psychoanalytic Study of the Child, 16*:449-63 (1961); R. Spitz and W. G. Cobliner, *The First Year of Life* (New York: International University Press, 1965); Bettleheim.

32. J. Scott and J. P. Fuller, *Genetics and the Social Behavior of the Dog* (Chicago: University of Chicago Press, 1965).

33. W. Sluckin, *Imprinting and Early Learning* (Chicago: Aldine, 1965).

34. A resolution of the organic-functional conundrum is suggested by R. M. Kahn in: "Both Horns of a Dilemma Are Usually Attached to the Same Bull," *Perspectives in Biology and Medicine 13*:633-35 (1970).

35. G. Bateson, *et al.*, "Toward a Theory of Schizophrenia," *Behavioral Science, 1*:251-64 (1956).

36. T. Lidz, S. Fleck, and A. A. R. Cornelison, *Schizophrenia and the Family* (New York: International University Press, 1965); Bateson, *et al.*

37. K. H. Pribam.

Why the Mind Is Not in the Head

HARLEY C. SHANDS

In beginning his *Philosophical Investigations*, Ludwig Wittgenstein (1953) quotes a passage from St. Augustine's *Confessions*, which seems to give two implicit theories of language. The first sentence states: "When they [my elders] named some object and accordingly moved toward something, I saw this and I grasped that the thing was called by the sound they uttered when they meant to point it out." This rather simple "see it and say it" theory is contradicted or at least greatly expanded by the next sentence, which reads: "Their *intention* was shown by their *bodily movements*, as it were the *natural language* of all peoples; the expression of the face, the play of the eyes, the movement of other parts of the body, and the tone of the voice which expresses our state of mind in seeking, having, rejecting or avoiding something" [Italics added].[1]

The first sentence gives an implicit "noun" theory of language, the second a "verb" theory. In discussing these notions I want to point to a number of bodies of evidence which suggest that not only is the "verb" theory far more easily supported

by the available evidence, but, in a considerable extension,
that all forms of mentation involve the whole body. Mentation resembles the circulation of the blood in that there is an
incessant flow of significant patterns throughout the entire system. The notion is by no means new. In a one-hundred-year-
old book recently made available to Western readers Ivan
Sechenov (1863) states that:

> The infinite diversity of external manifestations of cerebral
> activity can be reduced ultimately to a single phenomenon—
> muscular movement . . . To help the reader reconcile himself
> to this thought I shall remind him of the framework which
> has been created by the popular mind and includes all mani-
> festations of cerebral activity: This framework is *"word"* and
> *"action."* Under *"action"* the popular mind undoubtedly
> visualizes every external mechanical activity of man which can
> be accomplished exclusively with the aid of muscles, while
> *"word"* as the reader will readily appreciate, implies a certain
> combination of sounds produced in the larynx and in the
> mouth cavity also by means of muscular movement.[2]

To bring Sechenov's statement into the context of this essay,
it is only necessary to point out that the process he describes
is a circular one: the input of information from the muscular
actions into the brain is fully as important as the output in the
opposite direction. The contemporary situation is described
by another Russian interested in movement. Bernstein says of
the cybernetic view of mentation: "It is now beyond any doubt
that the most general and prevalent form of organization in
live organisms is not the reflex *arc* but the *reflex ring*."[3]
    Overwhelming evidence suggests that mentation involves
the whole body in ways which progressively change with progressive competence. Like any other skill, however, thinking
(as Bartlett notes, 1958) requires exercise and protracted effort
leading to a disciplined system.[4] Thinking exists only in time,
just as a motor skill exists in time—the miniaturization effect
in thinking allows us to ignore the exercise-discipline limitation. In another direction, thinking uses language, first as

overtly exhibited and more and more as implicit. Many of the traditional illusions having to do with thinking take origin in an inadequate grasp of the structuring effect of linguistic usage.

The theory of mentation we have inherited suffers from a fallacy of misplaced concreteness (Whitehead, 1960) that fallacy which assumes that process has a spatial location.[5] The concreteness evident in this kind of formulation has a poetic quality of appeal which, added to the simplification, makes the whole attractive to those seeking understanding. Shakespeare asks "Where is fancy bred?" and Emily Dickinson puts the same kind of problem in concrete imagery by asking, "Will there really be a 'Morning'? Is there such a thing as 'Day'? . . . Oh, some Wise Man from the skies! Please to tell a little Pilgrim where the place called 'Morning' lies!"

Thinking or mentation is a process involving sequential passage of patterns through a large number of combinations and permutations. Although it is essential that the process occur in some material setting, it becomes more and more apparent that many parts of the process can occur in a wide variety of artificial settings. In man the evidence indicates clearly that the whole human body is necessarily involved in mentation. With adequate learning, overt movements in the periphery can be minimized—in ways abstractly similar to those in which communication processes in contemporary machines are effected through progressive miniaturization of components. But the essential feature is that the process primarily occurs sequentially in time, and not in some static spatial localization.

Mentation in the broad sense is similar in its principles of operation to abstraction. In both instances it is the pattern which matters. The pattern is manifested in one or another of a myriad of possible substances and locations—the material context is irrelevant but essential. The *pattern of movement* establishes the basis of thought and communication. In its most private sense thinking is a process of communication to oneself. Human thinking is based upon a developed method of inner speech, much reduced in its overt manifestation by the shorthand techniques easily available to associates as intimate as "I" and "me".[6]

Western conceptualization has traditionally used a dichotomizing technique for describing. The basic reason is more closely related to the structure of language than to the structure of reality—whatever that may be. Reality is grasped only in communicational techniques, observational and descriptive, and reported only in linguistic-symbolic forms. When we compare sentence structure with physiological relations, we see that sentences are necessarily discursively linear, whereas physiological systems operate in circular feedback relations. In thinking of the pituitary as a master gland or of centers of control in the central nervous system, we are adopting linear patterns, suitable to the language, which implicitly ignore the fact that the pituitary gland is controlled by the level of circulating hormones emanating from its "target organs," while the central nervous system depends at all times upon the reflux inflow of data from the periphery.

When we separate a directing "mind" from a responding "body," we are perpetuating an ancient myth that the executive controls the system of which he is a central official. Even in the most autocratic of regimes the executive has to depend upon the consent of the governed, even if that consent is implicit and unconscious. A conspicuously inadequate executive tends to be overthrown even in a strongly authoritarian setting, as we find in English history in the cases of Richard II and Henry VI. The executive is supported by the kind of structure in which he finds himself, so that a great deal more tolerance for incompetence is found in highly structured settings, but this fact is far from absolute.

It is not unusual for parents to learn new dialects from their children. It is unusual, however, to learn from an inanimate "child," but this is one of the features of the contemporary scene as we learn from metallic "brain-children" who think, in limited ways, better than their parents. We can describe human mentation in computer dialect by saying that the human computer processes data only *on line,* in *real time.* The reason for this is easy to find in the extraordinary vulnerability of neural function. Any serious interference with the free supply of either fuel or oxidizer not only stops neural function but rapidly begins to injure the neural structure. Those parts of the nervous system most involved in complex kinds of thinking are those most vulnerable to this traumatic interference.

When we speak of "storage" in the nervous system, we are talking about a very active process. Data are recirculated in reverberating circuits, patterned into different forms of inter-connectedness between cells, somehow encoded in changes in molecular configurations, but however encoded they are maintained in a constantly active, living process. One fascinating indication of the electronic nature of some of the neural events is the notion that in some parts of the nervous system the storage function is attained through the formation of a "standing wave," incessantly renewed.

The time span of neural "reality" is measured in seconds or fractions of sections. In a curiously contradictory fashion, neutral existence is coterminous with the specious present presented as illusion by classical philosophers oriented to invariance and to eternity. From an understanding of the physiological fragility of neural integrity it becomes clear that all we can think we think *now.* Storage in the nervous system is active storage; each cell in which some part of the storage process is carried out has to remain in a state of physiological balance if it is to perform its function.

Because of this extreme lability and the temporary nature of neural physiological process, the invention of writing gives human beings storage methods far beyond the capacity of any other animal—and, indeed, far beyond the capacity of the illiterate human being. When philosophers early began to understand the power implicit in written records, they tended to celebrate this technique in a worshipful attitude. From the fact of durability beyond the life of any single human being it is easy to extrapolate to the notion of eternity. From the fact

of durability of the message written down in some form it is
it is easy to extrapolate to the ideal of invariance. From the
fact that records are kept in safety in specific buildings it is
easy to suppose that storage in the mind is equally static,
equally resident within the bony walls of the cranium. These
eternal verities turn out to be nonsense, however, to be replaced by a much more astonished wonder that so transient
and so pervasive a function as the data processing of thought
could take place so rapidly in so complex a fashion.

Animals think, if thinking can be construed as predictive
problem-solving. Some of the feats of animal knowing are astonishing, as for example the technique by means of which
bats flying in the dark unerringly find enough tiny flying in-
sects to keep themselves adequately fed. The human advantages in thinking depend upon the capacity to speak and upon
its derivatives in written language. While there is good evidence that a human being, once trained in linguistic method,
can think without having to go through detailed sequential
verbalization, there is no doubt that unless the human being
is trained to talk in the language of his peers, he will not be
able to think in human terms.

What we call a "word" is a shaped respiratory event, entirely dependent upon a skilled exhibition of muscular coordination as the respiratory muscles expel air which is shaped as
it passes through a series of organs which are themselves altered through muscular action. Learning to talk is learning a
complex motor skill shared in a common patterning of gram-
matical structure. The importance of the skill aspect can be
easily observed in watching a young child learn to cope with
words: he begins by saying them aloud, continues by mouth-
ing them, and ends by "thinking" them in implicit form. But
an expert speaker and reader of English often finds himself repeating this sequence in trying to grasp the significance of a
French or German sentence; to understand, he has to go back
to saying the words aloud to himself during the learning
process. When he does go from speaking to writing, he is
superimposing a subsequent manual skill upon an antecedent

respiratory patterning. Learning difficult new subject matter (especially in mathematics) requires going through the act of writing the symbols down.

When we think of seeing as a function of eye and brain, or hearing as a function of ear and brain, or touching as a function of sensory endings in the skin and cerebral connections, we ignore the facts of our own experience. In every case it is not only the activity of the special sensory organ which is involved alone; just as essential is the activity of muscular mechanisms which arrange for continuous movement in the relation of sensitive surface and system of interest. Only in the course of relative motion can sensing occur; the muscular movement which establishes the background of sensation tends to be unconscious in a most important sense of the term. Much of the training undergone in the course of developing sensory skills is training to regulate the muscular skill component so that it can be taken for granted.

Frederic Bartlett emphasizes throughout his book *Remembering* that perception is a transactional relation involving the special sense organ, as one party, and the "whole body responding," as the other party.[7] Bernstein comments that all peripheral receptors are equipped with "efferent innovation and a muscular system on which depend functions of optimal adjustment (in a very broad sense), and also the countless phenomena of search, guidance, haptic tracking, etc."[8] Arnold Gesell and his associates comment upon the formation of an "eye-hand system," noting that vision is the cue for the hands emancipated in man from a supportive function, while the hands direct the eyes in a manner in which "it is idle to differentiate between cause and effect."[9] They note that the human advantage is implicit in the increase of brain tissue, which allows human beings to exceed all other species in ocular and manual skills.

Jean Piaget and Bärbel Inhelder point out that: "From the rudimentary sensori-motor activity right up to abstract operations, the development of geometrical intuition is that of an activity."[10] Piaget notes that all perceptual processes depend upon a "centering," which makes the center of the field relatively more important than any other part. This centering relates closely to the visual technique of focusing, but it occurs (as Granit emphasizes) as well in the tactile and auditory spheres of sensation. The perceptual emphasis (which Piaget sometimes describes as a "distorting relativity") is subsequently altered by an integration of several different centerings into a general construct (in the "correcting relativity" of conceptualization). The important consideration is, however, that the retrospective integrative process of concept-formation has to depend upon a series of active centerings.

Granit sums up a wealth of observations (after discussing the well known experiments of George Stratton and of Wolfgang Köhler with inverting spectacles) that "the apparent plasticity of the psychological interpretation is an adaptation to the organism's needs. In this the conscious component *follows and agrees with reflex* motor performance. The psychological datum which we try to trap in psychophysiological experiments is an organized response to a large number of cues. If experience proves them unreliable a new and better system of interpretation is elaborated" (italics added).[11] The notion presented is that vision is "instructed" by motor activity: motor dominance is retained in what psychiatrists might call a "reality-testing" in action.

When we understand something of the powerful influence of peripheral muscular activity in relation to thinking, we can get a more significant view of the importance of the tiny muscles which control sensory organs from inside. The most significant experimental evidence available comes from work on the rapid-eye-movement-state (REMS) of paradoxical sleep in which dreams most probably occur. The clue which opened up this whole field was the chance observation of regular periods during sleep when the electromyographic evidence pointed to rapid movements of the eyes in conjoint fashion.

The tracing can be interpreted as indicating that the subject is "looking," although he can "see" only the backs of his eyelids (and he cannot in fact see them because they are too close). The interpretation given by Skinner is that these movements indicate "the behavior of seeing," separated from the "out-there" to which seeing is ordinarily oriented.[12]

In turn, we can assume that looking is subject to a separation of pattern from context such that after training the subject "sees" by looking, even though he is not "looking" at anything. To summon up "remembrance of things past" in "sessions of sweet, silent thought," it remains necessary to exhibit the minimum of the behavior of seeing. To see, even the dreamer has to look by converging. This impression is supported by the further observation that the behavior of the tensor tympani muscle associated with the eardrum gives the impression that the dreamer is listening. Further, the fact that the REM state is regularly associated in men with an erection of the penis indicates that even the unconscious experience of the dream has to involve at least minimal activity in the muscles intrinsic to sensory function in orientative, predictive behavior.

Not only is muscular activity essential in exploratory behavior related to the out-there, but it is equally essential in a different sense in relation to exploring in-here. The person trying to recall something or to think through a problem in a "brown study" may be observed knitting his brows and gazing at a distant point, even though when asked what he is looking at he will often (sometimes with a start, doing what we call "coming to himself") say, "Nothing."

Wittgenstein gives us an interesting description of his exploration of his own state of consciousness:

> When I . . . turn my attention in a particular way on to my own consciousness, and, astonished, say to myself THIS is supposed to be produced by a process in the brain!—as it were clutching my forehead. . . . But what can it mean to speak of turning my attention to my own consciousness? This is surely the queerest thing there could be. It was a particular *act of gazing* that I called doing this. I stared fixedly in front of me—but *not* at any particular point or object. My eyes were

wide open, the brows not contracted (as they mostly are when I am interested in a particular object). No such interest preceded this gazing. My gaze was vacant; or again *like* that of someone admiring the illumination of the sky and drinking in the light. [Italics added] [13]

The religious person seeking inspiration or help from his deity gazes upward again focusing even though he is not looking at anything in particular. The psalmist says: "I will lift up mine eyes unto the hills, from whence cometh my help" (Psalm 121). Mystics using meditational techniques often begin with the assumption of a gazing stance, oriented toward an object—but specifically concerned with ignoring the objectivity of the object. The central theme that to concentrate perceptual process one must focus vision appears throughout. The apparently extraneous activity of the extraocular muscles is a crucially important part of the processes of perception and even of conceptualization.

Pursuing the idea further into the ways of describing mastery of a concept, we repeatedly encounter the notion of "grasping." The metaphorical use of this term suggests that possibly the technique of grasping has something to do with the internalization of knowledge. When we watch a baby first coming to terms with his world, we see him reaching out to touch, grasp, mouth, push—he exhibits a full range of manipulative behaviors which he associates with special sensory investigation of tasting, smelling, and seeing.

We find repeated evidence that the basic structure of knowing involves a dualism allowing a dialectical method in which opposition is first posed, then resolved. It becomes a difficult, even an impossible question, to wonder whether this universal structure follows the lead of a "reality," which requires describing in this manner, or whether the series of descriptions structures the reality which we comprehend (note the derivation: we *prehend*, or grasp, *together;* for agreement, we have to resolve basic differences of opinion until we grasp the same thing).

In perception two separate lines of investigation are integrated into a single construct. In the usual case we can oversimplify by pointing to the importance of vision, on the one hand, and manipulation, on the other. For accuracy we must remember that the first category is actually that of the special senses, the familiar five. But abstract thinking in man is so predominantly a visually-based phenomenon that we can cover a great proportion of the field by looking mainly at the relation of vision and manipulation.

According to J. Z. Young, a demonstration of this kind of relation is apparent in as phylogenetically remote an animal as the octopus: "The octopus brain contains two anatomically distinct and localizable memory stores: one records the result of actions following visual events; the other the results of actions following the touching of objects by the suckers."[14] I would only suggest that it may well be more the grasping of objects than the simple touching of them.

In a series of studies relating to remote phylogenetic antecedents to the visual capacity of the human being, Richard Gregory points out that vision must always be informed or instructed by active exploratory movement. The retinal image, falling upon the two dimensional retinal surface, can only give the impression of three dimensionality by interpretation after the active participation of the limbs in exploration. Gregory states:

> Retinal images are symbols, like words in a language; however, like any symbols there must be a process of initial association to acquire significance, or the symbols are in a logical vacuum and cannot represent any reality. Furthermore, retinal images are but flat projections of a three-dimensional world and yet they give perceptions of three dimensions. There must be direct, non-visual, information of the third dimension. Other information comes from touch. It appears that any conceivable device for perceiving which relies upon two-dimensional images must use, at some state, direct touch information if it is to interpret its images in terms of three dimensions of surrounding space.[15]

He goes on to describe two kinds of touch: "which involve entirely different neural mechanisms. There are skin pattern touch and limb probe touch. Pattern touch involves the reception of patterns by contact with areas of skin, while probe touch is very different and requires exploratory movements of a limb. Pattern touch gives information only of structures lying on the two dimensional surface of the skin, while probe touch gives information in three dimensions, within the reach of the limb."

He comments upon the special function of the fore-limbs: "It is the fore-limbs, and especially their movements, which are available to vision but not pattern touch—which is hidden from the eye by (non-transparent) objects in contact with the skin. It is active rather than passive limb movement which gives visual learning."

When we compare and contrast the results of looking and grasping (including under grasping the notion of palpating or touching in an exploratory manner), we find that each approach modifies the other. In Marius von Senden's summation of the results of attaining visual competence in adult life, he notes that until the subject had an extensive experience of grasping round objects while looking at them, he could not *see roundness;* this ability is a derived and developed potentiality which has to be trained in action.[16]

Pursuing the notion further, Gordon Holmes reports from a study of brain-injured soldiers who had lost the capacity for spatial orientation: "It was only when they relied upon sight alone that they could not localize the positions of an object in space. If it touched any part of their own bodies they could always bring their hands to it immediately and correctly; touch gave them the necessary local knowledge that they failed to obtain from vision alone."[17]

Another British neurologist, Gordon Wright, comments: "The closer our physical relationships (this really means *tactual* relationships) with other people, whether by reason of kinship or by reason of our profession, the more intimate and thorough is our knowledge of them, and the more potent is the *manual* component of the images we have of them. . . . Manipulation is also of prime importance in constantly reaffirming the *corporeality* of ourselves and other people—in putting substance one might say into the body image."[18]

When we think of learning, we often use the rubric of the three R's—reading writing, arithmetic—with the idea that some record of a mostly exteroceptive perceptual experience is stored in the brain. This model is implicitly supported in the notion of a classical Pavlovian conditioning as a basic process in learning. In many of the classical procedures of neurophysiology the procedures begin with anesthetizing the animal subject or with the ablation of all of the nervous system except that part in which the experimenter is interested.

Perhaps the most dramatic demonstration available in recent years is that all of these procedures give an entirely erroneous notion of the basic processes involved (Livingston).[19] Only when it becomes possible to observe animals and human beings in effective action with others of their own kind is it possible to get a clear look at learning, as we know from many contemporary studies in ethology. The restriction is so great in any kind of simplification of animal life that it is possible to find a very pronounced difference between the learning processes of wild animals and those simplified by progressive domestication. Lee Kavanau, for instance, has studied wild mice and compared them with domesticated ones in a laboratory.[20] Wild mice show a remarkably expanded capacity for learning, even in situations requiring the simultaneous handling of several variables. In contrast, domesticated mice are markedly limited. In a laboratory environment the domesticated mice tend to be relatively placid, while the wild mice explore incessantly, playing with any kind of apparatus available to them in a continuous effort to get the better of the situation.

In a development of conditioning procedures derived from but considerably extending the scope of the Pavlovian variety, the Polish investigator Jerzy Konorski gives an interesting account of the extension of varied behavioral learning in conditioning experiments made possible when the exteroceptive stimulus used by Pavlov is combined with proprioceptive patterns introduced by movement of some part of the animal's body, whether that movement be passive, a response to a reflex stimulation, or somehow actively induced. He notes that the major difference of operant conditioning from the classical kind is that the former involves active participation of the experimental animal in the learning process.[21]

For example, if one trains a dog with a tone, he can be made to salivate with either meat or acid, thus showing a similar reaction to oppositely valued stimuli. With the type II conditioning procedure the subject can be trained to show oppositely valued reactions to oppositely valued stimuli—positive to pleasant, aversive to unpleasant. By varying the time of stimulation great differences in the result could be obtained. Perhaps most importantly Konorski showed that after appropriate intensive training, it was possible to remove the afferent signals from the trained limb while leaving the reflex movement possible. Since the deafferented limb was otherwise a "flail" extremity, the fact that it could be directed to carry out the appropriate action on exhibition of the conditional stimulus gives evidence that the integration of movement with perception of the exteroceptive stimulus makes fundamental differences in the way in which the memory storage is effected in the nervous system.

Available evidence indicates not only that motor activity is essential in learning, but that repetition of motor activity exhibited against consistent resistance is necessary for the maintenance of learned patterns. Richard Held and Sanford Freedman reviewed studies showing that unless the repetition of skilled actions takes place time after time in the context of a predictable resistance, the schemata which control those skilled actions are susceptible to deterioration.[22] This finding suggests that not only is it extremely important to carry out training in a situation which presents the appropriate resistance to the trainee, it is also necessary for subsequent exhibition of the skill to take place in the same context of resistance if the skill is to be maintained at a high level of competence. This result suggests that skills are stored in the form of schemata which are implicitly not so much *schemata of action* as *schemata of transaction*. The dialectical process is unavoidable even here. A properly performed skilled act represents a synthetic resolution of a conflict of thesis of action and antithesis of resistance. Neither can be ignored, although it seems possible, if we extrapolate from Konorski's finding, that in a highly skilled subject it may be possible to direct the performance of a skilled act without the immediate feedback of afferent information at the time.

These authors summarize their impressions, with special reference to the practical application of these findings in the space program:

> The maintenance and development of sensorily guided behavior depend in part upon bodily movement in the normal environment. Ordered information entailed in the motor-sensory feedback loop is responsible for the stable functioning of the plastic systems of coordination. It is found, from the results of experiments on vision and hearing, that the introduction of disorder into the motor-sensory loop changes the state of these systems and makes performance imprecise. In space, a freely moving astronaut will be exposed to a condition analogous to that of the subjects of these experiments. Consequently, he may lose his ability to perform certain tasks requiring precise sensori-motor control.[23]

Two further esoteric suggestions appear in material reported by introspective observers of great sensitivity. The first of these is a report by William James in the *Principles of Psychology*. There, reviewing the manner in which he finds himself, knowing himself, he says:

> this central part of the Self is *felt* . . . . It may be all that Transcendentalists say it is, and all the Empiricists say it is into the bargain, but at any rate it is no *mere ens rationis,*

cognized only in an intellectual way, and no *mere* summation of memories or *mere* sound of a word in our ears. It is something with which we also have direct sensible acquaintance, and which is as fully present in any moment of consciousness in which it *is* present, as in a whole lifetime of such moments . . . . But when it is found, it is *felt;* just as the body is felt, the feeling of which is also an abstraction, because never is the body felt all alone, but always together with other things.[24]

He goes on to describe his own feeling of the "central active self":

. . . I am aware of a constant play of furtherances and hindrances in my thinking, of checks and releases, tendencies which run the other way . . . when I . . . grapple with particulars . . . *it is difficult for me to detect in the activity any purely spiritual element at all. Whenever my introspective glance succeeds in turning around quickly enough to catch one of these manifestations of spontaneity in the act, all it can ever feel distinctly is some bodily process, for the most part taking place within the head . . . the 'Self of selves' . . . is found to consist mainly of the collection of peculiar notions in the head or between the head and throat . . . it would follow that our entire feeling of spiritual activity, or what commonly passes by that name, is really a feeling of bodily activities whose exact nature is by most men overlooked.*

A most interesting contrast to James' curiosity about how he knows himself can be found in a carefully reviewed experience by a Westerner learning a Zen Buddhist technique.[25] Herrigel spent a number of years in Japan, and while there he undertook a training process with a Zen master. The specific technique used was unusual, involving the learning of archery. Herrigel's fascinating report emphasizes throughout that the goal of his training is that of losing any feeling of an "I" directing or controlling; rather he was indoctrinated with the ideal that he learned so to participate in the larger process that when the arrow was released, there was a feeling of "it shooting." Like the utterly disciplined ballet dancer, who seems to be moving effortlessly without trying, the Zen archer is un-differentiated from his task. The method is so efficient in transcending the usual limitations that, according to Herrigel, the master once demonstrated that it was possible to shoot an arrow in total darkness and have it land precisely in the bull's eye.

The significant word in descriptions of Zen, of Yoga, and of many others of the mystical religious pursuits is *discipline*. Not by chance the route to the complete discipline involves incessant repetitive activity, both of action and of the controlled inhibition of action. The meditator has to sit in a given position for long periods without allowing himself to fall asleep. The yogi prescribes to his disciples that they undertake a complicated set of breathing exercises, the adoption of the lotus position, of standing on one's head, and the like. Those who practice these esoteric forms of self-discipline report universally that the subject gains a marvellous sense of mastery—paradoxically by totally giving up the goal of mastering anything except the physical exercises involved in the training procedure. One has to learn a skill with implicit perfection, then forget the whole process in the exhibition of that skill or discipline for its own purpose. The subject could be said to learn how to enclose himself within a discipline having no purpose, no outcome except that of perfecting the discipline. Once this is accomplished, an enormous sense of liberation occurs: "It" shoots!

To complete a review of a series of related ideas having to do with the participation of the muscular system and its related aspects in human mentation, studies of the rapid-eye-movement-state give further pertinent evidence. It was noted above that the muscles intrinsic to the special senses are active in the focussing process.

In diametrically opposite fashion, while these evidences of activity in tiny muscles related to orientation and preparation appear, there is an extensive relaxation of the large muscle masses of the periphery. The muscles which have the responsibility of taking action on the basis of the orientative preparation involved in sensory function are specifically relaxed. The internal state of the brain is of great activity, sharply contrasting to the inhibited state of the peripheral muscles. The contrast is so precise that it seems impossible that it should be without meaning.

A general characteristic of the activity of the brain is that its metabolism runs fast, no matter what it is going. The evidence from the REMS suggests that when the person apparently is sleeping, the brain may run fastest of all, while the great muscles are most relaxed.

The curious explanation that suggests itself for this internal physiological "contradiction" is that in the eye movements we observe the ultimate degree of playing. Liberated from the dreary restrictions of ordinary everyday reality and the necessity for making a living or demonstrating one's worth in some public way, the dreamer indulges in "ludic activity" (Piaget) with a maximal freeing of imagination. He evokes images at random and combines them with varying degrees of structure and meaning, putting impossible things together and separating the inseparable. In this ruminative play the main purpose is to give relief to the integrative function by allowing a comprehensive disintegration, with the dreamer protected from harm because he is incapable of action.

This idea, supported in depth by evidence from physiological studies, was suggested by Piaget from an entirely different line of reasoning. Piaget's basic description of behavior uses the unitary duality of accommodation, defined by him as a behavioral change imposed upon the organism by the environment, and assimilation, the structuring imposed upon the environment by the organism. Play is mostly assimilation because the playing child makes whatever he has be whatever he wants it to be. Imitation, an important method of learning in early life, is thus mostly accommodation.

Piaget comments about dreaming:

> Dreams are . . . comparable to symbolic play, but play which, by lack of consciousness of the ego, is itself analogous to the lack of coordination between the visual and the motor,

characteristic of the first year of life. The semi-consciousness of the dreamer is indeed comparable to the state of complete egocentrism characteristic of the baby's consciousness. In both cases there is a lack of differentiation between the ego and the external world, and the assimilation of objects to the activity of the subject. . . . The ego is unconscious of itself to the extent to which it incorporates external reality, since consciousness of the ego is relative to the resistance of objects and of other persons.[26]

When Piaget speaks of the lack of coordination of visual and motor components, we can remember that the REMS evidence indicates that even in the face of the loss of peripheral motor activity, the intrinsic muscular activity of the sense organs cannot be dispensed with if the experience is to occur.

If we try to come to a general formulation having significance in light of all these disparate bodies of evidence, we can suggest that learning is specifically dependent upon acting, with the clear implication that only in the course of overt activity does learning occur. Then a major task of human education becomes the training of human learners to *minimize* overt activity while *retaining* the capacity to be alert and to process data. The function thus described is that of exerting and maintaining discipline. Discipline then has a function—to make learning efficient. When we learn to concentrate, to read silently, or to think "in the head," we are learning a technique which bypasses much of the afferent input otherwise necessary. If we extrapolate from Konorski's finding, much of this would appear to be a matter of making intracerebral bypass connections, which, though dependent upon "operant" processing in establishment, allow bypassing and economy in exhibiting the learning involved.

In the most efficient instances of this kind of learning, however, there remains a limit to human capacity. Most of those who think in abstract contexts have to externalize the thinking as they go along if they are to move progressively through a problem in complex subject matter. Francis Bacon said that "writing maketh an exact man," and I would propose that the act of writing provides the minimal but essential muscular participation. Mozart supposedly was able to "hear" a complete symphony in his head before writing it down, but most people have to give themselves a great deal more help in working through to a solution or an artistic accomplishment. As we study reports of experience of those who involve themselves in mystical, meditative, or contemplative disciplines, the notion emerges that the final state has a significant connection with the training. Discipline progressively improves predictability: the highly disciplined human being knows precisely what to expect of himself. I propose that when predictability reaches some ultimate point of perfection, the control of muscular activity allows the human being to transcend the dualism of perception that separates the *me, in-here*, from the *world, out-there*. The illuminated person loses both the objectivity of the resisting world and the subjectivity of the yearning self. He comes to feel an undifferentiated continuity with "reality" or with "god" or "nature." The feeling is reported as ecstatically satisfying. If we extrapolate to ultimate states, we find the oceanic, undifferentiated experience of the infant in one direction, the unconscious consciousness of the dream in another, and the ultimate loss of self in death in still a third.

The ultimately paradoxical character of human experience comes through loud and clear: if overt muscular activity of the peripheral musculature is necessary to thinking or to remembering, then what cannot be experienced in muscular movement cannot be either conscious or remembered. The states of bliss which we approach by attempting to achieve an ultimate disciplined control of muscular activity, or the ultimate loss of muscular activity in the total relaxation of the dream, are necessarily states of blissful ignorance. The analytic activity of differentiation, which is the correlate of planned motor activity, is incompatible with intensity of feeling. Possibly we may all attain a new taste of the Garden of Eden from time to time in the REM state, but, as we are driven again from bliss upon reattaining the condition in which we can know good from evil, we lose heaven without ever knowing we were there again.

When we awaken, we can sometimes report, in a procedure

not too dissimilar from that of describing a receding seascape through a rapidly closing porthole, fragments of what we have been dreaming. But the limitation of this procedure is apparent to anyone who comes back to a record of such a report. What we remember is no longer the dream, but the report—I believe quite simply because we remember not the view but the muscular participation of writing it down or saying it to someone else. The dream would appear quite unrememberable, except in the derived and grossly reduced fragments that one can quickly grasp in the specious present in which the reverberations linger.

The suggestion is clear that human experience is necessarily circular in context after context. It involves a circulation of patterns out to the periphery, but equally importantly from the periphery back to the center; a circulation of patterns from the self to others and back and when we learn to internalize others (and a "generalized other"), in a constant circular communication in the form of an inner speech system; and in the broadest terms a circulation from a state of undifferentiation *in utero* through a detailed process of differentiation in an "object world" back to undifferentiation in dreaming and in the occasional but dramatic attainment of transcendental experience in mystic exaltation. Curiously enough, we only can understand this fact only after a long training in thinking abstractly, while the major purpose of the abstracting of patterns is to give human beings an entirely unjustified sense of spatial localization in a fallaciously misplaced concreteness. We live in a process which has a specifically spiral character, always coming back to a place from which we began, as Eliot put it, but knowing that place for the first time.

NOTES

1. (New York: Macmillan, 1953).
2. *Reflexes of the Brain* (Cambridge, Mass.: M.I.T. Press, 1965).
3. Nikolai Bernstein, *The Co-ordination and Regulation of Movements* (Oxford: Pergamon Press, 1967).

4. Frederic Bartlett, *Thinking: An Experimental Social Study* (London: G. Allen, 1958).

5. Alfred Whitehead, *Science and the Modern World* (New York: Mentor Books, 1960).

6. Lev Vygotsky, *Thought and Language* (Cambridge, Mass.: M.I.T. Press, 1934).

7. (New York: Cambridge University Press, 1954).

8. Bernstein.

9. *Vision—Its Development in Infant and Child* (New York: Paul B. Hoeber, 1950).

10. *The Child's Conception of Space*, (New York: W. W. Norton, 1967).

11. Ragnar Granit, *Receptors and Sensory Perception* (New Haven: Yale University Press, 1955), pp.

12. "Behaviorism at 50," *Science, 139*:951-97 (1963).

13. Wittgenstein.

14. *The Memory System of the Brain* (Berkely: University of California Press, 1966).

15. "Origin of Eyes and Brains," *Nature 213*:369-72 (1967).

16. *Space and Sight* (London: Methuen, 1960).

17. "Disturbances of Visual Space Perception," *British Medical Journal, 2*: 230 (1919).

18. "The Names of the Parts of the Body," *Brain, 79*:188-210 (1956).

19. Robert Livingston, "Some Brain Stem Mechanisms Relating to Psychosomatic Functions," *Psychosomatic Medicine 17*:347-54 (1955).

20. "Behavior: Confinement, Adaptation, and Compulsory Regimes in Laboratory Study," *Science, 143*:490 (1964); D. H. Brant and J. Lee Kavanau, " 'Unrewarded' Exploration and Learning of Complex Mazes by Wild and Domestic Mice," *Nature, 204*:267-69 (1964).

21. "Changing Concept Concerning the Physical Mechanism of Animal Motor Behavior," *Brain, 85*:277-94 (1962).

22. "Plasticity in Human Sensorimotor Control," *Science, 142*:455-64 (1963).

23. *Ibid.*

24. *Principles of Psychology* (New York: Dover, 1956). Originally published 1890.

25. Eugen Herrigel, *Zen and the Art of Archery* (New York: McGraw-Hill, 1964).

26. *Play Dreams and Imitation in Childhood* (New York: Norton, 1951).

Technology and Social Change

DONALD A. SCHON

It has become a cliché that we are experiencing an unaccustomed and accelerating rate of change and that this rate has something to do with technology. But it is not easy to specify the nature of this change, to determine whether its rate has in fact accelerated during the last ten to twenty years, or to explain the presumed uniqueness of our present situation.

Some persons argue that we are experiencing a rate increase which is in itself unusual, and uniquely tied to technology, and others (like De Solla Price) assert that there is no difference between the rate of technological change we are now experiencing and the rate of technological change characteristic of the Western world at any time during the last two hundred years.

The first argument rests on two forms of data. "Envelope" curves, for technological parameters such as velocity, numbers of elements discovered, strength-to-weight ratio of materials, and the like can be adduced to show straight-line, logarithmic growth.

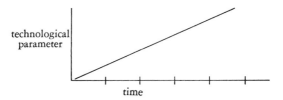

Diffusion curves showing the decreasing length of time required for technological innovations to penetrate their major markets suggest a logarithmic rate of shrinkage.

Time required for diffusion	*Years*
steam engine	150-200
automobile	40-50
vacuum tube	25-30
transistor	15

The time required for the diffusion of major technological innovations would appear to be approaching zero as a limit.

The problem with both sorts of curves is that they ignore the phenomenon of saturation. De Solla Price has argued that envelope curves in fact are smoothed out stop curves, such as:

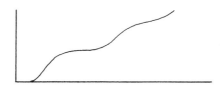

He contends that the overall level of technological activity is in our generation approaching a period of saturation, and that in any case rate of change—as distinguished from absolute level—has been little different in our own time than at any time in the last two hundred years.

The uniqueness of the phenomenon of technological change in our generation would appear to depend less on its rate of increase than on the nature of the changes and on certain critical levels reached. Technology-related changes have penetrated virtually all areas of social life in such a way that mature individuals will now have experienced several significant technology transitions within their own lifespans.

Among the principal features of technological change in the last twenty years are these: 1) The prevalence of industrial invasions in which the few science-based industries—chemical and petrochemical; electric, electronic, and communications; aerospace; nucleonics—have invaded traditional industries (formed during the late eighteenth and nineteenth centuries), such as textiles, paper, machine tools, and building. These invasions have induced dislocations in particular businesses, in whole industries, in regional concentrations of industry, and in occupational identity.

2) The broad-scale replacement, as a consequence of one invasion, of natural by synthetic materials.

3) The development of numerically controlled machine tools through which numbers arranged in programs and conveyed to a series of simple tools through paper or magnetic tape replace the direction of skilled operators. This invasion has been slower than anticipated, though it already represents more than 30 percent by dollar volume of all machine tool business in the United States. Its long-term, as yet largely unrealized potential, is in the ability to combine operational programs with a flexible array of simple tools so as to yield the economies of mass production coupled with the wide variety of finished products hitherto associated with custom manufacture. The magnitude of this change amounts, in effect, to a new industrial revolution.

4) The development of "systems" methodologies—at first through weapons and aerospace developments, such as the Manhattan project, the atomic submarine, Project Apollo—and their application, tentatively, but at an increasing rate, to areas of civilian concern. In its most dramatic form this is a trend toward the replacement of products by systems, both

as the unit of manufacture and as the basis for corporate identity.

The effects of these and related themes of technological development on American society is more complicated than any simple theory can account for. Clearly, however, these effects are of several different kinds and include: 1) Simple, direct effects on industry itself—as in the replacement of natural by synthetic fibers, and its chain of consequences, for instance, on the cotton economy of the South; or the multiple effects of the development of solid state devices on electronic products and systems; the varied effects on individual and organizational users of the new technology, for example, the changes in American life styles resulting from the wide distribution of products such as television, automobiles, prepared foods, and appliances; and 2) the more subtle influences of the new technologies as metaphors or models for human activity. It is in this sense, for example, that Marshall McLuhan speaks of a "new tribalism" among the young, centering on television; or of the emergence of network organizations, stemming from the model of the new electronic technology.

Clearly, too, the rapidity with which so large a number of technological changes critical to social organization and life style have occurred have influenced human response to them. The fact that these changes have occurred relatively precipitously within the easy memory of individuals at a rate that style has occurred have influenced human response to them. forces on us an awareness of change that undermines our faith in the stability of any future sociotechnical state.

During the same period (roughly the last thirty years) the United States has also experienced currents of social change. These include: 1) a growing awareness and intolerance of the imbalance in our society between the product-based consumer economy, to which the major thrust of the economy is devoted, and the critical public systems (transportation, housing, education, waste disposal), which have taken a poor second place. A rising intolerance of this imbalance (not necessarily related to the fact that public problems have been any more serious in the last ten years than in the fifty years before) pervaded the last two presidential administrations. The warcry of this awareness came in 1957 with the publication of John Kenneth Galbraith's *Affluent Society;* and 2) a growing dissatisfaction with the relatively powerless position in American society of many minority groups—not only racial (although the demand for decolonization of black society in America has been by far the most visible), but more broadly, the poor, rural families, the aged, the sick, criminals, and the mentally ill. It is as though we were now experiencing across the board an imperative for a righting of the balance of power. The expression of this imperative appears not merely in the demand for "our share" (as in the programs of the New and Fair Deals) but in demands for participation, decentralization, local control, and autonomy, that have in recent years taken on revolutionary proportions.

It may be, as Marshall McLuhan has suggested, that television, which provides for instantaneous confrontation of every part of our society with every other, has fueled these trends. What is clear is that they have accelerated in the last fifteen to twenty years; that they appear now to have reached critical proportions—at least in their energy and urgency. They combine with the multiple social and institutional effects of technological change to create our present social and institutional crisis.

As one consequence, no established institution in our society now perceives itself as adequate to its challenges. Institutions formed in the late years of the nineteenth century and the early years of the twentieth find themselves threatened by the complex of technology-related changes now underway. In some instances the very success of their adaptation to the period before World War II, or even to the 1940s and 1950s, makes them inadequate now. There is nothing local or parochial about this phenomenon; it cuts through American society.

The experience of business firms and of industry is particularly relevant, because industrial organizations respond to change in many ways in advance of other institutions. There has been a basic shift in what it means to be a corporation, in what "our business is," and in the form of organization and managerial style appropriate to the corporation. There have been shifts: 1) from the stable product line and market to the recognition of continuing product innovation as central to the firm. 2) From single-line, product-based definitions of "our business" to broader definitions, for instance, from "shoes" to "footwear," from "office equipment" to "information-processing," and then to process-based definitions. The 3M company defines itself as being "in the business of making money out of what comes from development." 3) A related shift from pyramidal forms of organization and management determined by simple corporate functionalism and spans of control, such as:

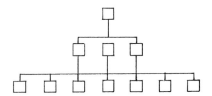

to the constellation form, such as:

These are multiply determined by the need to become research-based (in the sense of the 3M model, whose products bear only a family resemblance to each other); by the pressures of growth and the saturation of markets in the 1950s, forcing single firm entry into many markets as a means to growth; and by the multiproduct, protective response of companies to invasions from science-based industries. 4) A shift in requirements for managers and managerial style, from product line expertise—for example, in production (1930s and 1940s) or marketing (1950s); to network management, the management of product innovation and what has recently come to be called the management of change.

The American labor movement has in effect achieved its program of the 1930s. Its place in collective bargaining is assured. Its power in relation to management is secure to the point of being considered excessive by many elements in the general public. But, in the process, the broader social goals of the 1930s have been lost. Young workers who have forgotton or never knew the battles of that era tend to think in terms of job security, the acquisition of consumer goods, and the achievement of middle class status. The energy of the movement has been dissipated. Officials of the union on their way up tend to behave like members of any other large bureaucracy.

Leaders like the late Walter Reuther complained that labor has become middle class and has lost its sense of social mission. Reuther sought a new sense of mission in the as yet undeveloped concept of the "community union." Apart from his vision, the labor movement appears to be conflicted and unsure of its role or position in American society.

The federal government now faces severe pressure to bring resources to bear, quickly and effectively, on newly perceived problems—such as the problems of the decay of the cities, the poor, the inadequacy of our systems of public education, and the equitable delivery of health care. (What is new about these problems is not awareness of them, but the level of public intolerance for their continued existence.) Government has been seeking, in the broadest terms, to come to grips with these problems around or through bureaucracies which will in turn impede flexible response to still newer problems.

The U.S. Department of Agriculture, for example, came into being to attack problems of agricultural productivity in the late nineteenth and early twentieth centuries. The attack was successful—so successful that agricultural surpluses and their management have become our principal agricultural problems; yet the Agriculture Department continues on much the same basis (there are now approximately 70,000 extension agents in the field). Similarly, the Department of Labor grew up around the problems of unemployment and abuse of workers in the 1930s. The Federal Housing Administration and the Housing-Home Finance Agency grew up around housing programs of the 1930s and 1940s. The nation's problems have shifted away from these agencies, but the agencies continue much as before. Their "dynamic conservatism" is much like that of any other established organization.

On the other hand, any new problems—such as the problems of the cities—cut across most or these old institutions. The concerns of the cities, for example, relate to the distribution and consumption of food (agriculture), the use of labor (labor), the problems of public health (HEW), housing (FHA), and perhaps thirty or forty agencies. The obvious responses to this situation have been the creation of interdepartmental committees, reorganization of existing departments, consolidation of fragments within new organizations, and development of new agencies from scratch. But interdepartmental committees hardly ever function effectively; consolidation is apt to produce old wine in new bottles; and the creation of new agencies, in many ways the most promising approach (for example, Peace Corps, Office of Economic Opportunity), perpetuates the creation of bureaucracies, which tend to outlive the problems to which they were addressed.

There is a need to invent new roles for the federal government in relation to private industry and business, on the one hand, and to state and local government, on the other. Earlier notions of the proper relation between public and private sectors have eroded, and there has been a growing sense of urgency about public sector problems. The 1930s view of the proper relation between federal and local government suffers from demands for local autonomy and decentralization and from the generally perceived failure of large federal bureaucracies to carry out programs of service delivery.

The church in its various denominational guises finds itself forced to question both its role in society and its organization for carrying out that role. There are, on the one hand, pressures for ecumenism and, on the other, pressures for the same sort of local autonomy that individual neighborhoods and local governments are demanding. There is an urgent demand for moral wisdom, which internal conflicts have made difficult for the church to satisfy. Parochial sects have tended to dissolve under the technology induced inroads of the secular world, while more cosmopolitan sects seem diluted to the point of having little to offer. Many members of the church feel impelled to engage in the major battles concerning poverty, race, and urban problems; but to the extent that they do so, they tend to estrange themselves from the church. There is a general disposition to question and to attack the archaic bureaucracy of church organization. But attempts at reform run up against the fear that further liberalization will result in throwing out the baby with the bath water.

It is perhaps indicative that my organization (Organization for Social and Technical Innovations) has been asked to serve as consultant to church groups of several denominations and that the questions asked are almost identical to those raised by other organizations of business, government, or public service: How can we define our appropriate role? How do we work our way into our future? How can we both plan for and induce change? How can we overcome the resistances of our own organization to change?

These examples are only illustrative of what could be said about a wide range of established institutions—for example, systems of public education, the universities, and city government. In each of those domains, major spokesmen are calling attention to the inadequacy of the current system and requirements for change. But they illustrate in their own comments the confusion over the directions of change and over strategies for bringing change into effect.

This state of affairs is a present one, rather than one forecast for the year 2000, although a forecast of the year 2000 allows us a certain projective freedom to perceive present requirements for change even more clearly. What is required is not a new stable-state response—not an "answer" which is presumed to be durable to the year 2000 or beyond but a process through which institutions can be continually responsive to requirements for change.

What is true of institutions and institutional stability is true as well of individual persons and personal stability.

Consider the basic kinds of answers one can give to the question: who are you? These can be: 1) occupational: "I am a chemical engineer;" "I am a specialist in internal medicine"; 2) regional: "I come from Boston;" "I am a New Englander"; 3) religious: "I am a Roman Catholic"; 4) corporate: "I work at General Electric"; 5) normative: "I am a man who holds certain values."

But each of these bases for security in individual identity is in process of being threatened by the same forces that threaten institutional identity. Occupations are far less durable than they were fifty or even twenty years ago. A man who defines himself as a chemical engineer, a shoemaker, or a specialist in internal medicine runs an increasing risk of building identity on an unstable base. It is becoming less likely that occupational and professional identities will last throughout an entire lifetime. Traditional machine tool and textile crafts, for example, have been rendered increasingly obsolete by the technological invasions. A chemical engineer who grew up in the kind of chemical engineering proper to the paint or adhesive industry of thirty years ago finds himself in sharply decreasing demand today. Specialists at the frontiers of research medicine are having to retool at least every ten years in a way that almost reproduces in intensity their original research training. Regional stability is fast becoming a myth. Upward job mobility entails regional mobility, and the young American family is apt to move more than once. In addition, neighborhoods and regions that as recently as thirty years ago provided a well defined basis for regional identity, have been very nearly homogenized in large part through the technology of the automobile, television, and consumer appliances and the means of distributing and merchandising them. Distinctions are socioeconomic rather than in terms of the quality of region or neighborhood.

It becomes more difficult to cling to religious identity, as religious institutions grope for new roles in society. The same is true of such quasi-religious institutions of the 1930s as the labor movement.

The corporation is a far more salient institution for the men who work for it. But the corporation offers little basis for identity for most blue-collar workers; it is rather an organization to be tolerated or outwitted to have access to consumer goods. For white-collar and professional workers upward mobility requires mobility from job to job. These men may identify with their corporations, but they are likely to identify with several corporations in the course of a working lifetime. Even for a person who remains with his company over a long period of time, the nature of that corporation is apt to shift radically so that the effect is almost the same as if he were working for different companies.

Clearly values associated with particular jobs, regions, and religions will appear unstable as these institutions are challenged. But there are, in addition, cultural values—such as those associated with the concepts of modernity, progress, or the business enterprise—which must be considered separately.

The paradox of all this is that change in response to changed situations is extremely threatening. The more radical the change, the more it cuts into the concept of one's identity

("Who I am," "What business we are in"), the more threatening it becomes. I have pointed out in *Technology and Change* how this threat involves anxiety over confrontation with uncertainty—a sense of being overwhelmed by more information than we can handle.

Strength to undertake change comes from security. And security, whether for individuals or for institutions, demands a stable sense of identity. But it is precisely this stable identity that in many related ways is being undermined by the same factors that press for change. Thus, the central problems are: 1) how can we, as institutions, manage continuing flexible response to changed situations, without coming apart at the seams and 2) How can I, as an individual, retain self-respect and essential security, while in the process of change?

Responses to these questions cannot be mechanical. Our culture as a whole seems to be probing for transformations. We are in a period of search for new organizational forms, new processes of planning and action, new norms and values, and new bases for identity. Something of this underlies the present sense of disease in the United States, in addition to the urgent requirements of the black revolution, the Vietnam war, and the problems of American cities. There is an as yet implicit and confused sense of need for a shift to new forms, processes, and even languages for organizations and institutions, felt by the old as an uneasy confusion over events and by many of the young as an urgent demand for radical social change.

The nature of the transformations we are now groping for is still unclear, but seems to be expressing itself in a series of elemental shifts: from product to process, from components to systems and to networks, from static organizations (and technologies) to flexible ones, from stable institutions to temporary systems, to ways of knowing capable of handling greater informational complexity, from stable, substantive values to values for the process of change. Each of these shifts is critical and needs to be understood in its own right. But each is inextricably tied to the others. A particular example turns out to involve most or all of them.

Traditionally business firms have concerned themselves with particular products or component services. In the housing field, for example, American building suppliers have produced cast iron pipe, cement, lumber, glass wool, and the like; their involvement in housing has been a matter of producing, marketing, and occasionally modifying their products. In determining who has responsibility for the total house, or for systems of houses, we have needed to refer to the entire building industry, made up of architects, engineers, contractors, labor unions, building materials suppliers and distributors, code officials and inspectors, lenders, and speculators. No one organization has had responsibility for the whole. The whole house somehow got developed and built as a result of the interaction of many components of the building industry system, much in the form of a particular firm or agency. For a given company, growth took the form of extension of current market (horizontal integration) or movement forward toward end-use or backward toward raw materials (vertical integration). These were the only alternatives for expansion within the building industry.

One of the most significant effects of national involvement in weapons and space systems, however, has been the emergence into good currency of the concepts of systems and systems approach. An agency such as NASA in its Apollo mission or the Department of Defense in development and production of the atomic submarine set itself a broad function as a goal ("putting a man on the moon by 1970," "meeting strategic requirements") and then set about organizing to achieve that goal. This entailed: 1) development of performance criteria for achievement of the function in question; 2) development of quantitative measures of these criteria; 3) initiation of a research and development process designed to yield new technological approaches to those criteria; 4) organization of a development and production system related to particular subsystems; and 5) maintenance of an overall management and control function.

In such an approach particular products are subordinated to

subsystems goals, and these goals to systems requirements. Individual firms contract with the managing agency to supply component products and services against systems requirements.

As a result of the impact of military and aerospace systems, we are beginning to note "civilian systems." Firms have begun to define their goals in terms of broad human functions ("keeping clothes clean," "feeding people at minimum cost and maximum quality") and to grow in such a way as to incorporate within themselves or through contractual relations to others all of the component product and service firms required to achieve systems goals. This is the notion of the business system as a principle of corporate organization and growth. Its consequences for the corporation are as follows:

1) The corporation does not commit itself to a single product line or even to a single technology but its commitment is to a major human function and to the changing technologies and organizational relations to carry it out.

2) Separate corporate responsibility for different components of the system no longer serves as an obstacle to technological change, since the corporation maintains all relevant components under its control.

3) In housing, for example, the development of new wall paneling depended on new fasteners, as well as on new building standards and labor practices adapted to the new technology. As long as an individual firm had to persuade other elements of the building system to modify their contributions to accept its new technology, the process of innovation was long and slow and often too costly to be undertaken. As a single firm or consortium of firms (as in the present HUD-sponsored twenty cities project for low cost housing) gains control of all or most of the elements of the building system for a particular set of projects, it acquires the ability to develop and introduce the required system of supporting technologies.

4) A corporation may now take a variety of cuts at a business system. It can choose the set of component products and services it will aggregate as a basis for corporate identity; it

is no longer limited to horizontal or vertical integration or to conglomerate organization, which is in effect a random array of corporate entities grouped for fiscal reasons. Thus the raising of the level of corporate self-definition to business systems permits the management of continuing change in technology and in organization. What is held relatively stable is the function around which the business system moves and the performance criteria and measures related to it. Particular products, services, and organizations may change without disrupting the corporate structure. Moreover, in the case of housing, organization around business systems is a way of responding to user-related requirements for innovation, which had been difficult or impossible given the social system of the building industry.

The idea of network or infrastructure as a condition for innovation in business systems is crucially important. To permit continuing innovation in housing, for example, the design of a housing process conducive to innovation is required. For the firm or consortium of firms that takes housing functions as the basis for its business system, it is not the design of the house but of the housing process which is the major design responsibility. But such a process requires a network of relationships among elements of the housing activity—manufacture and transport of materials, assembly on site, housing design, control of construction, management of money, sponsorship of projects, maintenance.

This relatively stable network must provide for the flows of information, money, and people needed to generate a multiplicity of changing products and services.

Symbolically the shift from product to process is signified by the number of business managers who are saying that their principal function is the management of change.

For our present purposes we can draw a useful example from the field of urban and regional planning. Our model of urban planning has been something like this: the planner has been conceived as fulfilling a more or less independent function in relation to the machinery of government.

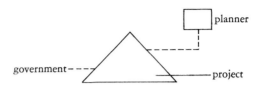

His function has been the production of a product, or a series of products—plans for action. The concept of that product has evolved significantly over the last thirty years, from a partial plan to a more comprehensive one, from a physical plan to a social-physical plan. But it has been an essential part of this model of planning that the planner produces his product, based on the generation and analysis of data, the internalization or imposition of planning goals, the techniques of his trade, and presents it to the city. Its implementation is left to others.

The inadequacy of this model is coming generally to be perceived as central to the inadequacy of our cities. Plans have a way of not being implemented, or of being implemented in highly distorted form. Moreover, our urban plans have been heavily criticized for being isolated from or irrelevant to the concerns of the various constituencies that make up the city and for being oriented to past events, such as past travel patterns, rather than to future eventualities.

Out of this critique has come a sense of a new role for planners as managers of a continuing planning process, rather than as producers of products called plans. Design and management of that process becomes their principal concern, just as design of the housing process becomes the principal concern of firms concerned with the housing system. Some of the features of the planning process include: 1) establishment of a continually updated data base for the city, which reflects not only the physical facts of the city (populations, housing stock) but the adequacy of facilities and services in relation to performance criteria; 2) concern for action and implementation as a central part of the planner's responsibility; the planner, then, becomes a "change agent" for his institution; 3) integration of the planning function with the rest of the machinery of government; 4) involvement of user constituencies (for instance, residents of poor neighborhoods, union members, business firms) not as disposers of plans through vote, but as participants in the formulation of requirements to which plans must respond; and 5) analysis of the social consequences of the development of physical facilities and of the social requirements which must be met to make physical facilities effective.

A planning process does not now proceed effectively in any city. But fragments of it are visible (for example, in the new Baltimore highway program; in the Rand Corporation work in New York City), and new schools of planning (at the University of California at Berkeley and at Los Angeles, at the State University of New York at Buffalo) are being developed around such a concept.

These shifts from component to network and from stable organization to temporary system are best considered together, and both can be illustrated by a physical analogy. In California, Ezre Ellenkrantz, a young architect, developed a school construction system known as SCSD. His purpose was to reduce costs and improve quality of school construction. He persuaded thirteen school districts to aggregate their purchases of schools, so as to create a market of some $30 million—adequate to attract industrial firms to invest in the development of new technology.

He worked with school administrators, manufacturers, teachers, parents groups, building code inspectors, and unions to select those subsystems of the school which would be most appropriate for innovation (internal structures, roofing, lighting, environmental control, partitioning were selected; plumbing and exterior brickwork were eliminated because of union resistance) and to formulate user criteria for systems based on the interests and behavior of the various user groups, including teacher, students, laborers.

A part of his purpose was to permit industrialization of

building through the use of standard components, but he discovered that a major requirement of user groups was flexibility, such as in lighting, environment, and use of space.

The consequence was a series of interlocking performance criteria which gave rise, in turn, to the development of interlocking flexible systems based on standard components. The total interior of the school, for example, could be redesigned in twelve hours. Air conditioning, adaptable to varied uses of space, could be installed with heating for the previous cost of heating alone. Floors could be carpeted for the previous cost of maintenance of hardwood flooring.

Critical to all of this was the design of networks—structural, electrical and means of aligning, connecting, or disconnecting—which permitted standard components to be realigned in a wide variety of relationships, cheaply and in line with user need. Standardization of parts, permitting industrialized manufacture, became consistent with demands for flexibility through the design of what might be called the infrastructure of the building.

It is not a great leap from this example to the problems of organizational and institutional design. If we think back to our discussion of the problems of governmental design, the principal requirement was a design for institutions which would be capable of relating themselves quickly to newly perceived problems and realigning themselves again as problems changed. The form of such institutions is what Warren Bennis has called "temporary systems."

One approach to the development of such institutions is network or matrix organization. An example of this, and, significantly, one drawn from industry, is the project system for the conduct of research and development. In this system research and development is conceived as a series of projects whose life cycles are relatively short. Projects draw on pools of competence which have a life cycle that is relatively long in relation to that of projects. Members of competence pools flow into project teams in shifting combinations, carry out their project-related tasks and flow back to competence pools for reassignment.

Project leaders manage for short-term performance. Overall program management determines what projects are to be undertaken, the relative allocation of resources, the initiation of new projects, the cutting off of old, and the like. Program management depends on a control tower or intelligence function, which handles information related to project requirements, competitors, project effectiveness, and resource availability.

The management of competence pools, on the other hand, is a kind of gardening function which involves attempts to recruit and develop resources with an eye to future requirements, professional development of people, training, optimum use of available resources, and management of movement in and out of projects. The system as a whole aims at flexible response to project need without the creation of a bureaucracy that will persist after project requirements have been met. It seeks to separate out requirements for security and stability and to meet these through competence pools.

Such a network organization is not limited to research and development functions. It has been broadly applied, for example, in aerospace firms (such as TRW Systems). It is currently used broadly in government in the areas of planning, evaluation, and policy-making—through the "task" force and "commission" systems—though not as yet in actual program implementation.

It is applicable whenever project life cycle requirements are short and changing in relation to relatively stable demand, cutting across projects, for skills and disciplines. The project team, though it may last anywhere from six months to four years, is a temporary system; the system of competence pools is relatively stable in relation to it.

The effective adaptive application of the entire system depends upon the network or infrastructure of the organization which connects competence pools with projects and with each other; manages the flows of people into and out of projects; and manages the flows of information on the basis of which projects come into being and dissolve.

The principal problem of organizational design, then, just as it was the principal problem of building design in SCSD, is the network which permits a flexible realigning of components responding to changed need and the process by which these flows of people, information, and resources are managed.

The interrelation of these shifts from the point of view of continuing adaptation to change is now somewhat more apparent. The shift from product to system, the movement upward in level of aggregation, permits a wider variety of innovations to come about under single management to meet basic functional requirements. With such a larger system, continuing adaptation to change situations requires the building of networks through which more or less standard components can be redesigned continuously to meet changing need, without loss of a relatively stable base for individuals. Attention must then shift from particular products to the planning management process by which information, people, and resources flow through these networks to particular but changing tasks. The focus on network and infrastructure, as well as on process, complements the movement to a higher level of aggregation as the unit of management and of organizational identity.*

But what has been said up to now relates primarily to the problem of design of adaptive institutions. It does not address itself as yet to the problems of value and identity for individuals, whose lives intersect many such institutions.

Clearly values based on ties to particular institutions, technologies, professions, regions, or to particular roles within institutions will be threatened and forced to change in the course of a single lifetime. What I have suggested earlier in this connection holds even for the more fundamental kinds of values associated in Western culture with the seventeenth and eighteenth centuries and with what I have called the Technological Program. (Paul Goodman, author of *Growing Up Absurd* calls it the "modern enterprise.") These are values of

---

*The notion of "planning" as a rational process of social change demands a new kind of organization or institution—in the manner of what is described above as a network organization. Then planning can be a process of sensing requirements for changing functions, presenting options and their consequences, or managing flows of information. In this way it can have a significant effect on the system.

work, individuality, freedom, peace, satisfaction of need. I will not reproduce here my attempt in *Technology and Change* to indicate the ways in which these values, too, have been significantly undermined by the progress of the technological program itself. The threat to them is not merely to a particular version of them, but to any enduring stable state.

We now generally share the views of Marx and Weber that our values derive from and depend upon our roles in the institutions and social systems of which we are a part. But the same changes in situation that force changes in the character of these institutions also force changes in the values contingent upon particular institutional forms. As a consequence, we experience the anxiety of the periods of transition, the problem of retaining self-respect while in the process of change, and the problem of self-respect and identity throughout a process of change, lasting over a lifetime, when it is no longer possible to believe that the next substantive value Gestalt will be any more stable than the last. The successful adaptation of institutions as well founders on these problems of value and identity for individuals within them.

A full discussion of these issues could not be accomplished here, but the directions in which the movement toward resolution may proceed can be indicated. The problem is the development—the real, "felt" development, rather than the academic formulation—of values for the process of change itself. These are, in a sense, "meta" or second-order values, rather than first-order values. They are values for the transitions rather than for the temporary stable states between transitions.

What is striking about values for change is that they must be related to the emergence of novelty—that is, values related to the deliberate, active involvement in the emergence of novelty rather than in its passive "suffering." But, understood in this way, we already have models for them. They occur in the values relating to artistic creation, to scientific discovery, and to invention. These include not the full range of values held by artists, inventors, and discoverers, but the values specifically tied to their own activity.

Unfortunately, we are generally not exposed to these values

or the processes of creation or discovery because of a tendency in our society to know artists or inventors by their products alone. The product alone tends to be public, with the process secret. Hence we get the stereotyped images of the artist in his studio or the inventor in his garret or laboratory.

But it is possible, nevertheless, to indicate some of the features of values for change as they emerge from these models. They include a prizing of the here-and-now (attentiveness to and involvement in what is going on now, rather than stereotypes of the past or dreams of future). This priority is an interpersonal matter, a here-and-now with others even when the individual is alone his stance and relation are to others.

It includes a faith in the here-and-now, a willingness to "come apart" with respect to old views, because of faith in the potentiality of the present. It implies an insistence on testing of views, theories, beliefs, in the here-and-now. There is, therefore, little reliance on what I have thought, or believed, and much generation of concepts out of the present situation. There is a willingness to maintain a viewpoint in the present, even while insisting that it is only a point of a view.

The prizing of the here-and-now is very much related to what has been called the existential present. The past is prized as metaphor or model for the future, rather than as a literal rule for it.

It is not uncommon to speak of rejection of the past as a necessary condition for the emergence of novelty. But total rejection of the past leaves no basis for invention of the future. The stock-in-trade of inventor or artist or creative scientist is his use of the past as projective model for the future, a familiar theory brought to bear on the present situation, transforming it and being transformed in the process.

The problem is shared by evolving institutions and nations. The pressures for change and the loss of the stable state press toward a variety of responses: revolt (an attempt at total rejection of the past, while letting in a literal or distorted form of the past through the back door); reaction (a futile attempt to return literally to the past); or diversions or attempts at escape from the problem—such as in the mindlessness associated with infatuations with machines, with violence, or with drugs. To the question what can I be if I am not what I am. the answer must always take the form a transformation of what I have been, not a rupture with the past.

Values for the process of change, of which the themes discussed above are only indications, do not take the place of substantive values. But they permit shifts in substantive values without major disruptions of the person by providing relatively stable values through which self-respect and identity can be maintained. The inventor need not stake his reputation or his identity on a particular invention if he has faith in and values the process of invention itself. The failure of a work of art does not undo the artist, if he is capable of engagement in and commitment to his own process of creation.

It is through a kind of static, product-oriented mentality that we have given relatively little prominence to these process values. Our point of view has tended to be retrospective and static (a "rear-view mirror" approach, as Marshall McLuhan says) even while we have spoken of progress.

But the changes now underway in our society, and the inadequacy of established institutions, forces us as individuals to develop values for change just as they force institutions to move toward definition of themselves around higher level systems, toward the design of networks and processes to manage change without total disruption.

Contributors

MICHAEL A. ARBIB
Stanford University

IRVING N. BERLIN
University of Washington

BARBARA L. DICKERSON
University of Michigan

LEONARD J. DUHL
University of California
at Berkeley

RUDOLF EKSTEIN
Reiss Davis Child Study
Center
Los Angeles

AMITAI ETZIONI
Columbia University

HOWARD E. FREEMAN
Brandeis University

ROSALIND S. GERTNER
Brandeis University

VICTOR GIOSCIA
Adelphi University

SAUL I. HARRISON
University of Michigan

ROY M. KAHN
University of California
at Berkeley

ELIZABETH W. KILLINS
University of Michigan

ROBERT J. KLEINER
Temple University

MORTON LEVITT
University of California
at Davis

DAVID LEVY
New York State Psychiatric
Institute

ROGER LITTLE
University of Illinois

JOHN F. McDERMOTT, Jr.
University of Hawaii

SEYMOUR PARKER
University of Utah

MARC PILISUK
University of California
  at Berkeley

ALICE S. ROSSI
Goucher College

BEN RUBENSTEIN
Marlboro College

HERBERT I. SCHILLER
Universtiy of Illinois

JOHN L. SCHIMEL
William Alanson White
  Institute for
  Psychoanalysis, Psychiatry,
  and Psychology, New York

DONALD A. SCHON
Organization for Social and
  Technical Innovations
  Cambridge, Mass

JULES SCHRAGER
University of Michigan

HARLEY C. SHANDS
Roosevelt Hospital,
  New York

JAMES T. TEDESCHI
State University of New York
  at Buffalo

DIANA TENDLER
Hunter College

NANCY E. WAXLER
Harvard Medical School

PAUL H. WENDER
National Institute of Mental
  Health

RICHARD H. WILLIAMS
National Institute of Mental
  Health

INDEX

ALI. *See* American Law Institute
Abortion: and contraception, technical distinctions of, 121; and maternal health, 122; and the Catholic Church, 130; in Asia, 121; open discussion of, 126
Abortion law, 132
Abortion law reform: and social change, 118-34; and legislative bills, 122; women's role in, 129
Abortion rate: in Catholic countries, 132; in other countries, 119; in the Soviet Union, 132; in the U.S., 119
Addams, Jane, 33
Adler, Herman, 37, 38
Adolescent, 292-303; anxiety of, 301; and desire to get along, 299; fun morality of, 297; intellectualism of, 297; learning style of, 278; and love, 302; and politics, 298; Puritanism of, 296, 297, 300; and sex, 303; types of, 295; "typical," 292; values of, 295
Adolescent rebellion, 49
Adoption, psychological effects of, 232
Adoption study, 228

Alienation: definition of, 69; psychological effect of, 74; reduction of, 75
Alienation school. *See* Conflict school
Alienation-anomie model, 206, 214
Alienation-integration continuum, 215
America. *See* U.S.
American Law Institute, state penal code, 122, 126
American Orthopsychiatric Association, 13, 19
American Psychoanalytic Association, 12
American Psychological Association, 11
Anxiety, adolescent, 301
Armed Forces: and community clinics, 99; basic training in, characteristics of, 92, effects of, 94; civilian criticism of, 107; control system of, 97; domestic intervention of, 112; education in, 90-100; effects of, negative, 103, 105, 107, on civilian institutions, 106, positive, 103, 105; information system of, 97; organization of, 95;

Morton Levitt is associate dean and professor of psychology, University of California at Davis.
Ben Rubenstein is lecturer, Marlboro College, Vermont.

The manuscript was edited by Linda Grant. Both the book and jacket were designed by Joanne Kinney. The typeface for the text is linotype Janson; the original dates from the 17th Century and was cut by Nicholas Kis. The display face is Eurostile designed by Aldo Novarese.

The text is printed on Allied's Paperback Book. The hardcover volume is bound in Columbia Mills' Riverside Chambray cloth over binder's boards; and the paperback volume is bound in Riegals Carolina cover. Manufactured in the United States of America.